CASH-RICH RETIREMENT

CA$H-RICH
RETIREMENT

Use the Investing Techniques
of the Mega-Wealthy
to Secure Your Retirement Future

JIM SCHLAGHECK

St. Martin's Press   New York

www.stmartins.com

Library of Congress Cataloging-in-Publication Data

Schlagheck, Jim.
Cash-rich retirement : use the investing techniques of the mega-wealthy to secure your
    retirement future / Jim Schlagheck. —1st ed.
        p.   cm.
ISBN-13: 978-0-312-37740-3
ISBN-10: 0-312-37740-1
  1. Investments.   2. Finance, Personal.   3. Retirement income.   I. Title.

HG4521.S3536   2008
332.024'014—dc22   2007043066

First Edition: March 2008

1   3   5   7   9   10   8   6   4   2

To Helen—

whose love, patience, and companionship

I value beyond measure

Contents

Part III: The Care and Feeding of Your Nest Egg

Acknowledgments

Grateful thanks to:

Lisa DiMona, agent extraordinaire; Phil Revzin, senior editor extraordinaire; and Larry Gadd, publisher and provocative thinker extraordinaire. I very much appreciate your guidance and help. I also wish to thank Drs. Jeremy J. Siegel, Robert J. Shiller, Robert D. Arnott, and Messrs. John C. Bogle, Benjamin Graham, Peter Grossman, Sreedhar Menon, and Peter G. Peterson for their vision, research, and good advice, which have helped me and investors everywhere.

Introduction

A CALL TO ARMS!

Congratulations! The fact that you are reading this book makes you one of a select group of people who are seriously concerned about their future. You want to learn more about and prepare more skillfully for retirement. Hats off!

This book is going to help you. It's going to cut through the confusing investment jargon and conflicting investment advice. It's going to help you choose among today's bewildering number of investment alternatives and—yes!—help you successfully achieve all the retirement income you'll need. It's going to help you weather a severe storm. And, count on it. An extremely severe financial storm is setting in.

At present, one of six Americans over the age of sixty-five is living in or near poverty. In twenty years, one out of four Americans over sixty-five will live in or near poverty because of gross ill-preparedness for retirement. You, however, are going to be one of the survivors coming out of the storm unscathed. This book is going to help you.

This book is a guide to help you build, enlarge, and protect your retirement wealth. Whatever your income bracket. Whatever your savings to date. This book is going to help you invest more skillfully and successfully build income for retirement.

In their publications about death and grieving, authors Elisabeth Kübler-Ross and David Kessler found that when people are told they have an incurable disease, they typically go through several distinct reaction phases. They demonstrate in succession (1) denial, (2) anger, (3) bargaining, (4) depression, and then (5) acceptance. I find that most people react to the notion of retirement in much the same way. In fact, most Americans are still in a denial phase. Most refuse to look at the hard retirement issues confronting them. Most refuse to realistically prepare for retirement or even acknowledge that their savings "opportunity clock" is ticking away.

For many people, retirement denial takes the form of spending whatever they have (and often *more* than they have), saving nothing whatsoever for the future. Buy another flat-screen TV! Buy that Lexus SUV! Buy! Buy! Buy! Because if you're never going to become a multimillionaire, at least you can live like one! So buy something Armani and watch reruns of *Lifestyles of the Rich and Famous*. Spend! Spend! Spend!

For others, denial hides in the creed that people should look forward to retirement with an emphasis on spiritual growth and fulfillment, not monetary obsession.

I agree. We should, indeed, champion the nonmonetary dimensions of our lives and look forward to retirement as an exciting phase when we can share our experiences and wisdom with others, give back to our communities, and enjoy and add to the warmth of our families and friends.

But I believe that having adequate funds for retirement is critically important, too. I believe that—more than ever before in the brief history of American "retirement"—*you* have much greater responsibility to prepare financially for the future.

So as much as I recognize the importance of the nonfinancial aspects of retirement, I foremost of all want you to be able to *afford* retirement and health care. I want you to enjoy the next phases of your life with bread on your table and the latest miracle drugs on your nightstand. I want you to have the financial strength and wherewithal to retire.

That means saving and investing right now *without any more denial or excuses.*

Most people are massively in "retirement denial." You, however, are not. That's why you're reading this book.

Once past the denial phase, many people move into anger. They express rage when they realize that they have not saved enough for the future. "I only have two years to go before my company pushes me out," one man told me bitterly, "and I'm furious with myself for not having saved more. I can't retire. I don't have enough savings. What am I going to do?"

More and more people are becoming angry as they wake up to the reality that traditional pension plans are collapsing and that their personal savings are nonexistent or pathetically low. They are angry because they have not invested wisely—or, in fact, not saved or invested at all. They are mad as hell as they take inventory of their predicament. They thought the government and their employers were going to take care of all their retirement needs. But guess what? That isn't going to happen. Get used to it.

Next are the people who want to bargain their way into a financially secure retirement. We are sure to see more employee groups and unions clamoring for better retirement benefits—even though many companies today can ill afford the long-term benefits they are already meant to pay. Nevertheless, many Americans will increasingly turn to unions, lobbyists, and their congressmen to bargain for better "entitlements" and benefits. But whoa there! Handing out more benefits just isn't going to happen magically or without cost. Get used to that, too.

And then comes retirement depression (as in "We give up! We're moving to Belize!") and acceptance ("So I'm going to keep right on working till I'm ninety—who cares?").

I'm here to help you translate whatever denial, anger, bargaining fever, or depression you may be experiencing into constructive action. I want to help you be one of the Americans who can and will retire securely and comfortably.

This book will help you. It will cause you to significantly change the way you invest and to get even more serious—deadly serious—about your retirement preparedness.

This book is a practical guide and *a call to arms!* It is a call to arms for a new, *income-focused* way of investing for retirement. It is a call to get back to fundamentals and common sense when you invest. And it is a call for *you* to take action to defend your retirement from the turmoil ahead.

TROUBLE AHEAD

Here are the sad facts. Most Americans are woefully ill-prepared for their "golden years." Mired in debt at home and in government, we are not saving for the future. Our pension systems are failing. Corporate retirement benefits are perilously underfunded. A "do-it-yourself" approach to retirement investing is not working. Millions of Americans do not participate in a 401(k) or any other retirement savings plan. Traditional wisdom about how to invest is often speculative and lacking in vision. Herd moves from one speculative bubble (such as technology stocks) to the next (such as real estate) happen again and again. And U.S. demographics portend a shock wave just ahead as a great surge of baby boomers gets ready to retire en masse and sell off assets.

The truth is that a great number of Americans will *not* be able to stop working. For many, retirement is an experiment gone sour. Many will never receive the full measure of retirement benefits on which they are counting. Many others—without adequate savings and retirement income of any kind—will simply never be able to retire.

So I see trouble ahead. Serious trouble.

This book is a wake-up call. It tells you how, after all, you will be able to retire with all the capital you need. And it gives you investment strategies that you can confidently implement—strategies based on extensive research and proven wealth-management expertise to sidestep the damage that may result from demographic changes.

MY EXPERIENCE WILL HELP YOU

For more than twenty years I have helped to create investments, set up mutual funds, and mind portfolios for everyday-Joe investors as well as mega-wealthy individuals, pension funds, and institutions. I have helped clients with *hundreds* of dollars and clients with *hundreds of millions* of dollars to invest. I did so as a senior executive at American Express Bank, Bank Julius Baer (the Swiss private bank), UBS (one of the most powerful wealth-management institutions in the world), TAIB Bank in the Middle East, and other respected financial groups. I have been responsible for hundreds of employees providing banking services, investment management, and advice. Hence, my experience has given me good insight into the fine art of investing in up markets and down.

My financial experience has spanned many different countries. I have worked extensively in Switzerland, Brazil, the Indian subcontinent, the Arabian Gulf as well as the USA. I have interacted with major investors and investment experts worldwide. And around the world, I have found that people often wrestle with similar investment issues, concerns, herd panic attacks, and risks. You are not alone.

I have an MBA from the Wharton School of Finance. I know investment theory and practice. But I also have long experience turning theory into practical success. I have helped some people enlarge great fortunes by investing prudently. I have seen others lose their shirts trying to double their money in record time. I have had the opportunity to learn and assess the investment views and "success formulas" of many experts and successful investors.

This book is a compendium of what I have learned about investing from my experience in a variety of investment categories, in a variety of different countries, and from a variety of distinguished employers and investment specialists over the last twenty-five years. It synthesizes the insights and investment theories that the Wharton School taught me, and the helpful investment tips and tactics I leaned as a private banker. It shares the "secrets" and skills I learned for building and preserving wealth. And it also gives you tips so that you, too, can avoid some of the investment risks and errors that have harmed others.

In this book we are going to look at a number of winning investment strategies together. We'll cut through the jargon, debunk today's harmful misconceptions about investing, and make skillful investing straightforward and simple.

PROVISOS

But before we move ahead, I want to make several important disclaimers. I want you to know, among other things, what *not* to expect.

First, this book is not *about how to become a multimillionaire by investing speculatively in stocks or real estate.* It is about how to *skillfully* invest for retirement. It is, consequently, strictly conservative in its approach. It is adamantly adverse to speculation. It is strictly against flipping houses or stocks for a fast buck. If you want to gamble or get rich quickly, try Las Vegas or Atlantic City.

There are recommendations in this book with which you may not agree. You may not agree with my diversification tactics. You may not agree that a serious retirement crisis is looming immediately ahead. You may not even agree that income-producing investments are the best kind for your retirement portfolio.

All of that is fine. I welcome your views and your own research findings. But if you do not have ideas that are better tested, better proven, and better substantiated than mine—step to the side!

Don't expect miracles! The recommendations contained in this book are not miraculous, foolproof, or without risk. There *are* no magic formulas for investment success. Not all of this book's recommendations may be suitable for you. You will have to carefully weigh them—and I hope you do so with a good financial planner by your side.

I cannot guarantee that you will have superior investment performance. I do not guarantee that you will even have positive investment results. I am not promising you riches or returns of any kind. No one can do that.

I base my recommendations on solid, serious, respected research—but it is not infallible. I always cite the academic and statistical research underlying my views so you know the bases for them. However, even the expert findings I use are not beyond debate. Long-term historical data is still statistically limited. The experts I quote cannot guarantee positive, "live happily ever after" results either. Past experience may *not*, after all, repeat itself. As the fine print says at the bottom of every investment prospectus, "Past history is no guarantee of future outcomes or success."

You must double-check my investment recommendations. I provide the names of specific funds, indexes, and other investments to consider. I invest in these same funds and indexes myself. By the time you read this book, however, the strengths and weaknesses of any funds or asset managers that I name here are sure to change. I repeat: *the strengths and weakness of the funds and managers I cite in this book are sure to change over time.* Consequently, the investments that I recommend may *not* be suitable investments by the time you read this. You need to do your own homework before making any investment—and I'll show you how.

You'll also need tax guidance. You are going to need personalized tax counsel when you set your investment plan, weigh the merits of different 401(k) plans or annuities, and actually begin drawing down your retirement capital one day (if you have not already done so). My suggestions may not match your personal tax situation. Be sure to check with a tax specialist before making investment decisions or taking drawdowns.

Okay. Are you ready to overhaul your savings and investment habits to build retirement income and security? Are you ready to adopt a radically different approach to successful investing?

Very good! Then our first step is to forge a common, factual, and incontestable view about (1) the retirement dangers before us, and (2) the incredible investment opportunities that are also just ahead so that you are truly motivated to take immediate, *without-fail* action.

It's time to get deadly serious about preparing for retirement. And you *are* going to be a secure retiree with ample savings and retirement income!

PART I

YOUR
RETIREMENT
IS IN
GRAVE DANGER!

Americans have many different, often inaccurate views about *what* retirement is, *when* they can take it, and *how* they must fund it. Long-retired Americans take it for granted that everyone can expect a gold watch and company pension when he or she retires. Not so! Younger Americans have been raised with a do-it-yourself responsibility for retirement funding—but many believe that they have all the time in the world to begin their own savings. Also not so! And in between are people who expect to retire at age sixty-five and for whom retirement means "maybe a pension" or "maybe a 401(k)." Or maybe not.

In this section we are going to explore why retirement in the United States means so many different things to different people. Golden years. Financial security. A Florida condo. Cocktails on the lanai. An IRA. Corporate pensions. Medicare, but only partial expense coverage. Pension cutbacks. Portfolio setbacks. Spiraling medical costs. "I haven't saved enough" panic.

We need to understand all of these associations and concerns to understand the American "retirement experiment." And *you* need to understand the financial underpinnings of retirement—what's paid for, what's not, and how much capital you will, indeed, need for a secure, cash-rich future. Let's get started.

1

IS RETIREMENT
A DYING EXPERIMENT?

Retirement is a modern experiment. It is a noble, strictly nineteenth-to-twenty-first-century "work in progress." And it is now in danger in the United States because of inadequate funding, extraordinary demographics, and generally poor financial preparedness.

Retirement is in danger in the United States because Americans like you and me are not saving enough, not investing wisely enough, and not insisting forcefully enough on safeguarding our benefits and nest eggs.

In contemporary mythology, "retirement" is the period of our lives when we stop working, relax, and enjoy the fruits of our labor. In the myth, we all enjoy "golden years" in good health and financial security.

Of course, that vision is bunkum. It is, nevertheless, a vision strongly etched in the minds of most Americans. It is the picture drummed into us after years of watching television programs like *Father Knows Best, N.Y.P.D. Blue, Law and Order,* and the like—programs that depicted average-Joe Americans working hard, building up their retirement savings, and giving loyalty to their employer in exchange for retirement security and "corporate care."

Not only is the myth romantic and fictional, but now retirement-the-reality is under siege. For thousands of years, people normally worked until they died, became incapacitated, or were pushed off on an iceberg. There was no organized system of "retirement." So if today's ideal of "a long and happy retirement" sounds like something too good to be true—it is! It's an experiment that some Americans will regrettably *never* enjoy in the coming decades and that few of our ancestors ever enjoyed to begin with.

BRIEF HISTORY

Let's take a moment to briefly survey the history of retirement. It's a fascinating saga.

In ancient Greece and Rome, people stockpiled jars of olive oil for their senior years. Olive oil stores well. So Greeks and Romans bought and stored jars of oil during their adult lives, which they eventually sold for income in old age. The ancients also bought income contracts called *annua*—-the world's original "annuity" contracts—to guarantee old-age income. A person bought such a contract with a onetime payment, and the contract guaranteed lifetime income beginning at a later age. The very same kinds of contracts are helping retirees even today.

During the Middle Ages, workers turned to guilds for old-age and disability benefits. Guilds paid income to members who became disabled or infirm. So the first pensions were initially "help your fellow worker" income programs aimed at solidifying guild membership. For example, one guild in England promised, "If any man or woman of the fraternity becomes so enfeebled through illness or old age that he cannot work or engage in commerce, then he shall be supported, at the cost of the gild, in a manner fitting his status."[1]

Barring incapacity, however, guild members were meant to work until they dropped. They were, as well, only a small part of the total population. Most people who reached old age at that time—the average life span was in the thirties[2]—primarily relied on the largesse of their families to provide for their later-age needs.

In colonial America, elderly people sometimes wrote wills and made them public, promising their heirs an inheritance if the beneficiaries provided old-age care—lodging, meals, and a specific amount of firewood. Referring to those times, one historian noted, "There is also . . . evidence that people viewed children and savings as substitute strategies for retirement planning."[3] Senior care primarily came from family members. The average life span was up to thirty-five,[4] but most people still worked until they could no longer do so.

Other than these rudimentary attempts to provide income or care, few societies organized "retirement" or "senior citizen" benefits on a large scale. Not, at least, until modern times.

For much of recorded history, in fact, there has long been one primary *"retirement planning" technique: people have traditionally had many children to care for them in old age.*

Americans never entertained the idea of "retirement" until the 1800s. Typically, our forebearers worked until they died or became disabled and had seven or eight children to care for them long term. In 1880, 78 percent of American men ages sixty-five and older were still working.[5] Among men age sixty-five and older in 1880, nearly half lived with children or relatives. Today fewer than 5 percent do.[6] So people at the end of the nineteenth century usually worked until they died and often lived with family members when they were older. Retirement then was quite different from what it is today. It was exceptional and "family-funded."

By the mid part of the nineteenth century, however, important changes began taking place. Pensions for U.S. Civil War veterans and railroad workers first took shape in the mid-1800s. The New York City police force set up the first public-sector retirement-income plan in 1857, and in 1875 American Express introduced for its employees the first corporate pension plan.[7] This plan benefited employees who had at least twenty years of service at the age of sixty. It rewarded employee loyalty. And many companies soon followed American Express's lead.

By 1882, the Alfred Dodge Company—a builder of pianos and organs—introduced a pension plan wherein workers contributed 1 percent of their pay to earn 6 percent interest paid by the company. The Dodge plan reflected America's "pay your own way" bias as regards benefit programs, a philosophical approach that underlies most of the country's retirement systems even today.

But an even more important retirement breakthrough took place in Germany in 1889 when Kaiser Wilhelm and Chancellor Otto von Bismarck established the first-ever *state pension system.* In this unprecedented national program, all German citizens qualified for a "retirement pension" when they reached age seventy. It was the first attempt by any country to provide income for its senior citizens.

The original German pension system equated age with disability; it set seventy as the official retirement age; and it equated old-age pensions with "state care." In the United States, the approach to pensions and senior benefits would undergo substantial modification on all three counts. The United States would emphasize "individual contributions" and frown on "it sounds like socialism."

America's nationwide social insurance program—Social Security— came into being in 1935. It was a response to the Great Depression and the widespread financial hardships of the 1930s. Provided you and your employer contributed to the program, Social Security paid you a small amount of money beginning at age sixty-five. Since the average life span for an American at that time was only fifty-nine for men, Social Security payments were originally meant to be *the exception* rather than the rule. In fact, most early Social Security benefits were actually paid to surviving spouses—not to workers themselves.[8]

Medicare, the national health insurance program, was established by Congress in 1965. It was designed to pay for some—but not all—of the medical expenses of disabled Americans and people sixty-five and over. Many Americans believe that Medicare and Social Security were avant-garde programs meant to guarantee a comfortable retirement and secure golden years for all workers. That is not so. By the time Social Security was established in 1935, thirty-four other countries already had national social insurance programs up and running[9]—ours was nothing new. Both Social Security and Medicare were designed to make only *limited* contributions to a person's financial and health-care well-being. They were not designed to cover all health-care costs or income needs. The emphasis has been and continues to be on personal savings and "pay your own way" retirement funding.

Following World War II, companies vied with each other to attract and retain skilled, loyal employees, and corporate pensions and retirement benefits became commonplace. Americans came to rely on them. And by the 1950s and '60s, an era of "corporate paternalism" had set in. Most workers could look forward to retirement with a handsome company pension.

That, however, was soon to change. Longer life spans and spiraling health-care costs eventually caused U.S. companies to rethink their pension pacts. A little-heralded but blockbuster shift took place. Beginning in the 1980s, many U.S. companies began cutting back retirement benefits and halting pension programs outright. Most companies directed workers to take full responsibility themselves for retirement funding via 401(k) and similar plans. From "corporate care," Americans were herded into do-it-yourself retirement-funding responsibility.

RETIREMENT TODAY

Today, Americans look forward to retirement supported by a mix of different programs, benefits, and funding mechanisms: (1) traditional employer pensions or "defined benefit" plans; (2) "defined contribution" plans such as 401(k), 457(b), and similar programs; (3) IRAs or individual retirement accounts; (4) Social Security; (5) Medicare; and (6) whatever other savings you can muster. As we will see, this mix of benefits and funding mechanisms is piecemeal and is not uniformly available to all.

Many Americans take it for granted that all workers have access to pension or savings plans and still cling to the myth that retirement is "a dazzling, decades-long vacation at the end of life."[10] The myth prevails, but the reality is starkly different.

Americans are retiring earlier—the average retirement age is now sixty-two.[11] Americans have also come to enjoy much longer lives. Instead of the average life span of sixty-one and a half years for both men and women when Social Security was created, today's younger Americans can now expect to live into their late eighties or nineties. Life spans are decidedly longer *and growing*. That means that individuals need more capital to fund their retirement at the same time that they are increasingly expected to amass that capital on their own.

So contemporary "retirement" is quite unlike that experienced by our parents or grandparents. Even as recently as 1985, *eight out of ten* American workers in medium-size and large private companies participated in a traditional pension plan.[12] Today, only *two out of ten* do.[13] In the 1960s and '70s, American workers could look forward to an average of ten years of retirement life supported by government payments and company pensions.[14] Today's workers have a much longer, *self-funded* retirement ahead.

In the past, Americans often retired—at least in the national mythology—with a farewell party and send-off gift at age sixty-five or a retirement age of their choosing. Today's Americans are often not in control of when they retire. Today, many people—more than one-third—are thrust into early retirement whether they are financially ready for it or not. Four in ten retirees report that they retired earlier than expected due to job loss, downsizing, poor health, or some other factor.[15] More than a quarter of the workers who recently retired before the age of sixty-five did so because of changes at their company "such as downsizing or closure."[16] And the retirement incomes of many Americans are not at all robust. Today, about one in six Americans over the age of sixty-five lives at or near the poverty level.[17]

So "retirement" is a modern, not necessarily carefree experiment. The "live happily ever after" picture of retirement in the United States is not true for many current retirees. And it is going to be much worse for people retiring in the future.

We are, in fact, in the midst of a developing crisis. We are moving from the security of traditional company pensions, which once guaranteed some retirement income, to do-it-yourself retirement savings that guarantee nothing at all. Our benefit programs, once solvent and sound, now suffer massive funding shortfalls. And many millions of Americans are about to enter their golden years with little retirement preparedness, minuscule savings, and little awareness of the precarious state of their benefit programs. *You,* however, can and will enjoy a financially sound and secure retirement. But to do so, you must understand what you're up against and why counting on government and corporate benefits *instead of personal savings* would be naïve.

DEFINED BENEFIT PLANS

A "defined benefit" plan—meaning a company pension plan—is a benefit program where your *employer* bears the risk of generating sufficient cash to pay you retirement income and/or other retirement benefits. Such plans were once the mainstays of American retirements. They are, however, dwindling in number today, and many are bordering on failure.

At present, only 21 percent of American workers in private enterprise have access to a defined-benefit pension or retirement benefits.[18] A much larger 80 percent of all government workers do.[19] Even if we add public- and private-sector workers together, however, the majority of *all* workers do not have access to any pension. This ratio of "haves" to "have-nots" is the inverse of what it was only decades ago.

Increasingly, fewer and fewer workers have access to defined benefit plans and fewer companies offer them. The *number* of pension plans plummeted 70 percent between 1983 and 2000.[20] Today, only one company in ten offers a pension,[21] and even that number is shrinking. Pension and benefit reductions are also becoming common. In its recent survey of retirement practices, the Employee Benefit Research Institute found that: "nearly half of workers report that recent changes to the employer pension system have made them less confident about the money they can expect to receive from a defined benefit (or "traditional") pension plan. . . . Seventeen percent of workers have personally experienced a reduction in the retirement benefits offered by their employer within the past two years."[22]

Whatever the access and cutbacks, defined-benefit payments may *not* materialize for many Americans because of pervasive underfunding. The little-acknowledged fact is this: of those companies or government agencies that offer defined benefit plans today, many have immense funding shortfalls. Underfunding is the pervasive cancer undermining defined benefit retirement programs nationwide. And many Americans counting on pension benefits may be in for a rude surprise.

The most recent data available shows that the majority of the country's largest companies—the five hundred that make up the S&P 500 Index—had less than full pension funding at the close of 2005. Their pension shortfalls alone amounted to $140 billion.[23] Add in the underfunding of other "postemployment benefits" such as promised medical coverage, and the total underfunding for *all* retirement benefits among S&P 500 companies was a whopping $461 billion.[24] *That's almost a half of one trillion dollars of funding shortfall just among the country's top companies alone.* For smaller companies the statistics are similarly dismal.

Of course, these numbers change from time to time depending on the investment performance of corporate pension plans. Even so, the *magnitude* of the problem is sobering.

According to the Congressional Budget Office, the total funding shortfall for *all* pensions and other "defined benefits" among *all* U.S. companies is now over *$600 billion.*[25] That staggering amount will not, in all likelihood, be replenished anytime soon.

The situation is just as bad, precarious, and inexcusable in the public sector. At last count, some *80 percent of the state retirement systems* that report data for the *Wilshire Report on State Retirement Systems* are also underfunded.[26] By 2003, at least nine states had pension fund liabilities that actually exceeded their total annual budgets![27] Of the municipal and county systems that report data to Wilshire, 77 percent were underfunded at last count as well.[28]

That, however, is just the tip of the iceberg. Many municipalities, states, as well as corporations are funding their pensions with limited contributions expecting their pension plans will generate high investment returns. Many of their return projections are unrealistic. In other words, many direct-benefit plans are counting on money that will simply not come in! So if the underfunding of defined benefit plans today is pervasive and dangerous, the situation is likely to become even worse in the future. We're in crisis territory.

Let me offer you two independent views about the state of affairs as regards direct-benefit pensions and benefits. According to Dr. Robert Arnott, a respected investment commentator and asset manager, "The U.S. economy may well be sitting on a trillion-dollar time bomb, in the form of unrealistic pension return expectations".[29] Harry Dent, author and investment-trend analyst, put it even more bluntly: "The level of payments promised to future retirees cannot possibly be paid, affecting not only private sector works but also civil servants. . . . Retirement benefits systems of all types are in crisis mode."[30]

So where does this leave us? Many of the country's top corporations are technically bankrupt because they cannot meet their direct-benefit liabilities. Many state, municipal, and public pensions are likewise in bad shape. I believe that many corporate and public-sector pension plans will *not* be able to meet their defined-benefit promises. And that means that all of us have to save more and invest smarter, ourselves.

If you are counting on a pension or other direct benefits, it's time to make sure those benefits are going to materialize. Visit my Web site, www .cashrichretirement.com. Copy the Letter Concerning Pensions. Send it to your employer. Use it to request independent certification that your pension plan is adequately funded, is realistically projecting long-term investment income, and can, indeed, honor its defined benefit terms. Do that today.

DEFINED CONTRIBUTION PLANS AND IRAS

Defined contribution plans—sometimes generically lumped together and called 401(k) plans—are also important funding vehicles. They are voluntary savings plans with tax advantages. There are many different kinds. And while "defined benefit" pensions cause *employers* to shoulder the risk of guaranteeing some amount of retirement income, a "defined contribution plan" has *you* bear the risk of saving enough and amassing enough capital to satisfy your retirement needs.

Today, many different "direct contribution" plans permit you to save money for retirement with tax advantage. The main kinds include (1) traditional 401(k) plans; (2) Roth 401(k) plans; (3) SIMPLE 401(k)s, for small businesses; (4) 403(b) plans, for employees of nonprofit organizations; (5) 457(b) plans, for state and local government employees; (6) SEPs or Simplified Employee Pensions; and (7) Thrift Savings Plans, for military personnel and civilians employed by the federal government.

There are also different IRAs or individual retirement accounts, which have similar characteristics: (1) traditional IRAs; (2) Roth IRAs; and (3) SIMPLE IRAs. Whew!

If you want more information about these programs and the maximum contributions you can make to each one, visit www.irs.gov for updated information or visit my Web site.

There are also Profit Sharing Plans, Money Purchase Plans, and Employee Stock Ownership Plans (ESOPs), with talk of a host of other plans and programs with complex acronyms. It's tax legislation gone mad.

So let's simplify things. In this section I am referring to tax-sheltered savings plans and accounts of all kinds—401(k)s, IRAs, and other plans— where *you* primarily fund the contributions and where *you* are solely responsible for the results. You should know several important things about them.

All of these different plans give you some tax advantage. You can use them to shelter your investment returns from taxes until drawdown—or, in the case of Roth accounts, forevermore once you contribute after-tax dollars. You should, therefore, use these tax-sheltered accounts to the fullest extent. They enable you to heighten the compounding of your savings. *In fact, most of your retirement savings should be lodged in tax-sheltered accounts of some kind. If you have access to such plans at your place of work, use them to the maximum!*

However, each of these different savings plans also has different drawdown or "distribution" requirements. For example, each has a time window during which you *must* draw down the proceeds or incur significant tax penalties. Be sure to read Ed Slott's *The Retirement Savings Time Bomb . . . and How to Defuse It* to properly make IRA and 401(k) drawdowns—he's the expert in the field. I also urge you to seek the guidance of a professional financial planner before withdrawing any 401(k), IRA, or other tax-sheltered money. The details are too complex to survey here, but Ed's books and a planner can help you.

Bear in mind, too, that not every American worker has access to direct-contribution or employer-related savings plans. According to the U.S. Department of Labor, *less than half* of U.S. companies now offer a 401(k) or similar plan, and *only about half*—54 percent—of all workers actually have access to one.[31]

But if access is an issue, so are participation rates and premature draw-downs. Here are several other vital facts:

- Only four out of ten American workers—43 percent—actually participate in a 401(k) or any other "direct contribution" plan at this time.[32]
- More than one out of five—21 percent—who could participate in such plans *opt not to*.[33]
- More than 90 percent of the workers who do participate in such plans do *not* contribute the maximum amount.[34]
- Approximately half of all workers draw down and spend their savings from 401(k) and similar plans prematurely when they change jobs.[35]
- Half of all 401(k) plan participants had account balances of less than $19,400 at the close of 2005, the most recent data available.[36] This included longer-term as well as newer investors. Among longer-term investors, half had less than $54,600.[37]
- The *average* 401(k) balance was higher—$58,328 for all participants and $102,014 for longer-term participants[38]—suggesting that a minority of well-off investors distort the "success statistics" often cited. And,
- Less than four in ten American workers report having an IRA.[39]

Most employees cite financial considerations as the reason they do not participate more fully or at all in such savings programs. For many, disposable income is simply not adequate. For others, the lure of consumer spending is too great or the financial burdens of paying for education, day care, medical insurance, or a house too onerous. Bottom line, these kinds of plans are *not,* after all, being universally used with much vigor. Many Americans are missing out on "the next best thing" after a traditional pension.

Here are the takeaways: A large percentage of Americans who are eligible to participate in direct contribution 401(k) or similar plans *do not*. Of those who do participate, the vast majority do not participate to the maximum. The balance in such plans is often low. Job changes often result in people cashing out these savings. *There has been, overall, numb acceptance of the "do-it-yourself" shift to funding responsibility and often mediocre results.*

In my view, defined contribution or 401(k) plans are failing for many people. IRA results are little better. These programs are not mandatory. They do not guarantee results. They are unnecessary if you are rich and not doable if you are poor. These plans will *not*, by themselves, give most Americans sufficient income in retirement unless you supplement them with other savings, conservative investments, insurance, and annuities.

SOCIAL SECURITY

Social Security is another important pillar of American retirement. It was established, we noted, in 1935 following the Great Depression. The first monthly retirement check—$22.54—was paid to Miss Ida May Fuller of Ludlow, Vermont. Miss Fuller lived to be one hundred years old and collected $22,888.92 in total Social Security benefits.[40]

Today, an estimated 162 million American workers are covered by Social Security, and nearly 54 million Americans are now receiving Social Security payments.[41] Social Security, it turns out, is *the* most important source of retirement income for a great number of Americans. The average Social Security payment for retirees in 2007 was approximately $1,048 a month.[42] Today, one out of five retired couples and four out of ten unmarried individuals derive *90 percent or more of their income* from Social Security.[43]

One common misconception—a core part of prevailing retirement myth—is that Social Security is meant to take care of us in old age. That, again, is not the case. As one expert put it, "Social Security wasn't even intended for that in the beginning. It was only to be an income supplement to your personal savings and other pensions. Under the most optimistic scenario, Social Security alone wouldn't allow you anything but genteel poverty when you could no longer earn a living."[44]

Another mistaken belief is that our "pay your own way" Social Security contributions are an investment in our own retirements. They are *not*. A team of economists who studied the system concluded that the contributions we make into Social Security are basically "transfer payments from . . . workers to nonworkers."[45] You are not paying for yourself. You are paying for the retiring beneficiaries drawing down *before* you.

That brings us to Social Security's design flaws: (1) Social Security was built with the expectation that beneficiaries would have a relatively short life span in retirement; and (2) it does not, after all, directly link the benefits that are *paid out* with the contributions that actually *come in*. Social Security has an inflow-outflow mismatch—and that is a serious defect. It means that as the surge of baby boomers nears the age to obtain benefits, Social Security will not have adequate long-term funding to pay them.

Social Security, we said, currently pays benefits to approximately 54 million American retirees, the disabled, and their dependents. That number will jump to 91.5 million in 2040.[46]

There is, consequently, an inflow-outflow mismatch of megaproportions taking shape. We can size up the problem as well by looking at the ratio of "funders" to "beneficiaries." In 1945 there were 41.9 workers paying *into* Social Security for each one beneficiary taking payments *out*.[47] There are currently 3.3 workers paying into the system for each Social Security beneficiary.[48] Within forty years, there will be only 2 workers paying in per beneficiary.[49] The ratio of funders to beneficiaries is shrinking dramatically.

You are sure to hear a great deal of debate about whether Social Security is, after all, becoming insolvent and even more ruckus about how to fix it. It suffices to note here what the Trustees of the Social Security Administration, themselves, have to say:

> Social Security's financing problems are long term and will not affect today retirees and near-retirees, but they are large and serious. People are living longer, the first baby boomers are nearing retirement, and the birth rate is low. The result is that the worker-to-beneficiary ratio has fallen . . . to 3.3-to-1 today. Within forty years it will be 2-to-1. At this ratio, there will not be enough workers to pay scheduled benefits at current tax rates.[50]

Longer life spans, the surge of an unprecedented number of baby boomers into retirement, and the dwindling number of funders relative to beneficiaries are all putting increasing strain on Social Security's coffers. The pressing question today is whether Social Security can continue paying out the same stipends. And the simple answer is that, as it is structured and funded today, Social Security *cannot*. Social Security will not have adequate funding to continue making the same payments beyond 2041 according to Social Security's own trustees, or beyond 2053 according to the Congressional Budget Office.[51]

Social Security will not be able to pay the same benefits in the future as now if it is not radically overhauled. And that's not my educated guess. It's the factual pronouncement of the people who run it.

The following question-and-answer exchange in the "Frequently Asked Questions" section of Social Security's Web site is insightful. Here's what Social Security's administrators are telling the American public:

> **Question:** I'm 26 years old. If nothing is done to change Social Security, what can I expect to receive in retirement benefits from the program?

> **Answer:** Unless changes are made, when you reach age 60 in 2040, benefits for all retirees could be cut by 26 percent and could continue to be reduced every year thereafter. If you lived to be 100 years old in 2080 (which will be more common then), your scheduled benefits could be reduced by 30 percent from today's scheduled levels.[52]

Take heed. Retirement security in the United States was once based on a much touted "three-legged stool": Social Security, pensions, and your personal savings. Today, pensions are becoming extinct, personal savings are pathetically low, and Social Security needs urgent fixing. Let me repeat: Social Security's problems are *not* likely to affect today's retirees or people close to retirement. In due course, however, the government will have to lower Social Security benefits, extend the retirement age, encourage people to work longer, impose heavier taxes, or do all of the above—there is no alternative. For all Americans, the Social Security picture is grim. It means that *you* have to take charge of funding more of your own future.

MEDICARE

If Social Security has large funding issues, Medicare has gargantuan ones. Medicare is the federal health insurance program that provides benefits to disabled workers as well as people age sixty-five and older. It is another important "pillar of American retirement." And it is beset by serious problems.

Medicare is a contributory insurance program. You are entitled to receive its benefits if you pay into the Social Security system while you are working. After you retire, you contribute to the program via taxes and premiums.

At present, Medicare consists of four parts, covering a jumbled mix of hospital, doctor, and prescription costs. There is also a program—Medicaid—for low-income families. You can visit AARP's Web site to learn what is and what is not covered by these programs. They are, simply put, a bureaucratic nightmare.

Entire books have been written on what Medicare will and will not pay. What I want to do here instead is touch on the most important facts about Medicare that impact your retirement preparations. The first is that Medicare only covers about *one-half* of a person's medical expenses.[53] You need supplemental insurance or deep pockets for the rest. And the second is that Medicare is also facing insolvency. It needs fixing, too.

We will look at ways of protecting you from the ravages of medical and health-care expense in a later chapter. Just make a mental note now that supplemental health-care insurance is important to have.

Medicare is also running out of funding. It has the same funding dilemma as Social Security—but on a significantly larger scale. In fact, Medicare's projected funding hole is estimated to be four times greater than Social Security's.[54] The magnitude is mind-boggling.

Medicare faces a long-term projected deficit of nearly $29 *trillion.*[55] The amount is so immense that it is often cited as a percentage of the country's gross domestic product. As the U.S. Department of Health and Human Services explains it, "Medicare trustees project that Medicare expenditures could rise from 2.7 percent of gross domestic product today to 9.6 percent in 2050 and reach 13.9 percent in 2080. . . . The Congressional Budget Office projects that Medicare and Medicaid combined could rise to 11.5 percent of gross domestic product in 2050. Expenditures of that magnitude today would represent more than half of the entire federal budget."[56]

So what does this mean for you? It means that health care—count on it!—is going to take a colossal bite out of your savings unless our health care system is radically overhauled. You are likely to incur increasing health-care and medical costs as you age. Medicare is designed to give only partial assistance and it is failing. You will need supplemental insurance and good savings to pay for it.

PERSONAL SAVINGS

Personal savings are, by far, the most important "pillar" of American retirement. Our country's benefit and national-insurance systems are meant to supplement—not supplant—personal savings. However, savings levels nationwide also show disturbing patterns.

Today, household and individual savings in the United States are pathetically low. Recent research of the Employee Benefit Research Institute reveals these chilling shortcomings:

Fact #1: Four out of ten American workers are currently *not* saving anything at all.[57]

Fact #2: One out of four adult workers—25 percent—have *no savings* whatsoever.[58]

Fact #3: Almost one-half—48 percent—of workers of all ages have total savings of *less than* $25,000 (excluding the value of their primary residence and any pension plan).[59]

Fact #4: More than one out of four—26 percent—of workers ages fifty-five and above have savings of *less than* $10,000 (excluding, once again, the value of their primary residence and any pension).[60]

These findings are not unlike those of past studies by the Federal Reserve Board. It found that the median level of household assets in 2004 was $172,000 *including* the value of a primary residence—and the median home value at that time was $160,000 for those who owned a home.[61] You do the math.

U.S. savings levels are dangerously low. Many Americans are not taking their "do-it-yourself" savings responsibility at all seriously. There is trouble ahead.

RETIREMENT IS IN GRAVE DANGER

Putting these facts together, the prospects for retirement in this country are not sunny and bright—at least not for about one-third of the people who are slated to retire over the next twenty years. In 1985, a full 91 percent of all full-time employees in medium and large companies in the United States participated in some kind of retirement plan—a defined benefit plan or defined contribution plan or both.[62] Today, only 51 percent do.[63] Retirement benefits are shrinking, short of adequate funding, and not universal. Participation in do-it-yourself plans is falling short. Most Americans are *not* saving enough for retirement. Our national insurance programs are in deep trouble. And many people are unaware of, indifferent to, or perhaps numbed by these facts.

Make no mistake about it. The retirements of most Americans are in grave danger.

Most Americans are likely to work until age seventy or seventy-three. Many of the country's retirement support programs will be cut. Social Security payments will have to be reduced or the taxes that fund the system increased because of the program's funding inadequacy. Health benefits may have to be cut or rationed. Many companies, government agencies, and municipalities will scale back on their "defined" pension benefit promises—in fact, it's already happening. We will see unrest and outrage, but these cutbacks are going to take place just the same. For a country that commands 59 percent of the planet's wealth, America's retirement systems and national health and social insurance programs are strictly second-class and disappointing.

All of these facts lead me to agree with the executive director of the Pension Benefit Guaranty Corporation, the government agency that guarantees many corporate pension plans:

"The broader issue we are confronting is retirement security. We have an aging population. Have we set aside enough resources to meet our future obligations and commitments? I think it is fairly clear that the answer is 'no.' Neither as a nation nor as individuals have we begun to tackle the looming fiscal and demographic challenges. . . . The retirement security mechanisms in this country—Social Security, occupational pensions, and individual savings—are inadequate to provide a secure retirement for our citizens in their elder years."[64]

This may sound negative and defeatist. But pessimism and self-defeat are not the reactions I want to provoke. Instead, I want you to squarely understand our retirement predicament and *do something* about it. I want you to take action! I want you to save more and invest differently.

America's retirement systems are in serious disarray. Fact after fact paints a pessimistic picture. But these facts should be wellsprings for *action*—not gloom, doom, or paralysis. They should jolt you into preparing for retirement differently and resolutely.

Is "retirement" a dying experiment? Not at all! Will *you* be able to retire? You bet! However, now more than ever it's up to *you* to take charge of funding and defending your future.

It's time to take saving and investing for retirement much more seriously— beginning right now! Whatever the shortcomings of the American retirement experiment, you can—after all—amass adequate capital for a comfortable retirement and financial security. But you have to save more, invest differently, and avoid speculation and losses at all costs.

ACTION STEPS

1. Visit AARP's Web site to learn more about Social Security and Medicare.
2. Read Ed Slott's book *The Retirement Savings Time Bomb . . . and How to Defuse It*. Learn the appropriate ways of drawing down your 401(k) and IRA moneys.
3. If you qualify for traditional pension or retirement benefits, ask your employer for independent certification that its pension plan is adequately funded and is projecting realistic investment returns. Download the model letter, Letter Concerning Pensions, from my Web site, www.cashrich retirement.com.
4. Locate your latest Social Security statement or request a new one. Ascertain the dates and amounts of your Social Security entitlement.

2

YOUR CORE INVESTMENT BELIEFS
ARE WRONG—*DEAD WRONG!*

N ot only are most folks indifferent to the issues confronting retirement in this country, most also have entrenched investment beliefs that are often harmful.

Let's take a look at a few of the prevailing investment myths that many U.S. investors hold dear. They may be sabotaging your retirement future.

Myth #1: "Investing in bonds is low risk and investing in government bonds is risk-free."

A bond is a kind of IOU or pledge of repayment that you get when you lend money to a company or government. Bonds have historically demonstrated less "volatility" or valuation choppiness than stocks. They are, indeed, less risky—but they are not risk-free at all.

Many investors and even bond experts misjudge bond risk. For example, most financial textbooks define U.S. Treasury bills as "risk-free." That may be a helpful analytical shortcut, but it disregards financial history.

Two credit-rating services—Moody's and Standard and Poor's—both give U.S. Treasury bills their highest triple-A rating (Aaa and AAA respectively). I highly respect the ratings of both groups and urge you to always check the Moody's and S&P ratings of any bond you consider. But the fact is that many sovereign governments have defaulted on their bonds in the past—very recently Russia (1998), Argentina (2001), and the Dominican Republic (2005), sometimes imposing large losses on their investors.[1] So, the fact that a bond is "sovereign government issue" does not guarantee that it is risk-free.

Let me be clear: I have complete confidence in U.S. Treasuries. They are excellent investments. However, *all* investments—even government bonds—have some degree of risk.

While U.S. Treasury bills are first-rate investments, the bonds of many municipalities, states, and corporations are not. Past defaults of municipal bonds have been rare—in fact, Moody's identified only forty-one instances of municipal bond defaults between 1970 and 2006 among the many thousands of bonds it analyses.[2] As we saw in the prior chapter, however, many municipalities, counties, states, and companies now have pension and retirement-benefit liabilities that are dangerously underfunded. There have already been instances of recent corporate bond defaults—such as those by Delta Airlines and Northwest Airlines in 2005—where pension liabilities contributed at least indirectly to the inability of the companies to honor their bond payments.

Going forward, the bonds of many other issuers may prove unsafe because of benefit underfunding. You should view municipal and state bonds in particular—as well as the bonds of U.S. manufacturers with large pensioned workforces—with caution.

Of course, corporate bonds with high Moody's or S&P credit ratings have historically had a low incidence of default or repayment issues. That is why it is important to always check on the ratings of any bond before you buy it. You primarily want bonds rated A and above.

At the same time, all bonds have inflation risk. If you invest $1,000 in ten-year bonds today and inflation begins to run up, the principal you get back in ten years may buy many *fewer* hamburgers or gallons of gas or TV dinners. That's "inflation risk." It's the risk that long-term investments may lose value if consumer prices in the economy climb.

My conclusion is this: Whether economists acknowledge the fact or not, *all* bonds—even government bonds—have risks. You must exercise caution with bonds as with any other investment. You must factor inflation risk into your investment thinking as well. When you invest in bonds, be sure to (1) diversify the parties you lend to; (2) avoid the bonds of corporations, states, and municipal governments whose retirement liabilities outweigh their finances; and (3) look for protection against inflation.

Myth #2: "Stocks are the best investment you can hold for the long term. Just buy and hold stocks for ten years, and you'll make a pile of money."

When you buy stock, you become a company owner. You become entitled to share its profits. And stocks have, historically, produced strong investment results. Over more than one hundred years of time, stocks have given investors an average return of about 10.1 percent per annum—substantially better than the average 4.8 percent return investors have obtained from bonds.[3] If you factor in inflation—and you should—the average return on stocks has been about 6.7 percent versus and an average 1.6 percent return for bonds.[4]

Research repeatedly shows that stocks have typically outperformed bonds, which have, in turn, typically outperformed Treasury bills over long periods. In popular mythology, however, this fact has been twisted into a belief that if you buy and hold stocks "for the long term"—for ten or twelve years—they are sure to give you positive, superior returns. As one extremely wealthy investor once told me, "As long as you count on holding 'em for a couple of years, stocks will never hurt you."

This view is misguided on several counts. Stocks do produce better returns in certain market cycles. But stock valuations depend on the overall economy, interest rates, business productivity and sales, as well as prevailing investor psychology and many other factors. At times, holding stocks can be dangerous or counterproductive. Between 1900 and 2000, for instance, stocks produced *negative* real returns (returns after inflation) in more than one-third of those hundred years.[5]

Likewise, in some ten-year and even longer periods in U.S and European financial history, holding stocks has resulted in losses. If you bought U.S. stocks in 1929, it took you twenty years to get back your original investment. And as investment author John Mauldin reminds us, "If you invested in the S&P 500 in 1966, it was sixteen years before you saw a gain, and twenty-six years before you had inflation-adjusted gains."[6]

Holding stocks "for the long term" is not always a surefire strategy for investment success. In their outstanding book, *Triumph of the Optimists: 101 Years of Global Investment Returns,* authors Dimson, Marsh, and

Staunton analyze U.S. and non-U.S. investments and make this startling observation:

"In the United States and the United Kingdom stocks have historically equaled or beaten risk free investment over holding periods of approximately twenty years or longer. We discovered that this is not the usual pattern. For equity investors to have beaten bond investors, it would often have been necessary to have an investment time horizon of forty years or more."[7]

It is misguided to believe that holding stocks for a decade is going to give you sure-thing, positive returns. You *could,* indeed, find yourself holding a bundle of depreciating stocks. There are periods when bonds outperform stocks, and there are periods when stocks produce losses.

I'm a strong believer in equities—provided you invest in them nonspeculatively and avoid overpriced markets. Stocks should usually represent a large part of your retirement portfolio, but stocks have substantial price volatility and risks. That's why it is wise to diversify your investments between bonds, real estate, and cash deposits as well as equities—and in ways very different, as we will see, than the top-heavy exposure in stocks that most folks have in their 401(k) plans today.

There are also periods when stocks are overpriced, speculatively risky, and dangerous—when you should hightail it out of the market! Investors learned that the hard way in 2000–2002, when the stock market corrected hard, causing investors to lose a whopping $7.4 trillion in stock value.[8] I will show that some *kinds* of stock—those that pay you real income—perform better with less propensity to sustain losses in down markets. I will also show you how to recognize the symptoms of a speculatively overvalued market and when you should cut back your stock holdings.

The important takeaway for now is this: Holding a lump of coal for ten years isn't going to turn it into a diamond. You need to invest in stocks mindful of their risks, true income potential, and propensity to periodically burn off price excesses.

Myth #3: "Real estate investments never lose. Real estate values are rock solid and keep climbing. So make your home your number one retirement investment and invest big-time in real estate."

Real estate holdings can be excellent investments—but *not* because "prices always go up." That is a fallacious view. Also, counting on windfall income from your home may prove to be wishful thinking.

Since 1998, U.S. real estate prices have surged. Investors are flocking into real estate investment trusts, or REITs. Television programs are encouraging the public to buy homes and "flip" them. Also, many families are spending their savings to remodel their kitchens and bathrooms so as to upgrade their houses for eventual windfall profits.

Sadly, most investors flat-out ignore the truth about real estate returns. In his excellent book *Irrational Exuberance,* Yale professor Robert J. Shiller shows that home prices increased by only 3.4 percent on average per annum from 1890 to 2007.[9] *That's right, only 3.4 percent (or 1.6 percent in real terms if you correct for inflation), including the recent spike!* There have, in fact, been only two periods when home prices increased by high percentages: immediately after World War II and the current era.[10]

We will explore the facts and learn more about Dr. Shiller's findings in chapter 11. For the time being I simply want to squash the "real estate always soars" myth. As Dr. Shiller explains:

"Why . . . do so many people have the impression that home prices have done so well? People remember the prior purchase price of a home from long ago and are surprised at the difference between then and now. In closing out the estate of an elderly person, one may be surprised to see that he purchased a house in 1948 for $16,000 and that the estate sold the house in 2004 for $190,000. The appearance is that the investment in the house did extremely well. But the consumer price index rose eightfold between 1948 and 2004, so the real increase in value was only 48 percent, or less than 1 percent a year."[11]

Take it from the recognized authority on "bubble" markets and U.S. real estate: "The notion that home prices always go up," Dr. Shiller tell us, "is very strong, and very wrong."[12]

Myth #4: "The object of successful investing is to buy 'low' and sell 'high' for capital gains. When it comes to stocks, forget dividends—they're paltry and don't add much to the gains you're looking for."

American investors are hooked on capital gains! Some broadcasting channels continually run ticker tapes showing the latest stock price fluctuations. When stock or real estate prices go up, most investors scramble to get in on the price swell. There are now umpteen television programs teaching us how to "Flip that house!" or make a killing by flipping stocks.

Most folks embrace this "get rich quick" philosophy and quest for windfall gains. Regrettably, many only jump on the bandwagon when prices are *already* sky-high. More often than not, they buy *high* and sell *low*.

Let's be clear: there's a lot more to prudent investing than flipping stocks or real estate for capital gains. In this book, I will show you that focusing on "gains" alone is not a success-prone way of investing your retirement capital. So let's begin setting the foundation right here.

Take stocks. When you invest in stocks, you are investing in a company's brand name, product line, management talents, and its ability to generate profit. *You are fundamentally buying an income stream.* You are *not* buying a lottery ticket that may or may not give you some windfall return. You're buying corporate earnings—or at least you should be.

Even so, most investors continually ignore the importance of earnings. When stock prices hyperinflated in the late 1990s, many investors pumped money into the stocks of technology companies that had never earned a red cent! Those buyers expected windfall returns. Instead they got a nasty market correction.

There are several ways of making money from stock investments— and "flipping" for "gains" is undoubtedly the most precarious. However, you can (1) acquire stock expressly to sell it for more than you bought it (that's the speculative approach frequently at play today); (2) earn real dividend income that you can reinvest; or (3) do both of the above together.

In chapters 4 and 5 we are going to talk about dividends in more detail. What I want to do here is debunk the "capital gains matter most" and "dividends don't matter at all" bunkum. So let's cut to the quick. Here are the views of some of the country's foremost investment authorities about dividends and gains:

"From 1801 to 2001, $100 would have grown to $700 million if you assumed all dividends reinvested. . . . If you take out dividends, however, you find that your $100 is worth only $2,099. . . . Conventional wisdom, which says equities get most of their value from capital appreciation, is false; it is based on recent experience and a bubble mentality."

John Mauldin, *Bull's Eye Investing:*
Targeting Real Returns in a Smoke and Mirrors Market[13]

"Do dividends matter? You bet. Unless corporate managers can provide sharply higher real growth in earnings, dividends are the main source of the real return we expect from stocks."

Robert D. Arnott, "Dividends and the Three Dwarfs"[14]

"If you had a hypothetical investment of $10,000 in S&P 500 stocks in 1984, it would have been worth $62,465 without dividends twenty years later. However, if you had reinvested the dividends paid on those five hundred stocks, the total would have jumped to $118,823, according to data from Ibbotson Associates."

American Century Investments,
"Dividend-Paying Investments Can Provide Benefits"[15]

"Dividend yields and earnings growth are the two fundamental factors that drive long-term returns in the stock market, and that's the beginning of wisdom."

John C. Bogle, founder, Vanguard Group[16]

I'd like these views to percolate into your thinking. Investing for income—for dividends in the case of stocks—*does* matter. It matters a lot. Whenever you hear anyone say that income is not important, don't be duped! Real income from an investment is *always* important. Earnings fundamentals *always* count. And dividends should *always* be the important component of the value you look for when you consider stock investments—you can reinvest them and make your nest egg grow!

We will convert these ideas into practical application in the next chapters. At this juncture, I want you to begin to question some of the "investment principles" that have guided you so far. Are you beginning to see flaws in the belief that "you can never go wrong investing in real estate" or that "dividends are too puny to matter"? I hope so. Because many of the "sound principles" that American investors espouse today are anything but sound. They're dangerous. They are not sound bases for building a sturdy retirement nest egg.

It's time to sober up and invest differently. It's time to get back to income fundamentals. It's very much time to invest your retirement savings *with the aim of achieving real returns that you can reinvest*—dividend *income,* interest *income,* and rent *income.*

I am going to explain a new approach to investing in the next chapters. But in addition to being clearheaded about our country's broken retirement systems, I want you to be clearheaded about prudent ways to invest. I want you to forget about chasing "gains" and focus on income. In fact, I want you to develop an income *fixation*. That is the first step in sharpening your investment skills and sheltering your savings from the turbulence ahead.

ACTION PLAN

1. Take a look at your most recent investment statements. Roughly what percent of your stock or equity-fund investments are invested in dividend-paying stocks?
2. Are you holding a large amount of municipal or state government bonds at this time? Do you know whether the issuers have pension liabilities that are significantly underfunded?
3. Take a look at last year's tax declaration. How much did you achieve in "dividends"? How much in capital gains?
4. Read the latest edition of Dr. Robert J. Shiller's *Irrational Exuberance*. Use it as a fact base along with this book for your investing efforts going forward.

3

THE COMING
DEMOGRAPHIC STORM

In addition to failing benefit systems and misguided investment beliefs, a serious storm front is also gathering momentum: U.S. demographics. Demographics have had a mighty impact on this country's consumer activity and investments. That impact is going to intensify acutely over the next twenty-five years. Here's the good news and the bad.

CHANGING DEMOGRAPHICS

The good news is—we're living longer! We owe great thanks to the doctors, nurses, scientists, food producers, pharmaceutical companies, clergymen, counselors, and significant others in our lives who are helping to extend our life spans.

We saw that the average life span in colonial America was about thirty-five years of age. It reached sixty-one and a half by the time Social Security was inaugurated. Today we're living much longer. A woman age thirty-five today who reaches the age of sixty-five has a 47 percent probability of living *at least* until the age of ninety.[1]

Longer life spans are causing American corporations great expense, making it much more costly for companies to fund retirement benefits.

Hence, pensions and benefits are being reduced or dismantled. In our new do-it-yourself approach to retirement funding, longer life spans mean that *you* have to amass a lot more capital for your "golden years."

So the good news is that we're living longer. The bad news is that longer life spans are severely straining our pension systems and funding abilities. *You* have to salt away more savings for a longer span of retirement time. *You* have to pay more yourself for health insurance and health care as life spans extend, medical costs escalate, and company benefits wither.

The bad news—the very bad news—is also demographic. An unprecedented wave of Americans is about to move into retirement and will soon pose a serious threat to the country's asset values and investment markets—and there is no way of stopping it.

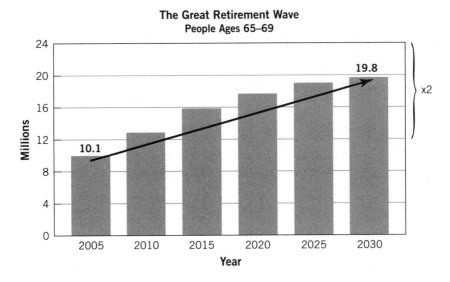

The Great Retirement Wave
People Ages 65–69

In the United States, an extraordinary surge of people—known as baby boomers—became economically active and financially powerful following World War II. A baby boomer is a person born between 1946 and 1964. There are 78.2 million of them.[2] More than one out of four Americans are boomers today, and they constitute a *megawave* of people moving closer and closer to retirement.

According to the U.S. Census Bureau, nearly 8,000 boomers began turning age sixty each day in 2006—330 every hour.[3] The number moving into ages sixty-five to sixty-nine (see above) will escalate mightily year by year. By the year 2030, just that subset of retirement-eligible people will be almost double what it is today. By 2030, one out of five Americans will be sixty-five or older, and 78 million baby boomers will be looking in earnest for retirement income.

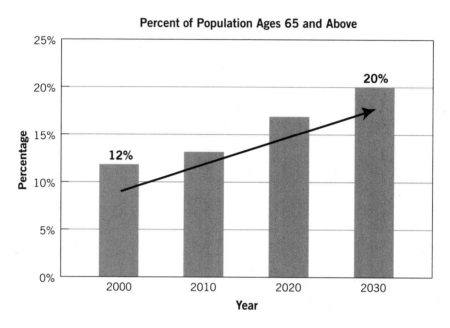

Percent of Population Ages 65 and Above

The Great Retirement Wave is not hypothetical or subject to debate. It will actually begin in 2008 when the first boomers qualify for reduced Social Security benefits at age sixty-two. Similar aging and mass migrations into retirement will also take place among the populations of other developed countries, such as Japan and the countries of Western Europe.

In the United States, this great movement of people into retirement may seriously strain our economy and retirement mechanisms. We saw, for example, that there will only be 2.1 workers funding Social Security for each Social Security beneficiary in 2031 by the time all the baby boomers pass age sixty-five. Boomer benefit claimants will bring Social Security to its knees unless that system is overhauled.

The bad news, too, is that many of our conventional ideas about investing and financial planning are completely blind to this retirement surge. The boomer retirement impact on the U.S. economy and on investments is going to be blockbuster. However, conventional wisdom tells us that "standard operating procedures"—such as moving out of stocks as you age— will work just fine *all the time* in every market cycle. That, we will see, may not hold true as more and more boomers retire.

THE BOOMER IMPACT THUS FAR

Boomers have already had an enormous impact on the U.S. economy and investment markets. For example, U.S. baby-food sales jumped 450 percent between 1941 and 1947.[4] By the mid-1980s, boomers were earning half of all personal income in the country.[5] And as investment expert Bill Gross noted about the boomer group:

"Their voracious hunger for consumer goods and the high life has propelled our economy forward, indeed kept it afloat. Where would we or the world have been without them. They bought homes, then second homes. They bought two cars, then added a four-wheeler off-roader. . . . They bought big screens, then flat screens, and now with the advent of cellular technology—mini screens."[6]

As they aged, boomers became our economy's prime movers, causing retail sales to skyrocket. They had a colossal impact on the U.S. stock and real estate markets as well. We can see that impact graphically.

For example, the chart on page 40 illustrates the historic movement of the Dow Jones Industrial Average, a widely used indicator of the U.S. stock market and a price-weighted average of some of the country's actively traded "blue-chip" stocks. I have added a dotted line at 1981—that's the year when boomers first began turning thirty-five and moving into "peak investing" years. Throughout this book, I use the term *peak investing years* or *peak spending years* to refer to the thirty-five-to-fifty-four age bracket. You might choose to add or subtract a few years to or from my definition, but the basic premise is nevertheless this: people in that age tier have tended to spend more and invest more than other age cohorts. As you can see in the above chart, the Dow Jones Index grew with a substantially more forceful upward thrust as boomers became active in the stock market.

Note that boomers ushered in an *unprecedented* era of higher stock valuations. It was not any minor "bump-up." It was not a onetime spike. It was a mammoth and extraordinary surge that changed stock valuations mightily over many years' time.

Boomers also sent shock waves through the real estate markets, hugely elevating home valuations. The graph on page 41 is from Yale University's Dr. Robert Shiller depicting home prices since before the turn of the century. In the latest edition of his book *Irrational Exuberance,* Dr. Shiller analyses real

Dow Jones Index Since 1930

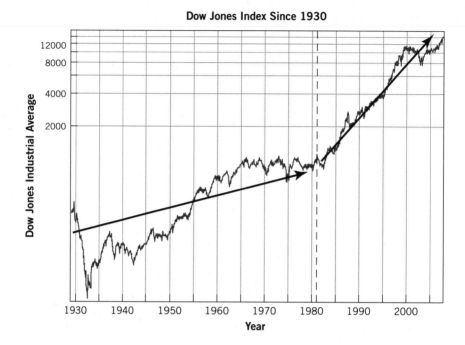

estate prices and explains the characteristics of speculative "bubbles." It's well worth reading.

If we add the "boomer entry" time line, we see that home prices also went north in a decidedly different and powerful way once boomers became economically active. (See chart on page 41.) *Once again, this is* not *"business as usual."* It is the result of an unprecedented surge of people looking for homes and "quick flip" investment opportunities as never before.

To be sure, a number of factors *other than* demographics contributed to these market shifts as well: (1) interest rates; (2) industrial production; (3) dividends; (4) tax policy; (5) corporate compensation practices and the proliferation of stock options, (6) the advent of 401(k) plans; and (7) the attractive returns of stocks and real estate, which, in turn, attracted more and more suitors.

Even so, most economists would agree that as the great wave of baby boomers moved into peak income and spending years, it has had an extraordinary impact.

Boomers have so far had a resounding impact on consumer spending, investing, and asset prices. They have been a powerful locomotive, con-

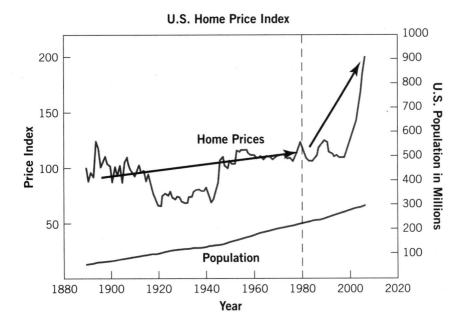

U.S. Home Price Index

tributing to strong economic growth and substantially higher investment valuations.

That, of course, brings us to the million-dollar question: What is going to happen when this same mass of people enters retirement and begins selling off assets to raise cash? How will mass boomer retirements impact asset values?

FUTURE SHOCK

Baby boomers control immense wealth in the United States. Boomers now own approximately $7.6 trillion of stocks, bonds, mutual funds, and other financial accounts and instruments.[7] They own an estimated one-third of all U.S. stocks and approximately 11 percent of all bonds outstanding in the U.S. market.[8] Pension plans own about 21 percent of all U.S. stocks—and they, in turn, are holding a large amount of these assets on behalf of boomer beneficiaries.[9]

Nearly eight in ten boomers own their own home—a number higher than the national average—and one in four boomers owns more than one property.[10] In fact, boomers own 57 percent of all vacation homes and 58 percent of all rental properties in the United States.[11] The numbers are stunning.

Whether we look at stocks, bonds, or real estate, then, boomer wealth is formidable. So when boomers begin to sell off assets or change their investment holdings as they move into retirement, will they rock the markets "on their way out" just as they did "on the way in"?

The coming boomer retirement wave poses several possible threats: (1) the threat of a slower economy if large-scale aging results in reduced consumer activity; (2) the threat of significant investment disruptions as boomers begin their gradual migration from stocks to bonds and cash; and (3) the threat of buckling asset prices because there will be a proportionately larger "investment sell-off" population when boomers attempt to convert investments to cash.

This is important. So let's take a moment to look at each of these issues.

On one hand, senior citizens have different consumer priorities. As we age, we will begin shifting our spending from cars, clothes, kitchen updates, and electronic ware to medical treatment, health insurance, smaller fuel-efficient homes, and perhaps more leisure-related activities. Just ask yourself, how many more television sets, SUVs, and iPods are you likely to buy when you reach age seventy-five? How much more jewelry? How many more paintings and silk scarves and Armani suits? (Okay, you can never have too many Armani outfits.) I believe that consumer spending will not necessarily *decline* as the American population ages, but it will *substantially change*. The aging of millions of Americans portends a *plateauing* of consumer spending for many goods and services such as flat-screen TVs and electronic gear and an *increase* of spending for other kinds of goods and services such as medicines, nursing care, and so on.

Meanwhile, most investment experts are preaching the same investment advice as though none of these changes were about to happen! They continue to tell us to invest heavily in stocks when we're young, then switch to bonds and deposits when we near retirement. Not surprisingly, Americans are heeding the advice. They are investing heavily in "target date funds," for example—funds that decrease stock holdings and increase bond holdings as people near a target retirement date.

The new financial products attracting public attention, however, are not addressing today's pressing questions: What kinds of investments are likely to perform successfully during the play-out of the boomer retirement wave? Will conventional investment advice work satisfactorily in the future? Does, after all, conventional wisdom take demographics into account?

News flash: Over the next two decades, 78 million boomers will try to exit from substantial stock and real estate positions to move more of their wealth into bonds, deposits, and cash. Many pension funds will do the same. Hence, a great amount of money is going to be coming out of the stock and real estate markets and moving into bonds and deposits. The migration will be unparalleled. The "boomer migration" could be monumentally disruptive. Stock, bond, and real estate prices *could* take a tumble. Will they?

WHAT EXPERTS SAY

A number of experts believe that these demographic risks are genuine and—yes—cause for concern. Here is a sampling.

"Demographics is the factor that has me the most worried. Here we're looking at a situation in which ten to twenty years from now we'll have more people than ever before selling assets to fund their retirement needs to a proportionally smaller population as a fraction of the economy than ever before. That's not good for asset values."

Dr. Robert Arnott, fundamental index expert[12]

"The boomer generation will demand goods and services, and because there are not enough workers . . . workers will demand more of the saved assets of retirees for what they produce. *This can come as increased prices for the production, as a drop in the value of saved assets, or both. That means either an inflation in prices or a deflation in wealth or a combination of the two.*"

John Mauldin, *Bull's Eye Investing: Targeting Real Returns in a Smoke and Mirrors Market"*[13]

"There are 80 million baby boomers who own trillions of dollars in stocks and bonds that in the next several decades will have to be sold in order to fund their retirement. . . . An overabundance of sellers could spell disaster for investors." "[But] the pessimists, who proclaim that the retiring baby boomers will bankrupt Social Security, upend our private pension systems, and crash the financial markets, are wrong."

Dr. Jeremy Siegel, The Future for Investors[14]

"To think that all the boomers have to do is sell their homes to pay for retirement and healthcare begs the legitimate question 'to whom and at what price?' If there are fewer X'ers and Y'ers to unload even their second homes to, rudimentary supply/demand curve analysis suggests prices must adjust downward to facilitate the transfer. . . . Similar logic applies to holdings of domestic stocks, bonds, or any other 'asset' which . . . must be unloaded to a smaller demographic of tentative buyers. It will be next to impossible to borrow or sell our way out of this one."

Bill Gross, investment and bond authority[15]

"When they reach retirement age and the time comes to sell off their mutual funds, where will all these boomers find enough willing buyers? At home, among the smaller and economically troubled Generation X following behind them? Overseas, in developed economies where younger households will be even scarcer? Or, in the emerging market and developing economies, like China and India—which will themselves be aging rapidly in the 2030s and which will in any case remain much poorer than America for several decades? Some financial analysts go so far as to predict that a 'great depreciation' in financial assets is likely to accompany the boomer retirement."

Peter G. Peterson, Chairman of the Blackstone Group[16]

Each of these commentators explains his views in books and online articles that are well worth reading. Collectively, they paint a mixed picture.

Professor Jeremy Siegel sees potential danger ahead with—"in the worst case scenario"—stocks and other assets plunging by as much as 50 percent.[17] However, Dr. Siegel is decidedly optimistic about the future. He does *not* believe any asset cave-in will take place. In his view and that of many other experts, investors from developing countries will help pick up the investments that boomers sell off. A number of countries, Dr. Siegel tells us, are likely to enjoy powerful economic growth. In turn, their growth and wealth formation will create a new cadre of international investors who will be eager to invest internationally. In the professor's words:

"As more and more of the doomsayers intone the coming economic and financial crises, remember the global solution: the young in the developing world will be the ones producing the goods and buying the retirees' assets. The economic success of these countries is not only good for these people but essential to the continued prosperity of our society."[18]

Dr. Siegel is right. While we experience "the graying of America," other countries will have many millions of people moving into peak investment and consumer-spending years. For example, between 2005 and 2025, the United States will add only thirty-two thousand—let me repeat, *only thirty-two thousand*—"peak investors/consumers" ages thirty-five to fifty-four.[19] By comparison, India will add 123 million. China will add 34 million. And Brazil and Indonesia will add 18 million and 22 million "peak consumers/investors" respectively over the same period.[20] The demographic changes that are taking place offshore are also remarkable.

Expectedly, the economic foment in many developing countries is going to be red-hot. There should, indeed, be huge demand in many countries for housing, transportation, energy, food supplies, basic materials, and natural resources.

So, many economists agree with Dr. Siegel that the likelihood of great economic growth in a number of developing countries will translate into larger global demand for U.S. assets. There is no need to fear U.S. boomer retirements, they tell us.

Here, then, is the conclusion that the U.S. Government Accountability Office drew in its report to Congress: "Retiring boomers are not likely to sell financial assets in such a way as to cause a sharp or sudden decline in financial asset prices."[21] Instead, the GAO says a number of factors are likely to defuse the impact of boomer retirements. Those factors, among others, include (1) the concentration of U.S. wealth in the hands of the top 10 percent of ultrawealthy Americans, who are unlikely to sell off assets when they retire; (2) the belief that—"as with prior generations"—boomers are only likely to liquidate their assets in slow, gradual doses; (3) the long, eighteen- or nineteen-year span during which boomers will enter retirement in staggered numbers—*if they retire at all*; and (4) the expectation we have already noted of rising demand for U.S. financial assets from developing countries.

So which is it? A crash? Foreign investors to the rescue? Or no real upheaval or sell-off at all?

AGING TRENDS MAY *NOT* PLAY OUT CALMLY

I am not a sensationalist, but I believe in the power of demographics. I also believe that aging trends in this country may *not* play out calmly.

We are, I believe, likely to experience a great deal of investment turmoil, for several reasons. One, a radical shift is about to take place in the number of U.S. "sellers" relative to "buyers." We're talking primal supply and demand. It will *necessarily* impact asset prices. Two, boomer sales of residential real estate will, in particular, cause home prices and "retirement wealth" to contract. Three, we cannot count on *gradual* asset sales "as with past generations." Four, even if boomer sales of stocks might be limited in volume and spread out over time, asset sales by pension funds, target date funds, *as well as* individual boomers will surely have a dampening effect. And five, it is not clear what magnitude of capital inflows we can expect from foreign investors wanting U.S. assets. The "global solution" may not, after all, pan out.

Let us briefly examine each of these views.

The fundamental issue we confront on the investment front is this: as millions of boomers try to liquidate their stock and real estate holdings, who is going to buy them?

Here are the facts. In the year 2000, there were 8.5 Americans ages thirty-five to fifty-four ("prime buyers" in their peak spending and investing years) for each one person sixty-five to sixty-nine (or "prime seller," who might try to sell down some of her or his investments for retirement income).[22] *Eight to one.*

By 2025, there will only be 4.4 prime-age "buyers" age thirty-five to fifty-four for each one prime retirement "seller" age sixty-five to sixty-nine.[23] *Four to one.* The ratio of prime buyers relative to prime sellers will drop markedly. There will, relatively speaking, be many more sellers. There will be, necessarily, a disruption of supply and demand. The shift will, unavoidably, impact asset prices.

Boomers are likely to trigger real estate upset in particular. Boomers have a high concentration of their wealth in real estate—specifically in the valuations of their own homes. Many must count on home equity for retirement income since their other savings are often paltry or nonexistent. Among yet-to-retire Americans ages fifty-five and over polled by *The Wall Street Journal,* for example, 20 percent said equity in their home will be a "primary source of income during retirement."[24]

I believe that many boomers will attempt to sell off real estate because of poor savings, the need for cash, and the likelihood of higher property taxes as states and municipalities scramble to offset Medicaid costs and their own pension underfunding. There also is evidence that many boomers have *already* bought second homes with the expectation of realizing retirement income from them or moving into them one day.[25]

Like Bill Gross, however, a number of economists are beginning to voice concern about the belief that home equity is the "quick fix" that will make up for lackluster savings. As one economic paper noted:

"Some have suggested that housing is [a] good way to finance retirement, particularly for Boomers who have benefited from widespread appreciation of home equity. Yet macroeconomic and monetary policymakers should be concerned with this reliance on housing values to finance retirement, since a sharp interest rate rise could induce a "hard landing" in housing values, and many Boomer households could then experience substantial wealth losses."[26]

Rising interest rates could, indeed, cause home values to buckle and harm boomer wealth, but interest rates are only one possible trigger. Higher property taxes and higher fuel costs might also impact home values, and property values will certainly decline if many more people attempt to *sell* homes than there are people around to *buy* them. This, I believe, is the foremost issue. There is fundamentally going to be less "take-out" demand relative to the number of boomers selling real estate. Many people may be counting on "homestead income" that may not, after all, materialize as planned.

Other analysts draw comfort from past history as regards "asset liquidation." Prior generations, they say, only sold off assets gradually when they retired. We don't have to worry about any "concentrated" asset sell-off or "meltdown" in their view.

I do not wholly agree with them. Past retirees could liquidate assets leisurely since many of them could count on traditional pension checks and company health-care benefits in retirement. Increasingly, those benefits are evaporating, and medical costs are climbing higher and higher. So the last boomers to retire in the years ahead will have substantially *less* pension income and fewer corporate health-care benefits— if any! With the dismantling of the corporate benefit system, don't count on the financial behavior of future retirees being at all like that of retirees past!

Then there is the argument that 10 percent of Americans control 90 percent of the country's wealth, so there is unlikely to be any "meaningful asset sell-off." That is an intriguing view. And it is partially true. We have already noted that boomers own about one-third of all U.S. stocks and 11 percent of U.S. bonds—but only 10 percent of all boomers own more than two-thirds of that generation's overall financial assets.[27] In other words, wealth is indeed concentrated in the hands of a few people, and those few may not, in fact, need to sell off assets for retirement.

However, *pension funds* will be stepping up their sales of stocks whether ultrawealthy individuals sell or not. Many boomers and companies will reduce stock holdings to buy bonds or build cash. And those who attempt to sell may *not,* after all, find adequate *domestic* market demand to "take them out" at today's prices.

Sorry, but wealth concentration does not make us immune to the laws of supply and demand. Whether or not America's most wealthy sold off stocks and contributed to the market correction of 1999–2001, the stock market nevertheless took a hard tumble.

That leaves us with the deus ex machina of offshore investors coming to the rescue. Dr. Siegel and others believe foreign investors will "pick up the slack" when boomers sell financial assets. The good news is that robust growth offshore is, indeed, likely.

Great economic growth is likely to take place in other countries because of their own demographic characteristics. We saw that other countries will be adding many millions of "prime consumers" or "prime investors" between now and 2025. They will have their own boom times, and their demand for energy, building materials, food stuffs, transportation, and consumer goods will represent investment and income opportunities for us all.

Unlike Dr. Siegel, however, I am not persuaded that "new capitalists" offshore will necessarily offset *all* of the contraction of our own investment markets. Here's why.

The countries demographically prone to exceptional growth are still extremely poor. Chartered accountants in India earn $487 on average a month and $770 on average a month in China.[28] Even well-paid professionals in those countries will not be able to afford large amounts of U.S. stocks anytime soon.

Today, Indian and Chinese nationals can already buy U.S. stocks, but most active workers in those countries are more likely to *first* use any extra capital or savings they amass to buy a bicycle instead of foreign equities.

Many foreign governments, treasury ministries, and overseas provident funds do buy U.S. securities—immense blocks of them. However, it is not clear that the population growth being projected offshore will necessarily stimulate more foreign government or institutional demand for U.S. financial assets.

As these countries gain economic power, *local* investments are likely to be more attractive, too. New Brazilian investors are sure to buy shares of their country's Vale do Rio Doce before they buy shares of Coca-Cola.

In my view, there is not an immediate investment culture in most developing countries to induce their own boomer populations to want U.S. investments anytime soon. There *will* be foreign demand for U.S. financial assets—but that demand will take time to build. Also, the prospect of large numbers of Brazilians, Chinese, or Indian nationals buying up U.S. residential properties is pure fiction. Foreigners are unlikely to prop up this country's residential real estate values when boomers begin raising cash.

Like Professor Siegel, I am confident that the prosperity currently building in other countries with "younger" demographics will create demand for U.S. investments. Nevertheless I believe we will experience investment commotion in the United States. It is not at all clear what amount of incremental foreign investments in U.S. assets will materialize over the next twenty years. Hopefully, large amounts—but don't stake your future on it.

Where does that leave us? Given no more than the *possibility* that mass boomer retirements might have some adverse financial impact, only one course of action is prudent and sane as regards our retirement savings. We must err on the side of caution. We must invest defensively, and we should also look at any sell-off or downward pressure on asset prices as a good opportunity to buy. Keep your powder dry!

BOOMER IMPACT IS ALREADY TAKING PLACE

Will massive boomer retirements impact U.S. investment markets? You bet! In fact, the process has already started.

Housing prices have escalated the sharpest over the last five years in California, Florida, Hawaii, Arizona, and the Northeast—in part because

boomers are beginning to lock into "retirement" and "investment" properties in those locations for their golden years.

The price surges we have seen in real estate have perhaps been one part
boomer, one part dissatisfaction with stock and bond returns after the
1999–2000 stock correction, and three parts speculation. But make no
mistake about it. We are already beginning to feel "boomer shock" right
now, and the effect is going to intensify. As index expert Rob Arnott recently noted:

"I would argue that the impact of demographics is *now* [his italics] and
that the breaking of the [1999–2000 stock market] bubble and the ensuing
bear market were the first lurch into a demographic-driven future. The immense bull market for 1975 to 1999—which turned every dollar invested
in stocks into $50—was also, most likely, largely demographics-driven. . . .
We baby boomers didn't produce enough kids to take care of us in our old
age; with fewer kids to support, we had more disposable income during
our peak earning years than any generation in history, and enough of that
made its way into the capital markets to fuel the biggest bull market in history."[29]

So boomers have already impacted the investment markets resoundingly. As they prepare to sell investment holdings, their "sell-off" impact is
likely to be every bit as strong.

THE SUPREME FALLACY

Demographics suggest that we could be headed for investment turbulence
and benefit withdrawal. Even so, we continue to trade stocks, comment on
mutual funds, buy and sell real estate, and discuss investments in general as
if there were no such threat at all. I call this the Supreme Fallacy.

*The Supreme Fallacy is the cataclysmic belief that we can invest over the
next thirty years just as we've done in times past without taking demographics
into account.*

It is the belief that you should primarily hold stocks and build capital
gains, then gradually move into bonds as you near retirement *without* considering demographics. It is the belief that you can buy real estate and
forevermore watch property values soar. Those tactics and beliefs worked
once upon a time. But they are doomed to colossal failure when 78 million

Americans—the surge of boomers who will begin to retire in 2008–30—move out of equities and real estate in a "let me get out the door first" frenzy.

Many investment professionals use sophisticated computer programs to find investment patterns and recommend allocations based on historic performance data. They see "clear sailing ahead." Of course, their beliefs are based on performance data that include the extraordinary surges caused by boomers in the investment and housing markets. The future will not be the same!

The belief that "it's clear sailing ahead" is foolhardy—even if boomer retirements only commence in staggered doses over eighteen to twenty years. In fact, I believe that traditional investment practices—and specifically the call to reduce stock ownership as you near retirement—are going to provoke great pain for many people for three reasons:

If, first of all, boomers heed prevailing advice and move more of their wealth from stocks into "more conservative" investments as they age, their investment migrations will pitch stock, bond, and real estate prices into disarray. There will be too many sellers relative to buyers. Stock and real estate prices will come down. Even those few wealthy Americans who control the country's assets aren't going to idly sit by holding on to investments for which there is less demand and price buoyancy. The sheer number of retiring boomers relative to the country's still-working population will cause upset—for Social Security, Medicare, *as well as* the investment markets.

Second, the "sell stock, buy bonds" strategy casts participants into less powerful income momentum as they age. If you're a boomer and heed conventional wisdom, you'll be migrating from stocks to bonds—from higher-risk, *higher-reward* investments to lower-risk, *lower-reward* investments. How, indeed, will *less stock* in your portfolio satisfy your need for strong streams of income over a possibly long retirement? In fact, most of us need to *maintain*—not dismantle!—prudent stock positions later in life for retirement income. Of course, we likewise need to avoid speculation, asset concentration, and hypervalued "bubbles" as well.

Third, the "sell stocks as you age" dictum completely disregards income fundamentals. It completely disregards the *kinds* of income and the *kinds* of risk that stocks, real estate, and bonds entail whether you are close to retirement or not. Conventional wisdom tells us to stay out of risky, higher-volatility investments when we have less time to recoup possible losses. *I would argue that you should always avoid risky investments with your retirement money—not just when you near or pass age sixty-five.* Selling off stocks as you age is not, by itself, an effective "loss aversion" strategy.

Many millions of Americans are about to march out of stock and real estate investments in a great wave. Will conventional investment advice still give us satisfactory guidance? Don't count on it! It's time to be even more prudent and much more cautious with your savings!

YOU MUST FACTOR DEMOGRAPHICS INTO YOUR PLANS

To quote one investment group, here in a nutshell is where we stand: *"The largest generation in American history is beginning the shift from asset accumulation to income distribution."*[30] You simply cannot ignore this epic shift and the demographics underlying it.

Of course, you may not agree that some turmoil in the investment markets is inevitable. Give the matter some thought. Read over Dr. Siegel's book. Read Dr. Shiller's. After that, perhaps we can at least agree that the coming boomer retirement surge *could*—I repeat, *could*—cause U.S. asset prices to weaken. That *possibility*, if nothing more, must figure into your retirement planning.

This much is clear: Great changes in real estate, stock, and bond ownership are going to take place for sure. A great lunge for cash is going to take place. The "sell" surge will be huge. "Buy" demand may be problematic. *Whatever the final impact, you must brace yourself for the possibility of a coming storm.* No, the sky isn't falling! However, prudence and new investment priorities will be increasingly important. The way people invested successfully in the past will not make for successful investing in the future. It's time for a fresh, risk-adverse, demographically savvy investment strategy going forward.

Unfortunately, few advisors or investment publications are telling investors what to do. Don't worry! In the next chapters I show you how you can capitalize on changing demographics. And I also show you how you can invest your savings with less risk and achieve better returns.

Right now, I simply want you to be mindful of the demographic storm setting in. I want you to appreciate the need for calibrating your investments to contemporary demographics. Some investments—in health care, energy, retirement housing, multinational corporations, and in countries where large numbers of people will be entering their peak investment years—are going to flourish. Others will not. *You* are going to capitalize on—rather than be punished by—contemporary demographics. Let's find out how.

ACTION STEPS

1. Make a list of all of your savings and investments. What percent is now invested in stocks or equity funds? What percent is invested in international or non-U.S holdings? Keep those papers handy.

2. Are you counting on "downsizing" income from your primary residence? If so, pay close attention to chapter 11.

3. Read Jeremy Siegel's book *The Future for Investors*.

4. Read Robert Shiller's book *Irrational Exuberance*. Look specifically for the last edition of that book containing Dr. Shiller's latest real estate commentary.

PART II

SIX STEPS TO BULLETPROOF YOUR RETIREMENT

$\mathcal{S}$o far we have seen that "retirement" is a modern concept that is under escalating attack. It is a social and economic experiment beset by do-it-yourself funding risks. A demographic tsunami is coming. Conventional investment beliefs are often wrong. Investments are all too often speculative. Savings are grossly inadequate, and many of our retirement-benefit systems are collapsing or in massive disarray.

What does all of this mean? It means it's time for *you* to take defensive action!

Wake up! Get the adrenaline pumping! *Your retirement is in grave danger!* You need to register—in a primal, gut way—a won't-go-away need to save much more, to invest less speculatively, and to become emphatically more proactive about building and protecting your retirement capital.

Can you do it? You bet! I am highly confident in your ability to make provisions for a sound future, but it's going to require a radical overhaul of your investment practices and beliefs. It's going to require saving and investing for retirement in completely different ways so that you defuse the challenges and threats ahead.

Five formidable kinds of risk threaten your retirement:

Accumulation Risk: The risk of not saving enough—of not amassing adequate capital to meet your long-term needs.

Market Risk: The risk of possible investment turbulence and capital loss—particularly in speculative markets.

Demographic Risk: The risk your retirement capital may sustain harm due to the impact on asset values of sharp population changes.

Longevity Risk: The risk of outliving your savings.

Inflation Risk: The likelihood of losing purchasing power because of inflation's corrosive impact over time on your savings.

In this section I am going to describe strategies that will help you offset these risks. I am going to explain tactics that will help you (1) better plan for retirement, (2) fundamentally improve the way you invest, and (3) get a lot more serious about defending and preparing for your future. I'm going to cut through the investment jargon and explain a research-tested and risk-smart way of investing for retirement. I'll give you all the tools you need to be a whopping success.

However, some of my ideas are unorthodox. They are sure to bring down the scorn of Wall Street and fuel debate. So as a service to my critics and, more important, to you, I am going to dedicate a separate chapter to each of the action steps I recommend so that you fully understand my views, are clear about the risks, and recognize the solid research underlying my recommendations.

I want to inspire *you* to take *without-fail* action to shore up your retirement nest egg. Let's get started!

SIX STEPS TO
BULLETPROOF YOUR RETIREMENT

1. Change your "automatic pilot."

2. Diversify your holdings in radically different ways.

3. Build out your investment plan with funds and objective research.

4. Get all the professional help you can.

5. Build income streams via a ladder of annuities.

6. Invest in health care insurance.

4

CHANGE YOUR
"AUTOMATIC PILOT"

Most folks are caught in a dangerous holding pattern. They believe they have all the time in the world to get ready for retirement. They do not routinely save. They invest for speculative gains. Their savings behavior and investment mind-set—their "automatic pilot"—are not geared for robust savings or a secure future.

To successfully prepare for retirement, *you* need to fundamentally overhaul your investment beliefs and behavior patterns. *You need to "rewire"— to think and act like a successful saver and cautious investor instead of thinking and acting like a slot-machine player.* You need to immediately *stop* I'll-start-tomorrow thinking about saving for retirement and discard the speculative investment practices that are causing you harm. You need to radically change your behavior patterns.

Bill Armstrong, a sports therapist and expert trainer I know in Maine, insists that it takes many repetitions to change behavior. For example, it takes about a thousand repetitions of a particular movement for it to become a "body habit." When a skilled athlete sets out to change body habits, the first four or five weeks of practice are the most important for locking in new patterns of behavior.

When it comes to preparing for retirement, *you* fundamentally need—*right now!*—new saving and investing habits, a new investment strategy, and a new sense of urgency. You need a new automatic pilot.

And you are going to set a different, success-oriented automatic-pilot beginning *immediately*.

GET SERIOUS ABOUT YOUR FINANCIAL FUTURE—
YOU DON'T HAVE TIME TO LOSE!

For most folks, saving for retirement is something you start doing "later on." Procrastination is commonplace. It is also extremely dangerous. If *you* believe you have all the time in the world to plan and save for retirement, change your thinking pronto!

The drivers of successful capital accumulation for ample retirement funds are to (1) save hard; (2) start as early as you can for long-term compounding; (3) amplify the compounding effect via tax-deferred accounts; and (4) invest in a nonspeculative, broadly diversified way so you don't lose what you accumulate.

"Compounding" is simply building up capital on the money you originally invest *as well as* on the returns that you make over time. The Motley Fool, a good financial Web site, explains what it calls "the miracle of compounding" this way: "Consider what happens to $1,000 growing at the stock market's average return of 11 percent per year. In the first year, it gains $110, and ends the year totaling $1,110. In year two, it gains $122. Year five, $167. Year sixteen, $526. Year twenty-two, $984. The remarkable thing occurring is that without your doing anything to your pile of wealth, it's growing—by an increasing amount each year."[1]

If you aren't familiar with the concept of compounding, go to the Motley Fool Web site for more information. What I'd like you to register right now is that *reinvesting the returns* you earn from your investments will cause your savings to grow larger and larger.

You can intensify compounding by beginning to save and invest early in life. That gives you a time advantage. However, you can also intensify compounding by sheltering your investment returns from taxes—and that's why tax-deferral accounts such as 401(k)s, IRAs, and annuities are so important.

Let me offer another illustration. Suppose you made the same onetime $1,000 investment earning 11 percent each year in a tax-sheltered account. Let's also suppose you are in the 25 percent tax bracket. You pay no tax on the money going in and no tax on the returns. After thirty years, your investment in the tax-sheltered account would be worth $22,892. Not bad on a $1,000 investment. In a *taxable* account, however, the investment would be worth $10,785—less than half. Compounding is significantly diminished when taxes take their toll.

If, on the other hand, you held this same investment for only twenty years, it would then be worth $8,062 in a tax-sheltered account and $4,881 in a taxable account.

I draw several conclusions from these examples: (1) compounding does, indeed, give you a "miracle" multiplier effect; (2) investing on a tax-sheltered basis is highly advantageous; and (3) a long holding time gives you compounding advantage, but it's never too late to start saving for a secure retirement—especially if you avoid losses and invest in tax-sheltered accounts. It's time to get cracking!

QUANTIFY YOUR CAPITAL REQUIREMENT

To change your savings and investing behavior in earnest, you need to start with a sober understanding of just how much retirement capital you really need.

Count On Having a Long Life

First of all, count on the likelihood of a long life. Here are the probabilities:

Life Span Probabilities

81%	Probability that a woman *now age thirty-five* who reaches age sixty-five will at least live until age eighty.
78%	Probability that a man *now age thirty-five* who reaches age sixty-five will at least live until age eighty.
41%	Probability that a woman *now age sixty-five* will be alive twenty-five years later at age ninety.
29%	Probability that a man *now age sixty-five* will be alive twenty-five years later at age ninety.
67%	Probability that one or both spouses of a married couple *age thirty-five today* who both reach the age of sixty-five will be alive twenty-five years later at age ninety.

Source: Ron Gebhardtsbauer, American Academy of Actuaries, using the fully projected UP94 mortality table, based on pensioner and group annuitant data.

As one expert concluded, "By the time pensioners reach their retirement years, they may be facing twenty-five to thirty more years with substantial probability."[2] What is more, life expectancies in the United States continue to show an upward trend. By 2003, American men lived on average *three years longer* than they did in 1990. Women could expect to live one year longer.[3] So not only are current life spans long by historical standards—they are pushing out further each decade as well.

As you plan for retirement, bear longevity in mind. There is a high probability that one out of every three of you reading this book will live at least until age ninety. You cannot know the exact life span you will enjoy. You must, necessarily, make provision for a maximum possible life span. There is a high probability that you will need retirement income for a span of *twenty years or more*.

Count on needing retirement income for a long time.

COUNT ON NEEDING A LOT OF INCOME

There is a lot of debate about how much annual income you actually need in retirement. Entire books have been written on the subject. Rather than speculate about the number or beat the subject to death, let's look at what expert financial planners and existing retirees have to say.

Most financial planners say you need 70 percent of your current income when you retire. You see this "rule of thumb" on most Web sites. Most of the big financial houses preach the same view. Even so, the "70% Rule" is *not* adequate.

A large number of Americans who have already retired—and a large number who have yet to retire—have quite different views.

According to a recent survey, one-half of the adults who are still working say they expect to need *70 percent or less* of their preretirement income to live comfortably in retirement. One out of seven workers is actually counting on needing *less than 50 percent*.

On the other hand, six out of ten people *already retired* said they needed *70 percent or more* of their preretirement income in retirement. *In fact, more than half of the retirees surveyed in one poll said they needed "95 percent to 105 percent or more" of their former incomes.*[4] In another survey, four out of ten retirees affirmed they needed at least the *same amount of income* when they first retired as they had earned beforehand.[5]

Make no mistake about it. People who have already retired are telling us to count on needing a lot of income!

At the same time, prevailing views about retirement income generally play down or ignore inflation. Here's the scoop: if inflation were to reach 4 percent per annum, your "income need" in fifteen years would be *double* what it is today just to maintain the same purchasing power.

My own conclusion is that conventional advice about the amount of income you'll need in retirement is kaput. You'll need a lot more than you think!

In fact, count on needing at least 80 percent of your current income— slightly more if you want to be conservative—in addition to medical insurance to protect yourself from the drain of health-care expenses.

That's right: 80 percent. Of course, each person's income requirement is going to be different. It's important for you to pinpoint *your* retirement income needs realistically so you have a crystal-clear income target toward which you are saving and investing. You can do so in several ways.

Homework. One, make a list of all your major expenses and outlays over the last twelve months. What amounts did you spend on food, shelter, utilities, transportation, health care, and so forth? Write down those numbers.

Online calculator. Next, use this history to make an "income need" tabulation. You can use one of these online calculators:

AARP: http://www.aarp.org/money/financial_planning/session seven/retirement_planning_calculator.html

Fidelity: http://personal.fidelity.com/planning/guidance_overview .shtml.cvsr?bar=c

These sites can help you make a rough forward projection of the amount of income you are likely to need.

Professional help. More important, hire a professional financial advisor to help you set a retirement Income Target and Savings Plan with more precision—and then coach you and help you select suitable investments along the way. *If you cannot afford a professional's help long term, at least pay for a onetime consultation to have a financial planner help you prepare* *an income calculation and rigorous savings plan.* I'll tell you how to locate such a professional in just a bit. It is one of the most important investments you can make.

At present, six out of ten adult Americans have never tried to calculate what retirement income they might need.[6] They have no income target. They have no savings goal. If *you* do not have a crisp Income Target and Savings Plan, it's time to get moving! Start by making your own retirement income projection.

COUNT ON NEEDING AMPLE SAVINGS

Okay, there is a good probability that you will enjoy a long life span. And over that long span, you are going to need ample income. This means you have to (1) save robustly; (2) produce steady, positive investment returns; (3) avoid losses; and, ideally, (4) start saving and investing early on or in large amounts for strong compounding.

Can you count on "big returns" on your retirement investments? Not realistically. Can you count on "steady, positive returns"? Perhaps not with the demographic trends that are building.

We don't know with any certainty *how* investments will perform in the future. *Necessarily, you have to err on the side of caution — on the likelihood of achieving only modest returns on your investments and on the need for a defensive, cautious posture when you invest.* Because there's no harm done if you *over*fund your retirement, but you cannot risk *under*funding it.

Count on needing at least 80 percent of your current income during retirement. Multiply your income by 80 percent, then write down the result on a sheet of paper. That's your Retirement Income Target.

Now confirm (1) the amount of annual Social Security income you can expect upon retirement, and (2) the actual date upon which you qualify for these full payments. This sets your compass. You now know the *amount* and *timing* of the government payments you can expect to receive. If you do not know these numbers, visit Social Security's Web site to request this information, and be sure to note that your Social Security payments will be higher if you postpone your retirement until a later age. Check what the higher amount would be. You may be wise to postpone your retirement to amass cash.

Next, ascertain the amount of any pension or "direct benefit" income you will receive. If you now work or once worked in a company that now has or formerly had a traditional pension or defined benefit plan, confirm the specific amount of your benefit, if you do not know this number.

Now you can compute your Do-It-Yourself Funding Requirement. That is the difference between the amount of money you plan to spend in your first year of retirement (roughly 80 percent of your current income) *less* (1) the annual amount you will get from Social Security, and *less* (2) the annual amounts you may get from any employer pensions. The balance is the Do-It-Yourself amount that you, yourself, need to fund.

Finally, you can ascertain your Savings Requirement. *As a crude rule of thumb, multiply the Do-It-Yourself number by 25.* That's right, 25! That is how much you will probably need to save by the time you retire in order to meet your income target and keep up with inflation.[7]

Let's take an example. Suppose your current annual income is $60,000. Your retirement income target is 80 percent of that amount or $48,000. If, hypothetically, you have no employer pension benefit but Social Security is going to pay you $12,000 each year, then you will need to make up the $36,000 difference ($48,000 minus $12,000). That's your Do-It-Yourself Funding Requirement. For that amount, you would need to save $900,000 ($25 \times \$36,000$).

This is strictly a crude metric. However, it gives you a high probability of having sufficient capital and being able to keep up with inflation over thirty years. You can analyze your savings needs with more sophistication using the tools at the Choose To Save Web site:http://www.choosetosave .org/ballpark/.

You should become familiar with this excellent site for savings ideas and support. It will confirm that the savings total you need for adequate retire-- ment income is likely to be huge if you do not have a traditional pension.

Most people are startled when they finally tabulate their savings requirement. It's a big number! So if you are *not* saving fervently and systematically at this time, it's time to hustle.

Get serious about stepping up your savings efforts! You still have time to save. You can still enjoy good investment returns on a compounded basis, whatever your savings to date.

Setting an Income Target and Savings Plan is the first step in setting your course to a sound financial future. You *are* going to retire securely and comfortably. Now save, save, save!

SAVE AT LEAST 20 PERCENT
OF YOUR PRETAX INCOME

We have seen that most Americans are not saving at all adequately for their future. The statistics are appalling.

We saw that 26 percent of workers ages fifty-five and over have total savings and investments for retirement (excluding the value of their primary residence and defined benefit plan) of *less than $10,000.*[8] Another study estimates that nearly 43 percent of U.S. households are at risk of not having enough savings to maintain their living standard in retirement.[9] Meanwhile, one out of five Americans working in organizations that offer 401(k) or similar savings plans do not participate in them whatsoever,[10] and 90 percent of the people who do participate in such plans contribute *less* than the maximum possible.[11]

In other words, savings are pitifully low for a huge number of Americans and the savings habits of many are outright defunct.

On the other hand, studies also show that people require different amounts of annual savings as a percentage of pretax income depending on when they first begin to systematically save. Here is what the Schwab Center for Investment Research specifically recommends (with sound effects courtesy of that organization):

Age at Which You Begin to Save	Percent of Pretax Salary to Save
20s	10%–15%
30s	15%–25%
Early 40s	25%–35%
45 and older	OUCH!

Source: Schwab Center for Investment Research

These percentages assume you have nothing in the piggy bank and are starting from scratch. They are crude guidelines. But they point to the need for a larger and larger savings effort the longer you postpone the start. I agree with them.

Since most of you reading this book are likely to be in your thirties, forties, fifties, or older, count on saving a large amount of your pretax income—at least 20 percent.

If you start saving 20 percent of your income in your thirties, you will not have to increase that percentage as you age. Maintaining a 20 percent savings rate from that age forward should be sufficient.

If you are older or your savings are lagging far behind, get a financial advisor to help you muster all the expense cuts you can. Read David Bach's *Start Late, Finish Rich*. I do not agree with all of David's investment ideas. But he describes a number of excellent, easy-to-implement steps that can help you change your mind-set and achieve good savings.

Whatever your age, it's time to roll up your shirtsleeves. Make a list of all of your savings over the last six months. Make a list of all of your expenditures over the same period. Compare the two, side by side. Which expenses can you cut in order to save at least 20 percent of your pretax income? That's right. At least 20 percent.

If you find yourself saying, "But I *can't* save any more!" then you may be in the wrong job *or* in a mind-set rut. It's high time to stop the excuses. It may be time, as well, to rethink your retirement plans and postpone your retirement until some later date. There's nothing wrong with that alternative.

Shocked by these exercises? Feeling demoralized? Don't be! The majority of the U.S. population is in the same boat. So rather than feel beaten or low, let these projections jolt you into action.

Find a good coach—a personal "financial trainer." If you cannot afford the services of a professional planner, then read up on saving techniques, join a savers club, and slash your expenditures to the bone. These resources may help you:

Savings tips: www.choosetosave.org
Join a savings and investment help group: www.meetup.com
Spenders Anonymous: www.spenders.org

Of course, clubs, online tools, and seminars aren't going to put savings in the bank for you. You have to do that yourself. And you should do so (a) automatically, and (b) with all the tax advantage you can muster.

HOLD YOUR SAVINGS
IN TAX-SHELTERED ACCOUNTS

As you amass savings, always invest them in tax-sheltered accounts for maximum compounding advantage. Investing in company-sponsored retirement plans—that is, direct contribution savings plans such as 401(k), 403(b), or 457 plans—is one of the *best* ways to save. So is investing in an IRA and then in annuities.

When you invest in a 401(k) or similar plan, you can postpone (or, in the case of Roth plans, altogether avoid) taxes on the returns on your investments. Rather than have your investment returns diluted by annual taxes each year, your returns remain intact and snowball with greater effect. You get a powerful compounding advantage.

What's more, many employers match some of the money that their employees put into these savings plans. *Obtaining the largest "match" is your first prize!* Matching contributions are free money that add to your return and fuel even more compounding. They are a significant benefit.

Whether your employer matches contributions or not, contribute the maximum amount to your 401(k) or similar plan. That is your first investment priority.

Individual Retirement Accounts or IRAs also give you powerful tax advantages. However, IRAs differ from 401(k)s on several counts. An IRA does not give you any matching employer top-up. An IRA will, however, often give you access to a much larger array of funds, indexes, and Exchange-Traded Funds or ETFs. A 401(k) or similar savings plan has substantially fewer fund alternatives.

Because they give you tax advantage but not matching employer money, investing in an IRA is your *next priority* after a 401(k). Open your IRA with a low-cost broker or major financial-services company such as Fidelity or Schwab so you enjoy low fees and the largest array of funds and indexes. You want access to the largest array of funds. If you do not qualify for a 401(k), invest in an IRA each year instead.

Many people ask whether they should invest in "traditional" or "Roth" 401(k)s and IRAs. Since entire books are available on the topic, we need not go into great detail here. Simply put, *traditional* IRAs and 401(k)s enable you to invest pretax money—money on which you have *not* paid income tax—into different investments, and the returns on those investments will not be taxed until you begin to draw down the proceeds after retirement. Then, yes, you will pay taxes. *Roth* 401(k)s and IRAs, on the other hand, enable you to invest *after-tax* money—money on which you have already paid income tax—but there are no taxes on your investments thereafter. The money compounding in and eventually withdrawn from a Roth 401(k) or Roth IRA is permanently exempt from taxes.

As a general rule of thumb, a Roth IRA or Roth 401(k) will usually be more advantageous because you will never pay taxes on the income from them.

Are Roth accounts right for you? Should you convert your traditional account to a Roth account? There is no pat answer. Since each person's tax status and income level are different, you will need guidance on the suitability of one kind of account over another. Call on a financial planner to assist you. Alternatively, use the tools available on SmartMoney.com and MoneyCentral. Those sites have further information and "calculators" that can help.

Whichever type of account you choose, saving in tax-sheltered plans such as 401(k)s and IRAs should always be foremost on your priority list. You want the tax-sheltering advantage they bring, but you are limited as to the amount of money you can put into such accounts each year. Once you bump up against those limits, move into annuities.

Annuities are investment instruments that likewise give you important tax and compounding advantages. We will discuss them in detail in chapter 8. For the time being, think of annuities as a kind of traditional 401(k) plan without funding limits. Annuities should also be a priority investment vehicle for you.

You want to keep in mind the "priority account hierarchy." You want tax advantage, compounding advantage, and matching contributions—so 401(k) plans come first. Next you want to use tax-advantageous accounts such as IRAs and annuities. Only after you have used these options should you lodge your savings in normally taxed accounts.

AUTOMATE YOUR ACCUMULATION EFFORTS

I'd like you to take a hard look at your savings behavior right now. Get out your payroll and investment statements. Then please answer these five questions: (1) How much did you save over the last six months? (2) What percent of your pretax income did these savings represent? (3) Are you contributing the maximum amount to your 401(k) or IRA? (4) Are you satisfied with your savings total vis-à-vis your projected capital need? (5) Were these savings *automatic* via systematic payroll deductions?

I believe that the best way of building a retirement nest egg is to save and invest automatically.

Many folks are not saving adequately because they have adopted a way of life and mind-set—an "automatic pilot"—that are all wrong. They continually spend everything they earn. They max out their credit cards. They borrow against their homes and spend more! And all the while they convince themselves that they cannot possibly save any money for the future.

If that's the way *you* think and behave, stop the defeatism before it causes you more harm. Stop making excuses and change your automatic pilot. Go from "I can't save" to "I save automatically."

Here's how to do it.

- Itemize all of your outlays over the last six months. How much did you spend on housing, transportation, cable television, lattes, cell phones, and so forth?
- Set a clear plan for cutting 5 percent of your total expenses this coming month and the next, then another 5 percent in months three and four. Divert that money into savings.
- If you need help, read one of David Bach's books. Implement his savings techniques. Take the need to save *seriously*.
- Tell your employer to automatically deduct money from your pay so you contribute *the maximum amount* to your company's 401(k) or similar plan. *Make savings deductions happen automatically.*
- When you "automate" your 401(k) contributions, also instruct your employer to automatically transfer some of your pay into your IRA (if you qualify), annuities, and any other investment account.

- Give your broker standing instructions as well on how to invest this money. *Always direct that the returns you receive on your investments be automatically reinvested.* Your money will automatically come in and will automatically be invested and compound. You can periodically change your standing investment instructions as market conditions evolve.

Now you're on an "automatic pilot" moving in the right direction.

Stop making excuses about saving and make saving and investing happen *automatically*. If you're having trouble saving adequately, join a savers club or compulsive spenders group. Find good "self-help" books that will make saving easy and painless. Most important, give standing *payroll-deduction, transfer,* and *investment* instructions so that you are funding different investment accounts *automatically* each month.

INVEST TO ACHIEVE REAL INCOME— NOT BOGUS "GAINS"

By far the foremost change of "automatic pilot" I want you to make is a fundamental overhaul of *how* you invest. *I want you to stop chasing speculative "gains." I want you to invest for* real income *instead.*

THE QUEST FOR PRICE GAINS

For most people, the aim of buying an investment—be it a stock, bond, or house—is to be able to sell it one day for a profit. If you're like most people, you're primarily investing for appreciation or capital gains. But setting your sights on price appreciation alone is dangerous.

According to John Bogle, founder and former chairman of the Vanguard Group, which now has more than $1 trillion of investment funds under management, you get two kinds of returns from investments: *investment* return and *speculative* return.[12] Investment return in the case of stocks, he relates, is the dividend return you get plus the earnings growth rate. In other words, investment return is intimately tied to income fundamentals: dividends and earnings. *Speculative* return, on the other hand, is the impact of the change in price that investors are willing to pay to buy dividends and earnings.

I argue that investors who ignore income fundamentals and primarily seek speculative "gains" open themselves to imprudent risk, set themselves up for correction losses, and derive inferior returns long term. We saw this with painful clarity in the late 1990s when investors bid up the shares of dot-com companies—companies that had often not produced any income whatsoever—only to incur sharp losses when the run-up stopped and the speculative "gains" quickly evaporated.

Speculative price run-ups are invariably followed by corrections and losses. That is *not* what you want to experience when you invest your retirement savings. Nevertheless, most investors are transfixed by rising prices or "gains." There are several reasons why.

Prior tax policy. Until recently, there have been heavier taxes on stock dividends than on capital gains. In the case of real estate, there is often no tax on gains whatsoever if you are selling a primary residence and your gains are within certain limits. Naturally, investors have sought the tax-favored kinds of returns. Today, dividends are taxed at a much lower 15 percent rate. That's outstanding! But most investors have been conditioned to ignore income fundamentals and look for price increases instead because of prior tax policy.

Executive compensation. Executive compensation has also encouraged "gain" fever. From the 1980s to the present, stock options have been a prominent feature of the compensation of many U.S. executives. Stock options give an executive the right to buy company stock at a fixed, often discounted price in the future provided the stock price increases. Not surprisingly, the recipients of these awards have done everything they can to boost the price of their company's shares. Dividends have been slashed. Up and up have gone stock prices.

Low dividend yields. Low dividend yields also contribute to "gain" fever. A "dividend yield" is simply the dividend payout of a stock divided by the stock's price. It's a good measure of the amount of income you're really buying when you buy equities. However, the current dividend yield on U.S. stocks is only 1 percent to 2 percent—about half of what UK stocks pay. That has led many U.S. investors and investment commentators to dismiss dividend income as "trivial." They're dead wrong! Almost half of the U.S. stock market's total returns over the last seventy-five years came from dividends, while pure "appreciation" accounted for less than one-third of total returns.[13] But the myth that "dividends are useless" prevails.

Media conditioning. All of us have also been conditioned by the media's relentless attention to stock prices and "advances." Every morning, afternoon, and evening news broadcast reports on the price ups and downs of the stock and real estate markets. By comparison, we hear little or nothing at all about dividend or rent trends.

The result is that most folks invest for gains with little concern for the income fundamentals underlying their investments. It's not smart.

Get-Rich-Quick-Itis

Most investors chase rising prices, not income. And the mind-set is unhealthy. It's part of what I call get-rich-quick-itis—the American mania for instant riches, speculative investing, and windfall returns. This mania contributes to the formation of bubbles and losses and has deep underpinnings.

In recent years, a series of speculative bubbles has formed in rapid succession in different asset classes.

1997–2002	Technology-stock boom, then meltdown
2000–ongoing	Real estate boom and correction
2001–2	Precious metals run-up
2003–5	Emerging-market funds run-up

Huge amounts of money have migrated from (1) highly speculative technology stocks to (2) overpriced real estate, and then into off-the-charts (3) emerging-market, (4) energy, and (5) precious-metals funds. As of this writing, we are in the midst of a real estate correction in many U.S. markets. In the words of Yale University's Robert Shiller, "The changing behavior of home prices is a sign of changing public impressions of the value of property and of a heightened attention to speculative price movements. It is the sign of a bubble, and bubbles carry within them the causes of their ultimate destruction."[14]

In short, we seem to be staggering from one speculative surge to the next. When real estate goes up, we scramble to buy houses with the expectation of flipping them for windfall gains. When a mutual fund or stock category shows red-hot returns, we buy in, too. And when an investment's annual appreciation shoots up so sky-high that it should set off "extreme danger" alarms, many investors pump in even more money!

Clearly, American investors are chasing gains that often have nothing to do with real earnings or income. It's a dangerous, pyramid-game way of investing. But look around you. Should this behavior come as any surprise?

Get-Rich-Quick-Itis

Flip This House	Becoming Rich Without	The Millionaire Real Estate
Flip That House	Cutting Up Your Credit	Mindset
Property Ladder	Cards	Become a Millionaire!
Move This House!	The Master Key to Riches	Retire Young, Retire Rich!
Sell This House!	The Weekend Millionaire	The Instant Millionaire
Cracking the Millionaire	How to Get Rich and Think	Millionaire Maker's Guide to
Code	Like a Millionaire	Wealth Cycle Investing
Why You Want to be Rich	Seven Years to Seven	Smart Women Finish Rich!
Think and Grow Rich!	Figures	Grow Rich!
Smart Couples Finish	Get Rich Buying Houses	Becoming a Millionaire
Rich	How to Get Rich!	God's Way
Secrets of the Millionaire	The One Minute Millionaire	Nine Steps to Becoming
Mind	The Millionaire Real Estate	Rich!
Real Estate Debt Can	Investor	Make a Million!
Make You Rich!	Zero Down Real Estate!	

Scores of television programs, books, and seminars all promise to help us get rich fast. We are urged to flip real estate, buy stocks on margin, and generally invest speculatively for big returns.

I see a dangerous pattern: We're chasing "hot returns" and "big gains" with greater fervor. We are ignoring income fundamentals and common sense.

> U.S. investors are becoming addicted to **follow-the-herd speculative** investing that disregards income fundamentals and is not risk smart.

Get-rich-quick-itis is an unhealthy psychology. It contributes to the expectation of unrealistic returns, herd buying sprees, bubbles (such as the technology-stock and real estate bubbles we have already experienced), and corrections. I want you to *stop* this speculative way of investing. I want you to select investments that put real money in your wallet instead of spurious "gains."

EXPERT VIEWS

Investing for price increases and windfall returns *always* results in corrections and inferior capital accumulation. Good research backs my claim.

A large volume of research shows that investing for income—not speculatively inflated "gains"—produces superior results.

For example, experts such as Benjamin Graham, Jeremy Siegel, Charles Babin, Glenn Hubbard, James O'Shaughnessy, Robert Arnott, Ned Davis Research, David Swensen, Ken Ziesenheim, and a host of others have found that dividend-paying stocks produce better returns. In his book *The Future for Investors,* Dr. Siegel offers a remarkable illustration. A onetime investment of $1,000 made in 1953 in an index of S&P 500 stocks, the broad index of the country's largest five hundred companies, would have grown to $130,000 by 2003. By comparison, the same investment put into the top 20 percent of high-dividend-yielding stocks and with dividends reinvested would have grown to $462,750.[15]

Dividend income makes a huge difference!

Study after study confirms that dividend-paying stocks and the reinvestment of dividends over time produces superior returns. Reinvest your dividends, and you own more stock, paying you even more dividends. With good dividend income, you know you are holding a sensible stock investment. You can likewise judge the sensibleness of real estate and bond investments by looking at their fundamental ability to produce income. If, for example, you pay such a high price for a house that its hypothetical rent return would be less than the return that you'd get from a bank deposit—that would patently *not* be a smart investment.

But there's more. Ample research also shows that investments rooted in income fundamentals are also more resistant to price corrections and losses.

Let's look again at the recent stock bubble. After running up stock prices in the late 1990s, investors sustained painful corrections. The herd woke up to the fact that their red-hot stock "gains" were nothing but speculative froth. The prices of stocks came tumbling down. However, *dividend-paying* stocks fared much better than non-dividend-paying stocks during the correction. The stocks of the 350 companies on the S&P 500 that paid dividends fell on average 13.3 percent in 2002. The stocks of dividend *nonpayers* fell on average 30.3 percent instead.[16]

All-in, income-producing investments fare better with less risk. An income focus when you invest outperforms "gain" mania time after time.

Still not convinced? Then take a moment to read the views of these respected gurus on the topic of income-paying stock investments.

"One may buy 100 shares of IBM at $75 per share hoping that someone will come along to purchase them from you at $100. But far less speculative estimates of value can be made by looking at the long-run flow of IBM dividends."

Burton G. Malkiel, *A Random Walk down Wall Street*[17]

"Over the long run, dividend-paying stocks do . . . better. A study by Ned Davis Research, a firm that advises institutional investors, found that from 1972 to 2005 dividend-paying stocks dramatically outperformed the market. Companies paying regular dividends returned 10.1 percent annually, compared with just 4.1 percent for those that didn't."

Don Durfee, Research Editor, *CFO* magazine[18]

In 2006, "the total return of dividend-paying stocks in the S&P 500 was 14.7%, versus only 9.6% for non-dividend-yielders. What's more, dividend-payers may be able to provide a defensive cushion for your portfolio, as they tend to perform relatively better than non-dividend-payers in declining markets."

Schwab Center for Investment Research and Ned Davis Research[19]

"Stocks of high-quality companies that paid reasonable dividends with a pattern of increasing those payments have historically experienced less volatility than those of non-dividend-paying companies."

Ken Ziesenheim, President of Thornburg Securities Corp.[20]

"Dividends provide the only real, tangible and bankable return of capital to investors. Investments that never yield cash can be very risky because the potential for capital appreciation may be transient, deceptive and often unfulfilled."

Wilson/Bennett Capital Management[21]

"I can't emphasize enough the importance of dividends and reinvesting those dividends."

Jeremy Siegel, Wharton Professor of Finance[22]

The conclusion to draw is this: you will derive stronger returns, amass more capital, and have less risk if you fundamentally change your investment habits and focus, a priori, on *income-paying* investments.

You want real, in-your-pocket returns instead of here-today-gone-tomorrow "gains." You want sober investments, rooted in fundamentals, that produce tangible income you can reinvest—interest *income,* dividend *income,* and rent *income.* Make income fixation the core driver of your new "automatic pilot" for saving and investing.

ACTION STEPS

1. Identify your Income Target. Project your retirement expenses and annual retirement income needs. Use these resources to help you:

   - www.aarp.com
   - www.fidelity.com
   - a professional financial planner

2. Contact Social Security for an updated benefit statement. Pinpoint the amount and start date of your *full* payments and qualifying date.

3. Contact employers where you qualify for a pension or direct benefits. Request confirmation of the benefits and amounts you will receive.

4. Identify your Savings Requirement. What amount of capital do you need to have in hand by the time your retire to produce your income target?

5. Determine whether you have adequate savings thus far for retirement. Use www.choosetosave.org to help you. (Go to "Ballpark Estimator.")

6. Read David Bach's *Start Late, Finish Rich* for help to improve your savings.

7. Set a disciplined savings plan. Itemize the expenses you can cut month by month. Cut unnecessary expenses and save *at least 20 percent* of your after-tax monthly income. Get a financial coach to help you.

8. Turn on a new "automatic pilot."

   - Make *maximum* 401(k) or IRA contributions.
   - Open up IRA accounts with Fidelity or Schwab.
   - Instruct your employer to *automatically* deduct and transfer your savings.
   - Give standing instructions to Fidelity/Schwab to automatically invest your funds and always reinvest income and dividends.

9. Set your sights on hard income from your investments. Stop speculating! When you make an investment, always ask yourself, *"How much dividend income, rent income, or interest income am I likely to get back?"*

5

DIVERSIFY YOUR HOLDINGS
IN RADICALLY DIFFERENT WAYS

To enjoy a cash-rich retirement, you need to broadly diversify your investments to protect as well as enlarge your nest egg and to produce a mix of different kinds of *income* instead of speculatively inflated, here-today-gone-tomorrow "gains." I want you to broadly diversify so that no one investment can cause you irreparable harm. I want you to invest with an aversion to "irrational exuberance," bubbles, and gambling sprees. Most of all, I want you to invest with a *fixation on income fundamentals* to achieve real returns, lower risk, and good performance.

You can accomplish all of the above by following a sound Investment Master Plan.

An Investment Master Plan is a diversification blueprint. It tells you how to split your money between deposits, stocks, bonds, real estate, and other asset categories. It's your big-picture strategy for investment success.

Investment professionals call this kind of plan an "asset allocation" model. I want you to create such a model that will guide your investment decisions in an objective, strategic way *across all of your investment accounts*—401(k), IRA, brokerage accounts, and all others. By investing with a clear plan, you will invest with discipline instead of emotion. You will diversify your exposure, heighten your returns, *and reduce risks*.

THE IMPORTANCE OF BROAD DIVERSIFICATION

Investment experts have spent a great deal of time analyzing the dynamics of successful investing. And wealthy people spend fortunes for the extra bit of performance that investment experts and highly sophisticated allocation software can help them achieve. Combined, all of the research and most of the world's experts recognize that *diversification* is one of the foremost drivers of investment success.

Most people understand the wisdom of "not putting all your eggs in one basket." However, loss avoidance is only part of the wisdom for broad diversification. For example, experts have articulated a formidable view of investing called Modern Portfolio Theory. It argues that asset allocation does, in fact, reduce investment risk, curb losses, and—yes—*improve returns.*

> Asset allocation—that is, how you diversify your savings between stocks, bonds, real estate, and other kinds of investments—is an important way to reduce investment risk and strengthen investment returns.

Modern Portfolio Theory is a Nobel Prize–winning view of investing that says that investors can reduce risk and enhance returns by diversifying their holdings so that a downturn by an investment in one category is offset by gains from investments in others. And the research that has evolved with this theory shows something quite remarkable: even mixing some higher-risk kinds of investments into a portfolio of otherwise low-risk holdings can actually reduce overall risk as well as improve overall returns. I'll show you an example in just a bit.

Hence, an "allocation blueprint" or Investment Master Plan is an important diversification strategy that tells you how to combine investments with different performance characteristics to achieve *higher returns* with *lower risk.*

Skillful asset allocation is a major contributor to investment success. However, many people do not take this truth seriously.

According to recent polls, one in four investors believes that asset allocation is "just an industry buzzword," and one in three "does not have any allocation strategy or rebalancing plan" of any kind.[1] Such beliefs and practices are foolhardy. In fact, I cannot overstate the importance of a skillful allocation master plan.

Of course, the idea of prudently diversifying your wealth is nothing new. Writing some seventeen hundred years ago, Rabbi Issac bar Aha recommended, "A man should always place his money, a third into land, a third into merchandise, and keep a third in hand."[2] Today that would mean splitting your money equally between real estate, stocks or inventory in your own business, and money market funds. Not a bad start.

In his Ph.D. research, Gary Brinson, who went on to become a director of UBS, one of the world's largest wealth-management institutions, found that asset allocation accounts for most of the volatility or up-and-down choppiness—good and bad—of investment results.[3] Put all of your money in one stock, and you stand a chance of suffering losses. Put all of your money into five hundred stocks, and your portfolio will go up when the stock market goes up, and down when the market contracts. However, if you put your money into a *mix* of stock, bond, and real estate investments, then one market's movement is less likely to harm your savings long term. Some investments will expectedly grow in value even if others lose ground.

Since Brinson's pioneering research, virtually all investment experts have come to see the formidable impact that asset allocation can have on returns—particularly for investors who maintain a consistent allocation strategy and do not practice frequent trading or market timing.[4] One survey of financial professionals estimated that "the right asset allocation plan would have added 68 percent to a portfolio's return over the past thirty years."[5] In other words, a skillful allocation or mix of investments can add as much as 1.6 percent *more* to your returns each year. And while that might not sound like much, just that small amount over your working life could give you as much as *ten years* of additional spending in retirement according to some estimates.[6]

A skillful allocation strategy can give you years of additional retirement income.

Moreover, eight out of ten financial advisors in the same survey said that a proper allocation plan could have cut investor losses "by at least half" during the market tumble of 2000–2002.[7] So broad diversification and a skillful allocation plan can help you significantly reduce losses as well as increase returns. Or as Marc O. Mayer, the chairman of one major asset-management organization, put it, "When it comes to portfolio performance, the three most important factors are allocation, allocation, allocation."[8]

CURRENT ALLOCATIONS ARE NOT SKILLFUL

When we examine 401(k) holdings, however, we see that typical investment allocations are often not skillful. In one survey of retirement savings plans, researchers found that the mean allocation into company stock (the stock of an investor's employer) was nearly 25 percent[9]—a dangerously high percentage as many Enron employees painfully learned. On the other hand, exposure in international equities was only 2.4 percent of a typical portfolio—a level, I would argue, that is quite low.[10]

Other researchers found that "some investors . . . divide their contributions evenly across the funds offered in the plan. . . . We find that the proportion invested in stocks depends strongly on the proportion of stock funds in the plan."[11] ". . . When plans add a stock fund, allocation to equities rises."[12]

In other words, some people divide their money between every fund in their 401(k) plan—forget about any strategy! Investors tend to put more money in stocks the more stock funds there are in a plan. And they tend to invest more in stocks yet again when they are shown "good news" long-term historical performance returns rather than more volatile short-term figures.[13]

In its survey of some 1.5 million 401(k) accounts, Hewitt Associates more recently found that a typical account is invested 49 percent in U.S. stocks directly, 19.5 percent in employer stock; only 9.3 percent in international stocks; and 34 percent in sundry kinds of "balanced," "pre-mix," "target date," and other funds that mix stocks and bonds together.[14] The allocations change somewhat month by month, but the following characteristics are typical:

- *Over*concentration in employer stock.
- High concentration in stocks in general, held in a myriad of fragmented "size" categories—large-cap, midcap, and small-cap funds.
- Low international exposure.
- Little or no real estate exposure (in fact, few 401(k) plans even offer such funds).
- Little or no investing rooted in income fundamentals.

One other predilection is also apparent—what I call "convenience investing." Perhaps bewildered by conventional advice and so many different investment options, many investors are putting money into "target date" and "balanced" funds. "Balanced" funds invest in a mix of stocks and bonds, and the fund manager—not you—decides how much to allocate to each category. With "target date" funds, fund managers decide how much to put into stocks or bonds for you, gradually ratcheting down stock exposure as the fund nears a particular date (usually your target retirement date). While the automatic "allocation changes" of such funds may be convenient, many target date and balanced funds have shortcomings. For example, these funds often give investors little international exposure and sometimes have surprisingly elevated exposure in higher-risk kinds of stocks and bonds. Convenience funds are anything but risk-free!

Likewise, most 401(k) accounts have little or no real estate exposure. So retirement savings are primarily concentrated in a few asset classes.

Here's what I see. The allocations investors currently make are often (1) top-heavy in employer stocks, (2) higher risk in bond content, (3) low in international exposure, and (4) generally lacking in real estate. Many invest in whatever funds are available in their 401(k) plans without any strategy whatsoever. Many are investing in target date funds believing they are low-risk holdings. And many tend to move into "higher-return" funds—the top performers of the day—setting themselves up for downturns when performance cools.

CONVENTIONAL ADVICE—YAWN—IS GETTING STALE

If de facto allocations show little skill, conventional allocation advice is outright musty. Conventional diversification advice is more often than not aimed at selling funds, not helping you avoid risk and losses! Nothing in conventional advice will put you off speculative investing. And conventional wisdom tells you to change your allocation strategy as you age, only adding to the consternation of most investors.

For example, one financial group recommended this particular mix for investors with five to ten years until retirement:

Investment Category	Percent of Portfolio
Stocks	
U.S. large-cap growth	7
U.S. large-cap blend	17

U.S. midcap value	19
U.S. midcap blend	13
<u>Foreign small/midcap equities</u>	<u>8</u>
Subtotal	64
Moderate Allocation	12
Bonds	
U.S. short-term government	8
<u>U.S. short-term corporate</u>	<u>16</u>
Subtotal	24
Total	100

There is no need to attribute this recommendation to a particular organization. Many groups offer similar advice. What I want you to notice instead is the emphasis on "investment subcategories"—large-cap stocks, midcap stocks, small-cap stocks, short-term government bonds, and so on. A bewildering number of these "cap size" funds and fragmented bond funds are available. Of course, the wonderful idea underlying these fragmented categories is that you need some exposure in *each and every one* of them to capture the next market surge. Let's hear it for Wall Street marketing!

You are also meant to change these allocations as you age. Conventional advice tells you to invest heavily in stocks when you're young since you'll still have ample time before retirement to offset any market downturn or damage. As you age, you are told to reduce stock holdings and increase bond investments to curb the risk of losses. Or as one financial writer explains it, "A traditional rule of thumb was to subtract your age from one hundred and invest that percentage of your assets in stocks, with the rest in bonds or cash. (A twenty-eight-year-old would put 72 percent of her money in stocks; an eighty-one-year-old would put only 19 percent there.)"[15]

That's the conventional, poor man's approach to low-risk investing. Had you been my wealthy client in Switzerland or the Middle East or New York, one of my teams would, instead, have used "optimization" software to analyze your investment holdings. Optimization programs are highly sophisticated computer analyses that evaluate the monthly performance of the stocks, bonds, and funds you own going back many years. The programs analyze the up-and-down performance movements of each investment and show how different mixes of investments might deliver "optimum" results—meaning give you the highest amount of return for a particular amount of investment risk or volatility.

Optimization programs show that conventional allocation advice is often crude and faulty. Of course, few investors have access to the world's best "optimization" tools. Private banks pay tens of thousands of dollars each year just to lease such software programs. Consequently, the use of such tools is pretty much limited to major pension funds, powerful institutional clients, and individuals of great wealth. Where does that leave you?

Rather than use conventional advice or the stale "subtract your age from one hundred" rule, *I recommend a radically different approach. I want you to invest to achieve a mix of different income streams.* Forget the many different *kinds of investments* in the market and focus instead on the foremost *kinds of income.* Because when you set your sights on hard income and real returns, all the subcategories and marketing bewilderment starts to fade.

You want income you can reinvest, not complexity! And you want the broadest diversification and least risk possible when you invest to safeguard your retirement wealth.

At the risk of sounding like a broken record, I want to repeat one important lesson I've learned from years of "optimization" analysis and practical experience in wealth management: investments that produce real income tend to generate higher returns in up markets and lose less in down markets. Income-producing investments exhibit less risk and deliver better returns! You can reinvest real income, but you can't reinvest "gains." Consequently, you are not well served by any allocation strategy that is rooted in Wall Street marketing hype or in investments lacking solid income underpinnings.

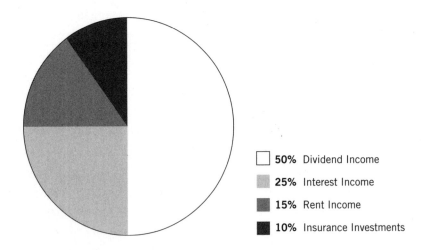

50% Dividend Income
25% Interest Income
15% Rent Income
10% Insurance Investments

Instead of chasing phantom appreciation, I want you to achieve a diverse mix of prudent, no-fluff-about-them income streams—dividend income, interest income, and rent income. I want you to capture and then reinvest that income. At its core, your Investment Master Plan should have the kind of income orientation shown in the pie chart on page 86.

INVEST FOR DIVIDEND INCOME

Dividend income is the income you derive when you buy stocks, become an owner of a company, and are paid a part of that company's profits. Please note that the payouts of some real estate investments are called "dividends" as well. When I use the term *"dividend income,"* however, I am solely referring to income from corporate ownership and equities.

The return on equities has historically been among the highest of all investments. That is why some advisors tell you to invest *more* than 100 percent in stocks when you're young—by investing all your money in stocks, borrowing against them, then buying more! To be sure, sizable exposure in equities will help you build capital for a long retirement. However, putting 100 percent or more of your money into stocks is simply not wise. And I want you to invest for prudent *dividend income* instead of stock gains. That is an important difference.

To begin with, dividend-producing investments have historically given attractive returns. Between 1900 and 2000, U.S. stocks in general delivered an average return of about 10.1 percent (or about 6.7 percent after inflation).[16] Bonds, by comparison, gave an average annual return of about 4.8 percent (or 1.5 percent after inflation) over the same period.[17] Over a long span, then, stocks have been the higher performers.

Stock returns are a combination of appreciation and dividends. And while many investors have become addicted to appreciation or "gains"—as in "I'll buy this stock for a dollar today and hopefully sell it for two dollars tomorrow"—the fact is that dividend payments are *the* most important component of stock returns. As one expert concluded, "From 1871 to 2003, 97 percent of the total after-inflation accumulation from stocks comes from reinvesting dividends. Only 3 percent comes from capital gains."[18]

Put this finding at the core of your investment strategy: Earning dividend income and reinvesting that income are irrefutably essential for portfolio success.

When companies make money, they can (1) use some of the profit to pay you dividends, or (2) use the money instead to make investments in plant, equipment, or acquisitions to spur more growth, or (3) do both of the above.

We saw that because of tax policy, executive compensation practices, and unhealthy investing practices and beliefs, most investors have become fixated on "stock gains" as opposed to demanding real earnings and dividends. Today, a fundamental reason for holding stocks—dividend income—has gotten lost in the shuffle. There's been a colossal disconnect. The convergence of misguided taxes plus corporate vested interests plus average-Joe greed has sabotaged prudent investment practices. And it has pushed the American public into a debilitating addiction. When we look at the recent tech-stock bubble, real estate bubble, and emerging-market bubble, it is clear that American investors are hooked on red-hot capital gains and flip profits whether they are realistic or not.

So break out the smelling salts and let's get back to common sense! When you invest in stocks and stock funds, I want you to do so for *dividend income*. Dividend-producing investments are critically important for several reasons.

Reason #1: Dividend-paying stock investments have historically produced better returns than non-dividend-paying stocks or the stock market as a whole.

Stock Market as a Whole (Traditional Index)	10.35%
Gross Dividends	12.01%
Revenues	12.87%

Source: John Mauldin, *Just One Thing: Twelve of the World's Best Investors Reveal the One Strategy You Can't Overlook* (Hoboken, NJ: John Wiley & Sons, 2006), 166–67.

Investment guru Rob Arnott tested the stock market's performance between 1962 and 2004. He found that a basket of the one thousand U.S. stocks selected and weighted on the basis of gross dividends or earnings (as opposed to a traditional stock market index) produced these average annual returns:

Arnott went on to build new indexes using dividends, revenues, and other measures of company size as weighting factors, and his funds are interesting. It suffices to note here that a mix of stocks that pay dividends—

that is, which actually pay you income that you can reinvest for more compounding—gives you better returns than the stock market as a whole. So do the stocks of companies with high earnings.

If You Had Invested $1,000 in 1957 In	Your Result in 2003
High P/E-ratio (high-priced) stocks	$ 56,661
Index of all S&P 500 stocks	$ 130,768
Low P/E-ratio (low-priced) stocks	$ 425,703
Highest dividend-yielding stocks	$ 462,750

Source:Jeremy J. Siegel, *The Future for Investors* (New York: Crown Business, 2005), 42, 43, 127.

Wharton's Dr. Jeremy Siegel undertook a similar study. He found, as we previously noted, that a *onetime* investment of $1,000 made in 1957 and held until 2003 would have given you dramatically better returns if you'd invested in stocks with strong dividend and income fundamentals:

If you haven't already done so, I again urge you to read Dr. Siegel's book *The Future for Investors* to learn more about the importance of dividends. You should conclude that the results of an investment approach rooted in income fundamentals are simply astounding. Dividend-paying investments give you superior returns. You also want to invest in stocks with low price-to-earnings ratios and high earnings.

Reason #2: Dividend-paying stocks tend to withstand market corrections better than non-dividend-paying stocks.

When the stock market corrects, dividend-paying stocks have tended to lose less money. For example, during the stock market's correction after the dot-com bloat in the late 1990s, dividend-paying stocks suffered substantially less damage. We saw that the stocks of dividend-paying companies among the S&P 500 fell by an average of 13.3 percent in 2002 while the stocks of non-dividend-paying companies fell by an average 30.3 percent instead.[19] Ouch!

Reason #3: Dividend-paying stocks may continue paying you income even if share prices sputter or fall—and you can reinvest the income.

When the stock market plummeted in 2002, some 191 companies actually increased their dividend payments.[20] That represented more money that investors could reinvest to accelerate the growth of their capital.

Today, more and more investors are returning to dividend-paying stocks because they are fed up with the seesaw corrections of "capital gains." There is renewed demand for dividend-focused funds. In the words of one financial commentator:

"The push on dividend funds reflects a radical change in investor psychology since the late 1990s, which were all about the rise of fast-growing stocks that generally paid no dividends and instead reinvested all their profits in the pursuit of more growth. Given how that turned out, small investors and big players alike have embraced dividend-paying stocks as a return to common sense."[21]

When you diversify your holdings, I recommend allocating half of your capital into dividend-paying equity investments. Foremost of all, I want you to obtain hard dividend income and then reinvest that income to buy more shares. Secondarily, I want you to invest in stocks that may not pay dividends, per se, but nevertheless have strong income fundamentals as measured by overall earnings and by a low price-earnings ratio. Companies may have good reason not to pay dividends from time to time. If you cannot get good dividends, at least get a claim on strong earnings.

A dividend-oriented investment strategy does, however, have risks. Companies that pay attractive dividends tend to be large-cap institutions, often concentrated in the financial-services, heavy-manufacturing, and utility sectors. If you focus on dividend-paying stocks, you may be concentrated in a few sectors.

There is, as well, tax risk. The favorable tax treatment for stock dividends is only officially in place until the end of 2008. The tax policy might once again change. And even dividend-paying stocks may *not* deliver positive returns. There is no guarantee of positive performance.

Notwithstanding such risks, stock dividends represent an attractive, commonsensical, and important income stream. Focusing on dividend-paying stocks will give you real income you can reinvest! And my excitement about dividend income is hardly new or revolutionary. Most of the country's greatest investment experts have long extolled the merits of dividend-oriented stock investments.

However, many experts also recommend reducing your equity holdings as you age. And as we've seen, some are beginning to caution about stocks going forward, saying that boomers may soon begin selling off equities for retirement cash, driving down stock prices.

I recommend a very different approach to stock investing. I argue that you should continually take a low-risk approach to investing in stocks *regardless of your age bracket*. I also believe that you should look forward to the boomer sell-off of assets over the next two decades as an important *buying* opportunity.

You are going to need income for many years of retirement. Significantly cutting back your stock holdings when you're age sixty-five or seventy will simply cripple the growth and income prospects of your savings. And if boomers do, in fact, sell off stocks en masse and cause stock prices to falter, that's your opportunity to buy more!

In future chapters, I name specific dividend-producing investments that you might consider and suggest when it might, indeed, be prudent to reduce stock holdings to avoid harm. But the changes of allocation that I recommend have little to do with your birthday.

First, let's agree on a fundamental strategy. Let's agree that it's prudent, pragmatic, and fundamentally sound to invest in stocks for *dividend income* that you can reinvest instead of chasing "windfall gains." Capital gains are great, but you want real income above all.

I therefore urge you to invest 50 percent of your nest egg in dividend-producing investments and to reinvest this income to buy more. Contrary to conventional wisdom, I believe you can hold this allocation as you age *unless* the stock market shows signs of speculative tumult or turbulence. You want income for a long life. You want income diversity. And you want to shield your savings from turmoil and loss. A steady dose of dividend-income investments can help you on all counts.

INVEST FOR INTEREST INCOME

Interest income is the return you derive when you *lend* money to a bank, a government, or a corporation. It is often associated with low- or moderate-risk kinds of investments.

You earn interest income by placing money in deposits or by buying bonds or Treasury bills. Bank deposits and bonds are actually loans that you make to a borrower who promises to pay back your money (called principal) with some reward (called interest) by a particular date (called the maturity date). You can make a number of different interest-income investments.

Bank deposits are perhaps the one kind with which people are most familiar. You can lend money to a bank simply by putting it on deposit for one month, three months, six months, and so forth. The bank pays you a return depending on its credit strength and prevailing interest rates. If the bank is a strong institution—meaning that your deposit has a low risk of default—then you are likely to receive only a limited amount of interest premium. There is always a direct link between risk and reward.

Bonds are a loan you make for a fixed time to borrowers such as the federal government, a government agency, a state government, a municipality, or a corporation. We noted that bonds have given investors an average annual return of about 4.8 percent (or 1.5 percent after inflation).[22] Depending on the historical period and the risk of the borrower, however, different kinds of bonds pay higher or lower rates of interest.

For example, Treasury bills are IOUs of the federal government. You lend money to the U.S. Treasury for some period of time and it agrees to repay you with interest. Many economists believe that Treasury bills are risk-free. I believe that is simplistic thinking, but U.S. T-bills usually pay the lowest amount of interest. Again—low risk, low return.

One kind of Treasury security called TIPS—i.e., Treasury Inflation-Protected Securities—periodically adjust your principal and interest returns if there is evidence of inflation. They are excellent holdings to have in your retirement portfolio because they offset the loss of purchasing power. However, you should only hold them in tax-sheltered accounts such as IRAs and 401(k)s. Otherwise you might have to pay hefty taxes on the inflation adjustments.

"Government agency" bonds are the bonds of a variety of different government groups and affiliates. They have a bit more risk because the borrower is often not, after all, the federal government per se. More risk, more return.

"Corporate" bonds are loans to corporations. If the borrower has strong financials and its paper enjoys strong ratings—specifically an "investment grade" rating of AA or better—then its bonds are said to be "blue-chip." On the other hand, "junk" bonds are bonds rated below BBB (Standard & Poor's rating) or Baa (Moody's). They have substantially more risk and therefore pay higher returns. For example, default rates on junk bonds can be high, surpassing 10 percent in some years.[23] "Emerging market bonds" are the bonds of countries such as Brazil, Malaysia, and Mexico, which pose as much or more risk and typically pay high interest.

A fundamental tenet of good allocation strategy is to hold a mix of these different interest-paying investments with an emphasis on high-quality borrowers, AA-or-better-rated paper, and the avoidance of unnecessary risk. Even so, many 401(k) and IRA investors are top-heavy in high-yield, emerging-market, and other higher-risk bonds. In large doses, that is not prudent.

All-in, interest-income investments give you one particular kind of income stream and have an important place in your portfolio. They have risks—default risk, interest-rate or opportunity-loss risk, inflation risk, and the like. You can limit these risks by focusing on high-quality borrowers, by sticking with short-term maturities, by avoiding junk bonds, and by putting money into TIPS. Most important of all, you can reduce the risk of losses and strengthen your returns by holding a *mix* of these investments.

Make note, however, of this distinction. Conventional authorities recommend a larger and larger amount of "low-risk bonds" in your portfolio as you age to offset the risk of losses. I encourage you to avoid losses *at all times* with your retirement money—not just when you're in your sixties or seventies.

I recommend allocating at least 25 percent of your retirement capital to interest-income investments.

They should be low-risk placements: TIPS, high-quality corporate bonds and short-maturity Treasuries. You should, moreover, avoid junk bonds as well as bond or deposit investments with long durations, since interest rates might gyrate. However, don't worry about continually increasing your exposure in interest-paying investments as you age. Be risk-adverse with your retirement money in every age bracket! Focus on generating real income as a fundamental way of curbing risk.

INVEST FOR RENT INCOME

Rent income is another cash stream that can meaningfully strengthen your returns and diversification. By *rent income* I mean income from commercial, medical, hotel, and industrial properties that you own via funds or real estate investment trusts, and, secondarily, appreciation on such properties and funds when you sell them. I do *not* mean the appreciation of your house. I do *not* mean buying a house, adding a Jacuzzi and birdbath, then flipping it—that's foolhardy speculation. And I do *not* mean investing in a "real estate fund" that actually holds a lot of high-risk mortgages.

Instead, I mean "rent" as in (1) you buy funds that hold a diverse array of income-producing properties; (2) you pick fund managers adept at securing tenants and locking into advantageous leases; and (3) you obtain real income each year that you can reinvest to heighten the growth of your retirement capital. Of course, the equity in your house is an important source of income, too. Right now, however, I want to focus on real estate investments that pay rent income.

Real estate is a distinct asset class. In investment jargon, we say that it has a "high correlation" with inflation, meaning that real estate values tend to go up when inflation does.[24] On the other hand, real estate does not move in tandem with stocks or bonds. The stock market may lose value while real estate prices actually climb—and that's exactly what happened in 2000–2005.

In fact, a good deal of historical evidence shows that real estate has often performed *independently of* and in ways *different from* stocks and bonds. That's precisely why you want rent-producing investment exposure in your portfolio. However, rent generation—as opposed to investments in mortgages or any other kind of "real estate"—is key. As David Swensen, chief investment officer at Yale University, put it, "High quality real estate holdings [can] produce significant levels of current cash flow generated by long-term, in-place lease arrangements with tenants. Sustained levels of high cash flow lead to stability in valuation, as a substantial portion of asset value stems from relatively predictable cash flows."[25]

Because rent-producing investments (1) are a distinct asset category that does *not* increase or decrease in value at the same time as stocks and bonds, (2) can help protect your savings from inflation, and (3) represent additional, stable diversification in your portfolio, they should be integral holdings.

You can invest in real estate through specialized vehicles as well as REITs. Real estate investment trusts are specialized kinds of trust funds that pool the capital of many investors to purchase and manage income-producing properties (which you want) or mortgage loans (which you *don't* want). They also pay out "dividends." But beware! Many "real estate" funds or trusts primarily contain mortgage content, hyperpriced blocks of residential properties, and/or the stocks of "real-estate related companies."

You have to check the content of any real estate fund or REIT carefully before you buy. Many do not have "rent" potential. When you invest in RE-

ITs, *you want the "equity" or rent-producing kind—and even then with content that is not price-inflated.*

Real estate investments have historically produced returns different from the returns of stocks and bonds. Unfortunately, many investors have been conditioned to expect double-digit performance from real estate— and that is not realistic.

Here are the facts. From December 1975 through December 2005, publicly traded REITs (the trusts) delivered an average annual return of 13.8 percent versus an average return of 12.7 percent for the S&P 500 stock index.[26] That is to say, real estate trusts outperformed equities in that period.

As we saw earlier, however, Yale University's Dr. Robert Shiller found that over much longer periods—from 1890 to 2007, for example—residential real estate prices more typically increased on average by only 3.4 percent each year.[27] *That's right. Residential real estate has a long history of only modest price gains.*

Compare that with the average 12.95 percent average appreciation that took place in U.S. housing prices from the fourth quarter of 2004 through the fourth quarter of 2005 alone.[28] This astounding valuation spike tells even the skeptics among us that we're knee-deep in another bubble.

Now here's reality. Given their risk characteristics, real estate investments should probably produce returns that are somewhat less than the return of stocks and somewhat more than the return of bonds.[29] Real Estate Investment Trusts—all kinds lumped together—have typically produced rather steady income returns of between 5 and 10 percent per year for more than twenty years.[30] In 2006, however, they produced returns of 35 percent.[31] REITs are, as I write this, red-hot high-risk investments.

All of which brings me to two conclusions. One is that real estate has historically demonstrated risk/reward characteristics much different from either stocks or bonds—so there is good reason to make provision for real estate exposure in your portfolio. However, many kinds of real estate investments are decidedly overvalued at this time. You need to consider any real estate investment with great caution.

Real estate investments have a variety of risks—the risk of property damage, tenant default, changing interest rates, and so on. They also have "speculation" risk—the risk that you may pay an inflated price for a property or fund, then see its value plummet when the market corrects.

So let me again urge caution: do *not* count on real estate to generate the kinds of windfall returns you saw in recent years up to 2006. We are currently in the midst of a speculative bubble. Many property values will fall. According to National City, a respected financial group, some seventy-one metropolitan areas representing more than four-tenths of all single-family housing value in the United States were already deemed to be "extremely overvalued" by the close of 2005.[32] By "overvaluation," the group meant that single-family homes were "overpriced by at least 30 percent."[33] Four-tenths of the market overvalued by 30 percent or more!

Today we are seeing an oversupply of condos in many markets, hyper residential pricing, residential corrections and subprime-mortgage defaults, commercial real estate flipping of unprecedented scale, commercial mortgages with terms just as foolhardy as the subprime residential ones, and valuations of commercial as well as residential REIT shares in "nosebleed territory."[34] There's danger ahead.

If you own U.S. real estate funds or REITs, it may be a good time to sell. In the long term, rent-producing investments at attractive prices *do* belong in your portfolio. However, use rent income as a barometer of value. A rent stream is a good determinant of the reasonable value of any real estate investment. You want rent return—real or hypothetical—that is better than you'd get from a bank deposit or bond.

As you set your Investment Master Plan, make provision for investments that produce rent income. Normally I would suggest a 20 percent allocation into rent-producing holdings. However, prevailing market conditions beg prudence, and I have lowered the percentage. There are still rent-oriented investments worth holding, but you want to achieve real income with reasonably priced investments, not "maybe gains" or speculative fluff. So avoid—at all costs—real estate investments in hyperappreciation locations. Do *not* follow the herd into bubble investments in California or Florida or Arizona. As one commentator put it about residential real estate today, "The real losers will be those who bought recently at inflated prices and are forced to sell, usually because they're taking a job in another city or can't make the payments when their adjustable mortgage rate jumps. And speculators who bought overpriced condos in the hope of a quick killing are going to get hosed."[35]

Finally, be sure to check out the *property content* and the *income yield* of any fund or REIT via its prospectus and Morningstar's research. The "income yield" is simply the income that a property generates divided by its purchase price. It's a measure of the income return you're getting back for each dollar you invest. As I write this, residential prices are correcting in many locations, and income yields for many commercial and industrial properties are less than you'd get from a time deposit. You, however, want investments that produce rent income at reasonable prices—not a boxload of subprime loans or a bundle of hyperinflated buildings. Be cautious.

MAKE PROVISION FOR INSURANCE INVESTMENTS

Even the best of investment plans can be derailed by market corrections, economic upheavals, or herd "panic attacks." So I encourage investors to keep a small part of their savings in "insurance investments" as well.

By *insurance investments,* I mean investments that can offset damage if your other, primary holdings take a plunge. Think of them as protection placements that may prevent larger losses.

Much of the protection you need is already built into our income-focused approach to asset allocation. Real income returns are your foremost shield. However, I additionally recommend several kinds of investments: (1) precious metals; (2) natural resources, commodities, or energy; and (3) Swiss-franc-denominated holdings.

Investing a small amount into precious metals is particularly helpful. Gold investments tend to move up in advance of inflation.[36] Repeat studies also show that a small amount of precious metals exposure can reduce a portfolio's risk as well as heighten its long-term returns.[37] Gold has a "negative correlation" with stocks and bonds,[38] meaning that it goes up in value when they come down. That's precisely why you want such exposure embedded in your master plan and portfolio.

There are good "insurance" and risk reasons to invest in precious metals. Moreover, demographics make such investments outright compelling. China and India have immense appetites for precious metals. Those two countries alone consume 37 percent of the world's gold production.[39] Their nationals often use gold as an important store of wealth. As hundreds of millions of people in those countries move into peak income and investing ages, the demand for precious metals is likely to increase.

Provision for energy, commodities, natural resources, or basic materials exposure in your master plan may also be prudent. With huge increases in the world's population taking place, the demand for energy, commodities, and basic materials may well soar. I expect valuations in basic materials—meaning chemicals, forest products, paper, building materials, iron, steel, and mining—to grow in tandem with the population surge. Such investments may give you inflation protection as well demographic benefit.

Alternatively, consider a small allocation into Swiss-franc-denominated investments. Switzerland's currency, the Swiss franc, is now informally pegged to the euro. Prior to 2002, however, the Swiss franc had gold backing. Its reserves are immense and exceptionally strong. Long political and economic stability plus advantageous banking-secrecy laws have helped Swiss banks attract vast amounts of "safe haven" capital from wealthy people around the world. That money isn't going away anytime soon! Switzerland's top corporations—such as Nestlé, UBS, and Novartis—are also among the world's most powerful companies. Hence, an investment in a Swiss-franc-denominated fund or deposit can be a powerful kind of insurance as well.

As you set your Investment Master Plan, I encourage you to allocate 10 percent of your capital into a mix of these kinds of insurance investments. They may not be particularly hot performers. In fact, I hope they aren't! But they may protect you from acute harm.

BUILD STRONG INTERNATIONAL EXPOSURE INTO YOUR PLAN

I also encourage you to ratchet up international exposure. At present, most American workers hold *less than 10 percent* of their 401(k) holdings in non-U.S. investments on average.[40] That is not reward-smart or demographically savvy.

If we add up the "capitalization" or market value of all the stock markets in the world, U.S. stocks represent about 46 percent of the global total.[41] So limiting your exposure to U.S.-only equity investments isolates you from a larger array of investment opportunities.

The same holds true for bonds. Measured by market value, U.S. bonds represent about 47 percent of the global total.[42] You'll miss out on good investment opportunities if you ignore non-U.S. bonds as well.

But "opportunity" is only part of the story. International investments have delivered attractive historical returns that have often been different from their U.S. counterparts. In recent years, U.S. and non-U.S. investments have tended to move more in tandem—and this is particularly the case when there is global turmoil.[43] In other words, international investments no longer give you much downside offset. When U.S. stocks come down, non-U.S. stocks often come down, too.

On the other hand, international exposure can help you broaden your diversification and reduce risk in some measure. One way of quantifying risk is to look at an investment's "standard deviation." Don't panic! That's simply a measure of performance choppiness. If an investment has a historical average return of 5 percent and a standard deviation of 3 percent, the deviation number simply means that the investment is highly likely to produce an annual return of between 8 and 2 percent (that's 5 percent plus 3 and 5 percent minus 3).

Looking at the period 1900–2000, U.K. analysts Dimson, Marsh, and Staunton found that the standard deviation on U.S. stocks was 20.2, while non-U.S. equities had a marginally lower risk of 19.5.[44] That's just a fancy numerical way of saying that non-U.S. equities had, past tense, somewhat lower risk characteristics.

Between 1950 and 2000, international equities had a standard deviation of 18.6, while U.S. equities had a lower 17.4 measurement.

But here's the important point: the researchers found that by combining non-U.S investments along with U.S. domestic equities in a 1950–2000 portfolio, you would have enjoyed an even lower risk measure *of 16.0 during the period. And the same held true for bonds.*[45]

We don't have to get bogged down in a lot of investment mathematics or jargon. But it is clear that adding international exposure can, indeed, help reduce portfolio risk.

There are strong arguments for international exposure. And demographics make such exposure vital as well. Millions of new consumers will emerge in parts of Europe, Asia, and South America. Millions of people overseas will be moving into their peak investment years. You want to tap this demographic groundswell.

We noted that the United States will only add thirty-two thousand "prime consumers"—people between the ages of thirty-five and fifty-four—between 2005 and 2025, essentially no growth at all.[46] I call that age group "prime investors" or "prime consumers" because they are the locomotives that have driven our country's economic and investment growth thus far. Going forward our growth may plateau.

By contrast, a number of developing countries will, we saw, be adding tens of millions of prime consumers—India, alone, will add 123 million and China 34 million by 2025.[47] That's a huge number of people becoming economically active.

Over the next two decades, then, we can expect immense demand in these countries for building materials, food supplies, energy, and natural resources. And that demand should translate into extremely exciting investment opportunities.

It is not clear how many Indian or Chinese nationals will actually become global stock and bond investors. Most may not. Even so, a number of Asian, Central European, and Latin American countries are likely to have vast numbers of people consuming more goods and services, contributing to economic growth, and investing in domestic as well as international markets. Demographics tell us that the *probability* of more consumption and investment activity in these countries is high.

Capitalize on the benefits of international exposure! Begin to look at investments from an *income perspective* and consider this: Coca-Cola is a U.S. company that produces more than half of its income offshore. Nestlé is a Swiss company that earns half of its income from the United States. The demarcation between "U.S." and "international" investments is becoming increasingly blurred. Diversifying your investments by *income stream* as well as by *geography* is an advantageous way of strengthening your portfolio. Don't be afraid of international exposure!

Of course, risks do come with international investments. They include foreign-exchange risk, the risk that non-U.S. investments will move more and more in tandem with U.S. ones, and the risk of political and social unrest overseas. Even taking such risks into consideration, I believe that international exposure is highly beneficial. As the Dimson-Marsh-Staunton team said, "Today, the United States has the world's largest equity market.

Your Core Strategy with International

	U.S.	Non-U.S.	Total
Interest Income	20%	5%	25%
Dividend Income	25%	25%	50%
Rent Income	5%	10%	15%
"Insurance"	—	10%	10%
Total Portfolio	**50%**	**50%**	**100%**

Even so, U.S. equities comprise less than half the world's total. U.S. investors who restrict themselves to their home market are thus ignoring over half the world's opportunity set, and forgoing the risk reduction benefits from international diversification."[48]

"So looking ahead, and while there are no guarantees, our best guess is that international investment will offer a higher reward for risk due to the risk reduction from international diversification."[49]

I would add that international exposure is also vital because of changing demographics. That is why you should make provision in your master plan for a full 50 percent allocation to non-U.S. investments along these lines:

DIVERSIFY SO THAT NO ONE HOLDING CAN CAUSE LASTING HARM

Finally, I want you to embed a diversification principle in your master plan so that no single stock, bond, or fund can cause you irreparable harm.

Many investors have a quarter or more of their wealth invested in a single company's stock or single mutual fund. That is usually dangerous unless the investment is a broad index.

When I worked in Switzerland and the Middle East, I was impressed that wealthy clients usually worked with four or five different banks. Not only did they insist on broad *investment* diversification—they even diversified between portfolio managers and banks! Wealthy investors diversify extensively to shelter themselves from harm. You should, too.

So build this guideline into your master plan: broadly diversify your holdings in each income category so that no single investment—stock, bond, real estate, or fund (with the exception of index funds)—represents more than 10 percent of your total capital.

USE THIS MODEL TO HELP YOU

Now let's put all of this together. To avoid losses and enhance returns, I'm encouraging you to invest with a strategic, income-oriented plan. You need to invest in a disciplined fashion, avoiding "follow the herd" moves into speculative markets and corrections. You want an *income-focused* approach to investing so that your holdings are rooted in genuine earnings and produce

Investment Master Plan

A Diversification Strategy to Protect
and Enlarge Your Savings

	U.S	Non-U.S	Total
Interest Income			
Short-maturity bank deposit	5	—	5
Short-maturity, high-quality U.S. bond fund	5	—	5
U.S. Treasury inflation-protected (TIPS) fund	10	—	10
High-quality international bond fund	—	5	5
Subtotal	20%	5%	25%
Dividend Income			
Dividend-weighted index of U.S. stocks	15	—	15
Fund or index of high-earnings U.S. stocks	5	—	5
"Value" or low-P/E U.S. stock fund or index	5	—	5
Dividend-weighted index of international stocks	—	15	15
Emerging-market stock fund	—	5	5
Actively managed international stock fund	—	5	5
Subtotal	25%	25%	50%
Rent Income			
REIT of U.S. nonresidential properties	5	—	5
International real estate fund	—	10	10
Subtotal	5%	10%	15%
"Insurance" Investments			
Precious metals fund	—	5	5
Basic materials, natural resources, *or* Swiss fund	—	5	5
Subtotal	—	10%	10%
Total Portfolio	**50%**	**50%**	**100%**

income payments you can reinvest. You want broad international exposure to
reduce risk, enlarge your income opportunities, and capitalize on contemporary demographics. And you want to avoid overconcentration in any single
investment or fund.

Here, then, is a more detailed version of the kind of allocation blueprint
I recommend. Copy it. Tape it to your computer screen. And use it to reconfigure your retirement investments across all of your 401(k), IRA, brokerage, and other retirement accounts.

In the next chapter we will identify specific funds and indexes that can help you execute this strategy. Right now, I simply want you to set a strategic *blueprint*—an Investment Master Plan—before you move into stock, bond, or fund details.

Take a close look at this strategy and customize it to suit your risk tolerance and personal views. One size does not fit all. For example, you may be substantially more risk-adverse and want even more interest income. Make that adjustment. Or you may want less "rent" exposure because of the price hype in the real estate markets. If so, make that adjustment, allocating more to interest income as well.

As for critics who find fault with this amount of exposure or that, my message is brief: Let's not debate whether a red extinguisher or white one works best when there's fire in the kitchen! A lot of people have *no* plan and *no* diversification strategy whatsoever. So let's get cracking with a real-return, get-back-to-fundamentals approach to investing. Let's stay focused on income instead of speculation. Modify the allocations in my plan to

---

ACTION STEPS

1. Obtain a list of your holdings in all of your retirement accounts—401(k), IRA, brokerage, and any others.

2. Identify each of your current investments as (1) interest-producing, (2) dividend-producing, (3) rent-producing, (4) "insurance," or (5) "I don't know."

3. Identify each investment as international or USA.

4. Add the amounts you currently have in each category, then compare your allocations with my model:

- Are you prudently diversified to achieve diverse streams of income?
- Do you have 40–50 percent international exposure?
- Do you have any single stock, bond, or fund position that represents more than 10 percent of your wealth?

5. Score yourself. What percent of your portfolio currently produces income that you automatically reinvest?

6. Set a customized Investment Master Plan of your own or adopt mine. Use it to diversify your holdings *across all of your accounts* to bolster returns and reduce risks.

meet your particular requirements or risk tolerance. But stay focused on the fundamentals that I'm recommending: (1) broad diversification so that no one investment category outright sabotages your future; (2) a focus on *income* instead of effervescent "gains"; (3) strong international exposure to capitalize on changing demographics; and (4) "insurance" investments to additionally strengthen your risk shield. And remember, with the strategy I propose, you need not make continual allocation shifts to "less risky" or fewer stock investments as you age. Instead, build risk aversion into your investments *at every age* by following an Investment Master Plan that is antispeculative and focused on good income fundamentals.

6

BUILD OUT YOUR INVESTMENT PLAN
WITH FUNDS, INDEXES,
AND OBJECTIVE RESEARCH

Y ou're on a roll! You now have an Investment Master Plan that will (1) help you broadly diversify your investments to protect as well as enlarge your nest egg; (2) specifically diversify your holdings so that no single asset category or single investment can cause you irreparable harm; and (3) help you achieve *real* returns that you can reinvest. In this chapter you will select investments to build out your plan, using funds, indexes, and good research.

THE ADVANTAGES OF FUNDS, INDEXES, AND ETFS

I have, I trust, convinced you of the great importance of diversification. A powerful way of achieving diversification is to use mutual funds, indexes, and exchange-traded funds or ETFs instead of individual securities. When you invest in a few individual stocks or bonds, you take on concentration risk—the risk that the volatility or performance of a single investment might put you in harm's way. You can achieve much broader, wiser, and lower-risk diversification with funds and indexes.

> Use mutual funds, indexes, and exchange-traded funds as the building blocks for a lower-risk portfolio. All three kinds of pooled investments are advantageous.

Why are funds and indexes attractive? A *mutual fund* is a kind of collective investment that pools money from shareholders and invests in assets in accordance with the fund's stated objectives. A fund may give you exposure in twenty, thirty, or fifty stocks or bonds at a time. Professional investment managers choose and monitor the securities for you. They collect the dividend, interest, and rent income on your behalf. You can usually buy or sell your fund position easily.

In other words, mutual funds give you important advantages: (1) expert management, (2) liquidity, (3) convenience, and, of course, (4) broad diversification. Unless you're an investment professional and have the time to do day-to-day research, trading, and investment monitoring, mutual funds are a highly advantageous and convenient way of investing.

Mutual funds are said to be "actively managed," meaning that professional managers actively screen and select investments for you. Funds put human talent to work on your behalf. In turn, the managers charge an annual fee for their services. On average, management fees run about 1.26 percent per annum for mutual funds industrywide.[1] However some funds charge as much as 2 or 3 percent each year. And that, of course, siphons money from your pocket.

Index funds can give you added diversification and cost advantage. An index fund attempts to match the performance of an entire investment index, market, region, sector, or asset class. For example, an S&P 500 Index Fund gives you exposure in all five hundred stocks of the large companies that make up Standard & Poor's 500 Index. An investment in a Short-Maturity Bond Index fund might give you a stake in more than seven hundred short-maturity U.S. bonds.

Index funds can significantly amplify your diversification. What's more, they often give superior returns over time. Research by Bogle, Ellis, Sharpe, McGuigan, Michelson, Hsu, Campollo, West, and others showed that index funds have given investors better returns than most actively managed funds over the long term.[2] As Warren Buffett, the master investor, himself concluded, "Most investors, both institutional and individual, will find that the best way to own common stocks is through an index fund that charges minimal fees. Those following this path are sure to beat the net results (after fees and expenses) delivered by the great majority of investment professionals."[3]

Thus, index funds give you exposure in a large number of stocks, bonds, or other assets—often with performance advantage. They are "passively managed" because investment professionals do not have to actively screen the content or select one stock over another. Instead, an index fund simply buys the same mix of stocks or bonds in the same proportion as in the underlying index. There's no need for a lot of decision-making or trading. There's no need for day-to-day stock picking by high-powered managers. And absent the need for decision-making and investment research, the management costs of an index fund are usually low. For example, Vanguard's 500 Index Fund charges only 0.18 percent—not even two-tenths of 1 percent!—in annual fees.[4] That's an immense cost advantage for investors.

Consequently, index funds give you the important advantages of (1) powerful diversification, (2) broad market participation, (3) liquidity, (4) low turnover, (5) low expenses, and (6) returns that are often better over time than those of many actively managed funds.

Yet another way of investing for broad diversification and income is via *ETFs or exchange-traded funds*. They are a new form of investing. An ETF is simply a fund—usually an index fund—that trades like stock. You buy shares of an ETF from a broker such as Schwab or Merrill Lynch. You pay the broker a commission as you do when you buy stocks. The price of an ETF fluctuates moment to moment like stock. And like stock, you can give your broker advance instructions to sell an ETF position at a preset price. So think of an ETF as a kind of index fund that is bought and sold like shares of stock.

Many ETFs have no minimum purchase amount. So with an ETF, you get the advantages of broad index diversification, the low cost of index investing, a low entry purchase, and the trading advantages of stocks.

You can advantageously build out your Investment Master Plan with mutual funds, indexes, and ETFs—all three. In the last chapter, I cited Gary Brinson's research and the impetus it gave to the view that asset allocation was one of the foremost determinants of portfolio performance. In effect, Gary's research helped firm up the view that index funds are better investments long term.

However, later research by William Jahnke challenged this view. Jahnke showed the merits of more fluid asset allocation, recognizing that expected returns for different asset classes vary with times.[5] He found that active fund management (meaning mutual funds instead of indexes) can, indeed, generate risk-adjusted excess returns over an index and reduce portfolio risk.

In other words, expert research shows that both index investing as well as active-management or mutual-fund investing can work advantageously in different circumstances. Forget all the doctrinaire articles about indexes versus active management. Both work! Hence I urge you to use a mix of mutual funds, index funds, as well as ETFs when building out your plan.

On the other hand, research also shows that fund costs and management fees do have a critical impact on performance.[6] Large management fees cause a drag on returns. They divert income from your retirement. When you invest in any kind of fund or index, therefore, you can heighten your prospects for better returns by selecting *low-cost* varieties.[7]

Let's go over the numbers once again. The average annual management cost of a mutual fund is about 1.26 percent—that is actually the composite of 1.42 percent for stock mutual funds and about 0.96 percent for bond funds.[8] By comparison, the average annual management fee for a stock index fund is about 0.18 percent per year and for an ETF about 0.12 percent.[9] Those differences represent savings that could significantly bolster the compounding and growth of your returns over time. So always keep costs in mind when you select funds or indexes of any kind. Investments via funds, indexes, and ETFs can *all* be advantageous. However, be sure to give priority to funds and indexes that have low costs and a decided real-return, *income* orientation.

FUNDAMENTAL INDEXES ARE PARTICULARLY POWERFUL

While mutual funds, conventional index funds, and ETFs are advantageous, new "fundamental" index funds may be even more so. Fundamental indexes are indexes that select and hold a large basket of securities using nontraditional weighting methods. They perform exceptionally well. In fact, research suggests that these new kinds of index funds may be hard-to-beat investments. Here's why.

Conventional index funds have a basic flaw.[10] They are usually structured or "weighted" on the basis of "market capitalization"—meaning the price of a stock times the number of shares outstanding. In other words, stock price is a key factor. The higher the price and the bigger the market cap of a particular stock, the more of a traditional index it occupies.

Suppose, for example, that the entire stock market consisted of just two stocks: Company A has a thousand shares of stock outstanding that cost $1 per share, and Company B has a thousand shares outstanding that cost $2 a share. A traditional index would hold a mix of both shares in a way tied to the stock price. For every $3 you invested in a traditional index, $2 would go to the higher-priced stock.

Don't worry about the mathematics or jargon. Just remember this: traditional indexes are price-sensitive. They have a bias toward high-priced securities. Whenever the stock market is speculatively inflated, a traditional index gives you more exposure in overpriced stocks. *And that is the exact opposite of what you want!* You don't want a collection of high-priced stock! You want the low-priced stocks of healthy companies that pay high dividends.

Let me repeat: you want to buy low-price stocks that pay high dividends.

Cutting-edge research by Arnott, Hsu, Moore, West, and Siegel focused on the price bias of traditional indexes.[11] They found that traditional indexes do, in fact, tend to overweight *overvalued* stocks and underweight *undervalued* stocks. In other words, *traditional "index funds draw you into every bubble going."*[12]

These researchers also found that indexes that are price-indifferent—or at least that are not built on the basis of high stock prices—perform substantially better. We saw in a previous chapter that Arnott tested several new indexes—he called them "fundamental" indexes—that select and hold stocks, giving equal weighting to four factors other than market capitalization: (1) income, (2) dividends, (3) sales, and (4) book value.

Arnott and his colleagues back-tested this fundamental four-weight index approach for both U.S. and international stocks. They found that their fundamental indexes of U.S. stocks outperformed traditional indexes by as much as *2 percent* each year with slightly lower risk or volatility.[13] That's astounding!

What's more, fundamental indexes produced even stronger results internationally. Arnott's international fundamental stock indexes actually delivered *2.5 percent more return* on average each year than traditional indexes—again with slightly lower volatility.[14] That difference, over time, could represent many years of retirement income!

We also saw Wharton professor Jeremy Siegel's remarkable finding. His research demonstrated that different kinds of fundamental indexes weighted by (1) high dividend yield or (2) low price-to-earnings ratios could result in many hundreds of thousands of dollars of incremental investment returns for you. This is so important that I'd like you to look at Dr. Siegel's conclusions once again:

If You Had Invested $1,000 One Time in 1957 In	Your Result in 2003
Index of high P/E-ratio (high-priced) stocks	$ 56,661
Traditional index of all S&P 500 stocks	$ 130,768
Index of low P/E-ratio (low-priced) stocks	$ 425,703
Index of highest dividend-yielding stocks	$ 462,750

Source: Jeremy J. Siegel, *The Future for Investors* (New York: Crown Business, 2005) 42, 43, 127.

Amazing, isn't it?! On one hand, index funds of all kinds give you powerful diversification. They reduce your risk. They have often performed better than actively managed funds over time. And they often have substantially lower costs—savings that can represent a lot of retirement capital for you.

But *how* an index is structured is also important. *Fundamental indexes—the ones that avoid price bias by selecting and holding stocks on the basis of high dividends or low price-to-earnings ratios or even a mix of other measures of value—produce the best results with lower risk!* They can help you achieve real income and avoid speculative overpricing. Over time, they appear to produce returns that simply cannot be beat.

But let's not kid ourselves. There is no magic. Not even specialized indexes are always going to perform in a superior fashion. Even fundamental indexes have drawbacks, too. For instance, dividend-weighted indexes underperform in red-hot markets and result in sector concentration. Nevertheless, I urge you to use *fundamental index funds* for broad diversification and real income returns you can reinvest. I'll name some particularly good fundamental indexes in just a bit.

THE IMPORTANCE OF OBJECTIVE RESEARCH

That brings us to an important question. *How* can you pick suitable mutual funds, indexes, or fundamental indexes? It's best to go with the top performer—right? Wrong! Sky-high performance often means that you already missed the boat. High returns may represent *correction risk* that you want to avoid. So top performance is most certainly *not* the sole or foremost criterion for picking a suitable index or fund. If you buy a top performer, you may be "buying high" and setting yourself up for correction losses.

To prudently select a fund or index, you need to consider a number of factors: its investment objective, risk characteristics, fees, performance history, and—most important of all in the case of actively managed funds—its human talent. Understanding the strengths and weaknesses of any fund, ETF, or index *before* you put money into it is vital. You have to do your homework! And you need objective, trustworthy research to do so.

Unfortunately, the investment recommendations of many experts are not always objective or helpful. Many groups that provide investment commentary also have investment funds, newsletters, stock lists, or fund recommendations they want to sell. Some earn commissions by recommending one fund or investment over another. And many are unable to offer objective investment advice because of conflicts of interest.

Brokerage houses, in particular, have a decidedly checked recommendation record. They have repeatedly demonstrated conflicts of interests when they offer investment views. They have, in fact, recommended stocks or funds on many occasions when the investments were mediocre or outright dangerous.

Brokers are working hard to change this reputation, and many brokers certainly do have excellent advice to offer. But that still leaves you in a predicament. Where can you go for *strictly* objective advice about the funds, ETFs, or index funds that are suitable for your plan?

I recommend Morningstar. It delivers strictly objective views in a convenient way. What's more, its research is free.

Morningstar publishes concise, objective, and *free* overviews of stocks, ETFs, and funds. Morningstar does not sell or manage funds of its own, so its views are independent. It publishes an "overall rating"—the so-called Morningstar Rating of one to five stars (five is the highest)—to help investors compare the strengths and weaknesses of different investments and funds. Many investment professionals find great fault with the "star" system. And I agree with the substance of their views. Picking a fund solely because it has five stars instead of two or three is overly simplistic. Don't fixate on the stars.

Nevertheless, Morningstar gives you access to useful information when you are screening investments. In particular, it is a good tool to help you size up a fund's *management* strengths, overall size, fundamental investment strategy, expenses, and operating issues.

Go online to www.morningstar.com and kick the tires. Enter a fund's name or symbol. Then spend a few minutes becoming acquainted with Morningstar's data. Take a look at a fund's (1) management (have there been any recent changes?), (2) size (humongous can be problematic), (3) risk factors, (4) returns, and (5) fees.

If you can afford it, consider subscribing to the following two information services as well. They can help you even better screen and appraise investments.

Morningstar's Premium Service is a for-pay service that gives you access to analyst commentary on the strengths and weaknesses of many funds and added fund views. It is a particularly straightforward way for laymen to obtain *objective* commentary about the management talents, risks, content, and fees of most funds. To obtain further information, contact Morningstar at 866-229-9449.

Motley Fool's Dividend Investing Newsletter does a good job sizing up dividend-focused funds and indexes. Subscribing to *Dividend Investing* is a convenient and relatively inexpensive way of checking for new funds with a dividend or income focus. Check it out online.

When you use these databases, look for funds, indexes, or ETFs that focus on income fundamentals, dividends, and earnings. In all cases, check out the fee structure. How much will come out of your return? In the case of mutual funds, pay close attention to the management talent as well. Is the management team stable? How much are you paying for it?

It's up to *you* to assess the strengths and weaknesses of any investment you consider. Do so using objective, trustworthy research. Try Morningstar's free research as a first step.

NEXT STEPS

Now let's go back to your Investment Master Plan and incorporate these recommendations about broad content diversification and income focus.

The allocation model I posted in the previous chapter lists fourteen different funds or investments. Don't panic! Think of your Investment Master Plan as a paint-by-number blueprint—you're simply going to fill in the blanks by selecting suitable funds and indexes to execute your income strategy. And you're going to diversify using different funds so that no single one holds too much of your retirement capital and has the ability to cause harm.

If you do not have large savings, you may use fewer funds. You may actually use five, ten, or sixteen different funds to complete your plan. You may hold them in a single account or in several different accounts. For example, you might hold several funds in your 401(k) plan and several others in some other account—but they will all be components of your one master plan. Or you may gradually build to fourteen different funds across accounts. That will depend on the size of your savings and the minimum entry requirements of the funds you choose.

The important thing is that when you choose investments for your master plan, primarily use *funds and indexes* instead of individual stocks and bonds. I also want you to use *objective research* that is easily available online *and free,* investing just twenty minutes of your time each quarter to screen and monitor your fund selections. And I want you to execute your master plan across all of your savings accounts.

One issue, of course, is that funds are often categorized in a mumbo-jumbo fragmented way by "size" (as in "large-cap" and "small-cap" equity funds) or by "quality" (as in "blue-chip" stocks or "investment-grade" bonds) or by "maturity" (as in "short-term" or "ultrashort" bonds). And these conventional labels often have little or nothing to do with the income focus I want you to insist upon. In fact, many funds that call themselves "income" funds or "dividend" investments produce little dividend or real income.

To help you, I've used Morningstar fund-family research and other sources to identify a number of preliminary fund prospects for you. They are listed in the same order as in your investment master plan. However, let me make several comments before we get into specific names and details.

The funds and indexes I name are strictly "prospects." They may change managers or suffer performance reverses by the time you read this book. So you yourself need to check out every one carefully *before* you actually invest in it. You need to do your own homework.

That a fund or index is cited here is no guarantee of positive performance or happy results. There *is* no surety of good or positive performance. And there are, as well, many other good funds and indexes not listed here. Don't be afraid to look into them as well.

That said, let's take a look at some funds and indexes that may help you.

INVESTMENTS FOR INTEREST INCOME

When you invest for interest income, you are looking for a mix of low-risk, high-quality deposit and bond investments. You want to steer clear of higher-risk securities, which represent unnecessary risk.

SHORT-TERM BANK DEPOSIT: 5 PERCENT

First, keep a small amount of your savings in a short-maturity bank deposit. This is "emergency money." It should be kept with an FDIC-insured bank—meaning that you should not lodge more than $100,000 (the insurance cutoff) in any one deposit with any one bank. Be sure the bank has FDIC insurance. Since we continue to enjoy a low-interest-rate climate, your deposit should be limited to three-month or six-month maturities. Should interest rates eventually rise, you want to capitalize on the opportunity to earn more interest.

SHORT-MATURITY, HIGH-QUALITY U.S. BOND FUND: 5 PERCENT

Symbol	Fund
OLTYX	Oppenheimer Limited-Term Government
SNGVX	Sit U.S. Government Securities
TCTRX	TIAA-CREF Short-Term Bond II
VSGBX	Vanguard Short-Term Federal Bonds
GGIFX	Victory Fund for Income R

You also want to invest in bonds of high quality. You do not want junk bonds or even municipal bonds in large doses. They can be unnecessarily risky.

The funds cited above hold shorter-maturity corporate and/or government bonds of investment grade and high quality. Consider putting a small amount of your capital into one such fund. I particularly like Oppenheimer's and Vanguard's funds, which have a government-bond focus, good track records, and low fees.

U.S. TREASURY INFLATION-PROTECTED SECURITIES (TIPS) FUND: 10 PERCENT

Symbol	Fund
FINPX	Fidelity Inflation Protected Bond
MPSAX	MassMutual Premier Inflation Protection
PRRDX	PIMCO Real Return Bond
TCILX	TIAA-CREF Inflation-Linked Bonds
TIP	iShares Lehman TIPS Bond
VIPSX	Vanguard Inflation-Protected Bonds

Treasury Inflation-Protected Securities, or TIPS, are the U.S. Treasury bonds that are periodically adjusted for inflation. There is a lot of debate about them because of their sometimes low returns. Don't let that stop you from making a savvy interest-income investment that protects you from inflation! In fact, I believe 10 percent of your savings should be lodged in this kind of bond fund. *However, only hold a TIPS fund in a 401(k), IRA, or some other tax-sheltered account.* Otherwise you will pay taxes on the inflation adjustments. And while there are many funds to choose from, there is (at least at this writing) only one ETF with this kind of bond content—the iShares Lehman TIPS fund. It is a low-cost way of achieving broad, indexlike exposure in the inflation-protected-bond sector.

HIGH-QUALITY INTERNATIONAL BOND FUND: 5 PERCENT

Symbol	Fund
BEGBX	American Century International Bond
FNMIX	Fidelity New Markets Income
OIBAX.LW	Oppenheimer International Bond
PFODX	PIMCO Foreign Bond Dollar Hedged
PREMX	T. Rowe Price Emerging Markets Bond

We also noted the importance of factoring demographics into your investment decisions. There are several ways of capitalizing on demographic trends. One is to hold the bonds and stocks of countries poised for strong demographic and economic growth. Many foreign countries will have huge numbers of people moving into adult economic activity, family formation, and peak consumption years. The economic growth of these countries will require funding. Hence, holding international bonds should be attractive.

Some investors are leery of so-called emerging-market bonds because of the past bond defaults of countries such as Argentina and Mexico. In fact, emerging-market bonds have only had a 2 percent default rate and deliver attractive returns.[15] Consequently, I am listing international bond funds that have good ratings, sound risk characteristics, and sometimes emerging-market content. Take the time to learn more about them.

INVESTMENTS FOR DIVIDEND INCOME

When you reach the point of selecting *dividend-income* investments, the quest for real income becomes much more exciting. Today, a number of fundamental indexes—some of which are still little-known—enable you to invest for dividend income with great advantage and powerful diversification. They are excellent investments. It's time for you to learn more about them as well.

DIVIDEND-WEIGHTED INDEX OF U.S. STOCKS: 15 PERCENT

We saw that indexes are baskets of stocks or other assets that mimic the returns of an entire market or some part of it. Indexes have, over time, often outperformed actively managed funds. Consequently, indexes in general are excellent core investments for your portfolio.

As we have also seen, traditional indexes have a "high-price" bias because they are market-cap weighted. They give added weight to higher-priced securities. On the other hand, "fundamental" indexes are baskets of stocks selected and weighted on the basis of factors other than stock prices. We saw that a fundamental index may use dividends or earnings or some other weighting criteria. And fundamental indexes have historically outperformed traditional indexes—at least thus far.

So let's recap. Indexes in general are good investments because they give you extremely broad diversification and they often outperform mutual funds. Fundamental indexes do not have the price bias of conventional indexes and outperform conventional indexes. Hence, I urge you to invest in fundamental indexes of dividend-paying stocks as a core investment in your portfolio.

You want the low-priced stocks of healthy companies that pay attractive dividends you can reinvest.

You can, therefore, invest in dividend-weighted indexes such as these:

Symbol	Index	Weighting
DTD	WisdomTree Total Dividend Index	Dividends Exposure in 1,467 Stocks
DTN	WisdomTree Dividend Top 100 Index	Dividends Exposure in 100 Stocks
DHS	WisdomTree High-Yielding Equity Index	Dividend Yield Exposure in 400 Stocks
DVY	iShares DJ Select Dividend Index	Dividend Yield Exposure in 117 Stocks
PFM	PowerShares Dividend Achievers	Market Cap Exposure in 332 Stocks

These indexes give you exposure in the stocks of many different companies and I have indicated the number of stocks at the far right. The number of shares, of course, may fluctuate over time. I have also noted how each index is weighted. Some are weighted by *dividends*—so stocks that pay more dividends in total have a stronger weighting and take up more of your investment. Some indexes are weighted on the basis of *dividend yield*—so stocks that have strong dividend payments *relative to a low stock price* get more weighting. And some indexes are weighted by other factors.

Each approach has advantages and disadvantages. Indeed, you may wish to invest in different kinds of these indexes because of their weighting differences and because of the 15 percent total allocation to such exposure in your plan. *However, I strongly recommend investing in a dividend-weighted and/or dividend-yield-weighted fundamental index. WisdomTree's broad DTD index is particularly attractive.*

Whatever your selections, dividend-focused indexes are an exceptional way of investing. And when you invest in them, be sure to give instructions to your broker *to reinvest the dividends.* That will accelerate the compounding of your capital.

> Use fundamental *dividend-weighted* indexes as the primary way of producing equity income. Invest in them, obtain dividend income from them, and automatically reinvest the income.

A word of caution, however. Many funds and indexes have the word *dividend* in their name. You may be tempted to use them instead of one of the dividend-weighted indexes I am recommending here. That would be misguided, as many *dividend*-named mutual funds deliver little or no dividend income. As *Money* magazine noted, "Mutual fund companies are slapping the word *dividend* on seemingly every new fund they trot out these days."[16] You have to be cautious.

On the other hand, you are likely to enjoy large diversification, better long-term results, and true income-bearing stocks using *fundamental index funds* at the core of your investment strategy. Invest in *dividend-weighted* and *dividend-yield-weighted* indexes for the best dividend-income results.

INDEX OF HIGH-EARNINGS U.S. STOCKS: 5 PERCENT

Symbol	Index	Weighting
EXT	WisdomTree Earnings Index	Earnings Exposure in 2,336 Stocks
EPS	WisdomTree Earnings 500 Index	Earnings Exposure in 500 Stocks
PRF	PowerShares RAFI U.S. 1000 Index	Sales, Dividends, Book Value, and Cash Flow Exposure in 1,000 Stocks

We saw Arnott's finding that an index weighted on the basis of revenues produced higher returns than a traditional stock index and, in fact, higher returns than even a dividend-weighted index. Good earnings are an important "value" measure, too. However, earnings do not give you any compounding advantage unless you actually receive dividends and reinvest them. So first prize goes to dividend-paying stocks and indexes that pay you income you can reinvest. Secondarily, I recommend allocating some money to a "high-earnings" fundamental index such as the ones cited above.

You can invest in the equities of high-earnings companies in several ways. The WisdomTree group recently launched several fundamental indexes expressly weighted on the basis of high earnings. They are excellent choices.

You might also consider the fundamental indexes designed by Rob Arnott and his colleagues at Research Affiliates. These Research Affiliates Fundamental Indexes, or RAFI, funds function a bit differently. They are the indexes I mentioned earlier that select and hold stocks giving equal weight to four factors: (1) dividends, (2) sales, (3) cash flow, and (4) book value. These measures clearly focus on income fundamentals, and the RAFI funds have, past tense, outperformed dividend-weighted indexes. Be sure to check into Research Affiliates' other offerings as well.

"Value" or Low-P/E Stock Fund or Index: 5 percent

Symbol	Fund or Index
EZY	WisdomTree Low P/E Index (Index Weighted by Low P/E Ratios)
SSHFX	Sound Shore (Mutual Fund)
VIVAX	Vanguard Value Index (Market Cap Index)
WPVLX	Weitz Partners Value Fund (Mutual Fund)

We noted Dr. Jeremy Siegel's research showing that an investment in a broad array of low price-to-earnings stocks also gave superior returns. "Value" funds and indexes have this same orientation. They focus on underpriced or low-priced stocks. And that focus makes good sense. Because a fund or index that has a bias toward low price-to-earnings stocks gets us back to income and earnings fundamentals. Research by Dimson, Marsh, and Staunton confirmed the "superior long-term performance in the United States of value stocks, namely, those with a high dividend yield and/or a high ratio of book to market value of equity."[17] After analyzing more than a century of stock statistics, those analysts concluded that "value stocks have performed markedly better than their growth-stock counterparts."[18]

This gives you several alternatives. You can invest in an actively managed value mutual fund, which will give you the advantage of professional management. You can invest in a conventional value stock index (such as Vanguard's) that has a low-P/E orientation but a high-price bias. Or you can invest in a fundamental index expressly structured and weighted on the basis of low-P/E ratios, such as WisdomTree's. I like the WisdomTree approach.

DIVIDEND-WEIGHTED INDEX OF INTERNATIONAL STOCKS: 15 PERCENT

Symbol	Index	Weighting
DOO	WisdomTree International Top 100	Dividends Exposure in 100 Stocks
DWM	WisdomTree DEFA Index	Dividends Exposure in 2,350 Stocks
DTH	WisdomTree DEFA High-Yielding Index	Dividend Yield Exposure in 670 Stocks
DND	WisdomTree Pacific ex-Japan Dividend	Dividends Exposure in 402 Stocks
WTY	WisdomTree Emerging Markets High Yield	Dividend Yield Exposure in 218 Stocks
PID	PowerShares Int'l Dividend Achievers	Market Cap Exposure in 60 Stocks

Fundamental indexes are also available for non-U.S. stocks. Again, up to 15 percent of your capital should be allocated to this type of investment. In particular, dividend-weighted indexes focused on Asia-Pacific (excluding Japan), Latin America, and nonindustrialized Europe may be advantageous because of demographic trends. Hence, I have cited the names of dividend-weighted indexes having broad international content as well as ones with a specific regional focus.

WisdomTree has a number of international fundamental indexes that are weighted by dividends and by dividend yield. Its DEFA fund—standing for Dividends Europe, Far East Asia and Australasia—gives you exposure to more than two thousand non-U.S. stocks selected and weighted on the basis of their dividend payouts.

EMERGING-MARKET STOCK FUND: 5 PERCENT

Symbol	Fund
GEMAX.LW	Goldman Sachs Emerging Markets Equity A
LMEMX	Legg Mason Emerging Markets Prime
MAPTX	Matthews Pacific Tiger
ODVYX	Oppenheimer Developing Markets Y
PRMSX	T. Rowe Price Emerging Markets Stock

We saw that the United States, Western Europe, and Japan have aging populations, while many so-called emerging-market countries—such as India, China, and Brazil—will have large numbers of people moving into peak investment and peak consumer years. For example, India alone will add hundreds of millions of people to its head count over the next twenty-five years, and its population of prime investors/spenders—folks in the thirty-five to fifty-four age bracket—will increase by more than 123 million by the year 2025.[19] This is a huge number.

As demographics play out, we can expect to see more economic growth and investment vibrancy in developing markets. *Demographics favor investments in emerging markets.* Hence, an investment in an actively managed fund or index of emerging-market stock markets should be a part of your portfolio, too.

I am only citing actively managed fund alternatives in this particular table. A number of good emerging-market equity indexes—the traditional market-cap, high-price-biased kind—also exist. Since emerging-market investments entail more risk, however, it may be advantageous to invest via actively managed mutual funds in addition to a dividend index so that professional managers can select stocks and monitor the choices for you. I recommend having both kinds of holdings.

ACTIVELY MANAGED INTERNATIONAL STOCK FUND: 5 PERCENT

Symbol	Fund
ARTIX	Artisan International
DIVTX	DFA International Value II
DODFX	Dodge & Cox International Stock
GCIAX.LW	Goldman Sachs Structured International Equity A
QIVAX.LW	Oppenheimer Quest for International Value A
TIERX	TIAA-CREF International Equity

A *mix* of mutual funds and index funds can be helpful, and many actively managed international funds produce laudable results. As you check out fund offerings, make sure that the fund managers have the same views about global demographics and opportunities that you do. Funds that exclusively invest in Western European or Japanese stocks may not be particularly wise since the populations of those regions will be aging and consuming differently. Funds that have a broader mandate and give their managers freedom to invest as and where they see opportunity may be better choices. The funds above have demonstrated that kind of agility as well as good performance.

INVESTMENTS FOR RENT INCOME

Rent-producing investments—as distinct from "real estate" investments of all kinds—also feature in your plan. Your allocation blueprint calls for two kinds.

REIT OF U.S. NONRESIDENTIAL PROPERTIES: 5 PERCENT

Symbol	Real Estate Investment Trust	Concentration
FRT	Federal Realty Investment Trust	Shopping Centers
HCP	Health Care Properties	Health Care Properties
NHP	Nationwide Health Properties	Health Care Properties
PCL	Plum Creek	Timberland
VNO	Vornado Realty Trust	Government Tenants

When you invest for U.S. rent income, you want to consider REITs that have true rent-producing content. As we've already noted, you don't want mortgages! They can be dangerous these days. You don't want funds holding the stocks of building-material companies. And for that matter, you don't want residential content either. Because of overpricing in many residential markets, REITs focused on residential properties may be risky. You only want to invest in residential REITs when prices ease back and when interest rates substantially rise, making rentals more attractive.

In other words, you want rent income from *nonresidential* properties that you can reinvest. That gives you a number of good alternatives. For example, you might consider investments in industrial properties, warehouses, office buildings, malls, or even timberland. Barring a severe economic downturn, they should be good choices.

Likewise, real estate gives you an opportunity to capitalize on "the graying of America." This may be a good time to invest in REITs that have a health-care orientation, specializing in clinics, hospitals, and specialized-care facilities. Exercise caution, however, with REITs that primarily own nursing homes that rely on Medicaid income. They could be vulnerable to Medicaid's own funding issues long term.

With this caveat, health-care REITs are well worth considering. So are REITs that invest in properties having long-term, locked-in leases signed by prime commercial or government tenants.

As I noted in the previous chapter, however, you want to limit your total exposure in real estate and invest with caution at this time. Let prices simmer down and avoid REITs or funds having content concentrated in high-appreciation locations. Curb your exposure in real estate until we see more cool-off.

INTERNATIONAL REAL ESTATE FUND: 10 PERCENT

Symbol	Fund
EGLRX	Alpine International Real Estate
GIRAX.LW	Goldman Sachs International Real Estate A
IGLAX.LW	ING Global Real Estate A
IRFAX.LW	Cohen & Steers International Realty
RWX	streetTRACKS Wilshire International Real Estate

Several funds that invest in *non-U.S.* real estate have strong performance records. They're good! However, they do not necessarily invest for rent income. And residential bubbles exist in many offshore markets as well—particularly in Western Europe where demographics are akin to ours. Consequently, you need to look at the content of any international offering carefully.

There is, moreover, one other issue. We can expect growing demand for housing and office space in many foreign countries—meaning that prudent, diversified non-U.S. investments should be quite attractive in the years ahead for American investors. Indeed, wealthy investors already have access to private placements that earn attractive returns from real estate investments in Asia, parts of Europe, and Latin America. However, such opportunities are usually only open to people with large amounts of money to invest. There are, in fact, few *rent-focused* international funds for "average-Joe" or mass-affluent investors.

Check my Web site, www.cashrichretirement.com, for news about other international real estate offerings. A number of international, rent-oriented funds whose managers have strong track records are in the pipeline. I'll keep you posted about them.

"INSURANCE" INVESTMENTS

Let's now consider the "insurance" component of your portfolio. Your plan calls for at least two kinds of exposure.

PRECIOUS METALS FUND: 5 PERCENT

Symbol	Fund
BGEIX	American Century Global Gold
OPGSX.LW	Oppenheimer Gold and Special Minerals A
TGLDX	Tocqueville Gold
UNWPX	U.S. Global Investors World Precious Metals
USAGX	USAA Precious Metals and Minerals

I recommended investing a small amount of your capital in *gold* or *precious metals* as a hedge against risk. The prices of gold, silver, palladium, and the other metals tend to move up *before* and with inflation. They tend to move up in times of crisis. And two of the countries that will have massive numbers of people moving into peak investment years over the next two decades—India and China—have a high social and economic regard for gold. For many Indian and Chinese nationals, gold is *the* "safe harbor" holding of choice—much like a Swiss bank account is for wealthy people elsewhere. So (1) the promise of inflation protection, (2) further diversification, and (3) the likelihood of strong long-term demand collectively make a small allocation into a precious metals fund particularly suitable. The above funds stand out as strong performers.

Basic Materials, Natural Resources, or Swiss Fund: 5 percent

Symbol	Fund or Index
DBN	Wisdom Tree International Basic Materials Index (Dividend-Weighted Index. Invests in 166 Stocks)
PRFM	PowerShares RAFI Basic Materials Sector ("Rafi" Index. Invests in 51 Stocks)
FNARX	Fidelity Select Natural Resources
IGE	iShares Goldman Sachs Natural Resources
EWL	iShares MSCI Switzerland (Market-Cap Index)
PRPFX	Permanent Portfolio (Mutual Fund With Swiss and Gold Content)

For your final selection you might choose a basic materials fund, a natural resources fund, or a Swiss fund. Just one of the three.

A basic materials fund invests in the shares of companies that produce iron, steel, minerals, forestry and paper products. A natural resources fund focuses on oil, natural gas, electricity, coal, timber, pulp, paper, and mining. And the rationale for holding either kind of fund is to have an additional offset to inflation.

There is demographic reason for such an investment as well. Because the world's population will grow mightily over the next twenty-five years, the demand for natural resources, commodities, and basic materials is likely to soar. Hundreds of millions of people will, we saw, be moving into adult economic activity and peak consumption years. That surge is going to translate into immense demand for energy, metals, steel, and timber. In tandem with this demand is an important investment fact: investments in commodities—such things as gold, copper, crude oil, and the like—generally have low correlations with stocks and bonds, offset inflation, and "provide . . . superior returns when they are needed most."[20] So it may be advisable to put a small amount of your money into a high-quality fund with these kinds of specialties.

Alternatively or additionally, consider exposure in a Swiss equity fund or a Swiss-franc-denominated time deposit. Switzerland continues to attract the money of the world's wealthiest people. Swiss equities include the stocks of some of the world's most powerful multinationals, and its currency is often a "safe haven" in an international crisis. Hence, funds such as those cited above can be reasonable performers in "good" times and help you hedge against portfolio damage in "bad."

ABOUT THESE SELECTIONS . . .

As you consider different funds and indexes, bear in mind several things.

One, remember to execute your Investment Master Plan *across accounts* so that your diversification strategy covers all of your savings. You might build out your master plan in sections—perhaps using your 401(k) savings for the "interest income" part of your plan and your Schwab IRA for "dividend income." Start by deciding how to allocate your 401(k) capital in accordance with your overall plan. Check whether your plan's fund offerings match the funds I've named here. Pick your 401(k) investments first. Then make fund decisions for your other accounts.

Second, I myself invest in many of these funds and indexes. I am obligated to tell you that. However, I have named these particular funds because I truly believe in their income potential and attractiveness.

Three, my fund recommendations are not definitive. Many other good funds and indexes exist. *I hope that you will challenge, confirm, and enlarge the lists of prospects I have provided.*

Four, the funds and indexes I have listed are sure to change management-wise, risk-wise, content-wise, and performance-wise by the time you read this book. So it is important for you to check each fund's or index's strengths and weaknesses *before* you invest. Read the prospectuses—they're available online. Consult Morningstar for information about each fund's performance, management, and risks. Do your own homework.

And five, some of the funds I have listed here may not, after all, perform satisfactorily. Even the best funds do not always shine. There is no guarantee of positive results. So it's important to broadly diversify and to check on the *current* performance, focus, and management of any of the funds you consider.

Once you do your homework and check out different indexes and funds, select ones to build out your Investment Master Plan. Use the model at the end of chapter 5. You need to make fourteen basic U.S. and international investments for a well-diversified portfolio—perhaps a few more or less depending on your savings, your access to good funds, and your tolerance for risk.

However, I would urge you to diversify broadly and invest in at least four- teen funds to limit concentration risk. I also urge you to use new "fundamen- tal indexes" for income focus and breadth.

If your employer requires you to hold company stock as its matching contribution in your 401(k), treat it as a dividend-income investment and try to limit such exposure to a maximum of 5 percent of your total. When- ever possible, restrict any single stock position to no more than 5 percent of your total holdings in all of your accounts.

IF YOU DO *NOT* HAVE ACCESS TO THESE KINDS OF FUNDS IN YOUR 401(K)

Okay. What if your 401(k) or similar savings plan doesn't offer these funds or indexes? What then?

Fundamental indexes are relatively new and may not be available in your 401(k) or similar plan. They are, nevertheless, extremely important. They can significantly add to the retirement capital you amass—strong re- search confirms it. You want access to such investments!

If your 401(k) or similar plan does not give you access to the kinds of fundamental indexes or funds I've named, then go to my Web site, www .cashrichretirement.com, and download the "Model Letter to Your Em- ployer." Copy it. Submit it to your employer. Let your employer know that you want access to income-producing indexes and funds. Name specific ones. Get vocal! Speak up! Your future depends on it.

On the other hand, your employer may not offer any 401(k) plan at all. If so, you can open up an IRA with Schwab or Fidelity to have access to the broadest possible array of funds—including the ones cited here.

If you have a 401(k) account with a *past* employer, consider moving it to Schwab or Fidelity or a similar company, so you can invest in the broadest array of funds and fundamental indexes. Contact Schwab's or Fidelity's 800 numbers to discuss the advisability of moving your old 401(k) into an IRA account with them for access to a larger fund menu. *However, do not attempt to move any money or draw down these funds on your own. That would trigger tax penalties. Get the broker to make the transfer for you.*

All in, look for ways of using your 401(k) plan's offerings as you build out your plan. Ask your employer to add fundamental indexes and high-quality funds to your plan so you have access to the offerings of OppenheimerFunds,

T. Rowe Price, Vanguard, Goldman Sachs, and other superior management groups. And use a Schwab IRA and other non-401(k) accounts to invest in the funds and indexes you cannot reach via your 401(k).

CONCLUSIONS

Investing in a broad array of dividend-producing, rent-producing, interest-producing, and "insurance" funds and indexes will give you important advantages: (1) diversification, (2) protection, and (3) show-me-the-money real returns.

I urge you to use "fundamental" indexes for broad diversification and real income. I urge you to focus on low-priced investments that produce real returns you can reinvest. And I urge you to give standing instructions to your employer (as regards your 401(k) investments) and to your broker (as regards your IRA and other accounts) to *automatically* reinvest all of your dividend, interest, and rent income.

Turbocharge the compounding of your savings! Always invest for income. And always reinvest that income automatically.

At the same time, build broad global exposure in ways that enable you to capitalize on—rather than be penalized by—worldwide demographic changes. And hold, as well, a mix of "insurance investments" that will help to shield you from harm. Using the kinds of funds and indexes I have recommended here will help you on all counts.

ACTION PLAN

1. Go to morningstar.com to become acquainted with its research and fund information. Key in a fund symbol in the top left "quotes" box and explore the data available.

2. Use Morningstar's research and fund prospectuses to identify the strengths and weaknesses of any investment you consider.

3. Use my fund ideas and your own homework to make a list of the funds and indexes in which you want to invest. Discuss your choices with a financial planner to tailor a portfolio of income-oriented funds and indexes that are suitable for you.

4. Make a list of the funds and indexes available in your 401(k) plan. Do any of them match the funds cited in this chapter? Decide how to utilize them to build out parts of your master plan.

5. Make a list of the funds and indexes *not* available in your 401(k) plan. Use the "Model Letter to Your Employer" on my website, www .cashrichretirement.com, to request access to these investments.

6. Use brokerage accounts for the investments you cannot make in your 401(k). Build out your Investment Master Plan across a *variety of accounts.*

7. Give standing instructions for the *automatic reinvestment* of the interest, dividend, and rent income your portfolio produces. Produce income and reinvest it!

7

GET ALL THE PROFESSIONAL
HELP YOU CAN!

The preparations you make for retirement are some of the most important you will ever undertake. Ever! Americans are increasingly being handed do-it-yourself responsibility for retirement funding, yet most folks are operating with little financial education, little guidance, and often little help. It's like being told that the pilots of the 747 jumbo jet in which you're a passenger have just parachuted out of the plane and—oh, yes—would you mind climbing into the pilot's seat and preparing for landing.

PROFESSIONAL HELP IS VITAL

The adage that "*you* are the best person to make investment decisions on your own behalf" is bullroar. You may, indeed, be a skilled investor. You may be an investment professional with extensive experience in the field. But it's much more likely that you lack the time, research tools, or experience to make well-informed, 24-7 investment decisions. It's highly *unlikely* that you have the time or inclination to continuously track changing economic developments, changing tax rules, investment opportunities around the globe, new funds, and day-to-day risks to successfully invest and curb losses.

Investing skillfully is a full-time job. And there's no shame in admitting to having less than full time to devote to it or having an investment skill level that is less than a pro's. Indeed, *few Americans have any financial planning or investment education.* And for many, that is the particularly disturbing starting point.

Here are the facts. At present, about half of American workers receive educational materials or have access to investment seminars via their employer or 401(k) plan provider to help them invest.[1] However, study after study shows that poor financial education is a national handicap. Few high schools or universities offer much in the way of practical financial training. Many high school graduates lack even rudimentary financial skills, including balancing a checkbook. Most, according to one national organization, "simply have no insight into the basic survival principles involved with earning, spending, saving and investing."[2]

In the words of one Social Security publication, "Most Americans demonstrate a clear need for financial guidance. Only 33 percent of surveyed adults understand the basics of compound interest, and 42 percent do not know why federally insured certificates of deposit have a lower rate of return that privately held mutual funds."[3]

A later study, referring to a poll of hundreds of professional financial planners with more than five years of experience, found that "more than half (51%) of all advisors say their typical client would be more likely to be able to explain the rules of Texas Hold 'Em Poker than they could the principles of asset allocation."[4] In fact, about half of the professionals surveyed in that poll said their clients were "not too knowledgeable" or "not at all knowledgeable" about the great impact that asset allocation has on investment performance.[5]

When it comes to saving and investing fundamentals, many Americans are functionally illiterate. Many—perhaps *most*—are *not* prepared for do-it-yourself retirement funding.

Meanwhile, successful investing and retirement planning are becoming more and more complex. For example, the latest "help guides" from the IRS provide 295 pages of small print on the preparation of individual tax returns and another 80 separate pages on "Investment Income and Expenses (Including Capital Gains and Losses)" to explain the taxes due on investment returns.[6] No wonder ultrawealthy Americans hire teams of high-powered accountants for help!

At the same time, the kaleidoscope of investment funds and investment opportunities is fast changing. During the stock market boom in the late 1990s, hundreds of new mutual funds were launched each year.[7] Over the last decade, new Roth 401(k)s as well as Roth IRAs have come into being—and, again, you have to read more small print in the tax codes to understand the differences of these new accounts.

Make no mistake about it. In today's world of complex tax rules, changing investment opportunities, and shrinking retirement benefits, you need all the professional help you can get! That's why I urge you to tap four kinds: (1) online educational tools; (2) seminars about investing; (3) professional asset management; and, foremost of all, (4) the guidance of an objective, experienced, professional financial advisor.

ONLINE TOOLS AND EDUCATION

There are many good educational materials and analytical tools that give you access to expert advice and are available online. Schwab's and Fidelity's Web sites, for example, have good arrays of educational articles, investment commentary, and useful planning tools. Such sites permit you to tap the wisdom of many different expert investment professionals *free of charge*.

AARP, MassMutual, and Morningstar also have particularly good tutorials and "help centers." Here is a list of some online resources that can help you tap first-rate expertise and expand your financial education.

AARP

WWW.AARP.COM

Exceptional library of educational materials in the "Money & Work" section. Covers all facets of retirement, investing, and financial products. Helpful. Comprehensive. A "must-visit" site.

BETTER INVESTING

WWW.BETTER-INVESTING.COM

This not-for-profit organization has helped millions of Americans to sharpen their investing skills. It offers a broad array of educational materials and good information on investing courses, clubs, and other resources.

FIDELITY

WWW.FIDELITY.COM

Large array of educational materials that explain "the basics" of smart investing. Particularly helpful savings tips and calculators. A site you should visit if you're serious about successfully funding your golden years.

MASSMUTUAL FINANCIAL

WWW.MASSMUTUAL.COM

First-rate educational materials and calculators in this site's "Learn" section. This is an excellent resource center. Visit it to polish your retirement plans and learn more about asset growth and protection.

MORNINGSTAR

WWW.MORNINGSTAR.COM

Click "Help" at very bottom, then "Investing Classroom" at bottom middle. Morningstar offers comprehensive, first-rate tutorials in all facets of investing—for novices and experienced investors alike.

SCHWAB

WWW.SCHWAB.COM

Top-notch resource center in the "Planning & Retirement" section. Advice from professional financial planners and investment experts. Another "must-visit" site.

YAHOO®FINANCE

FINANCE.YAHOO.COM

Good investing advice. Tips about investing clubs. Good educational materials about investment basics.

When you finish reading this chapter, take a few minutes to visit these sites just to become acquainted with the free educational materials they provide. Pick two sites for frequent visits. Use them to look up any financial jargon you do not understand. And by all means, use their good advice to help you invest more skillfully. Of course, these sites will only give you limited help when it comes to income-focused investing, as they generally offer conventional guidance. Tap their insights to become a better investor—but invest *for income* as I've recommended.

INVESTMENT SEMINARS

Investment seminars can also help you sharpen your skills. There are many seminars to choose from. When you consider one, just make sure it is *not* about flipping houses or "day-trading." That's just more of the dangerous "let's speculate and get rich" claptrap. Forget it!

Instead, look for programs that explain investment diversification, asset allocation techniques, and demographic as well as investment trends. For example, you may be able to join a skill-building meeting or a seminar hosted by an investment expert via www.MeetUp.com. Also check with Better-Investing.com to learn when and where seminars are scheduled in your area. And give preference to seminars and discussion groups that are free of charge—that will help you avoid the get-rich-quick programs that usually only enrich the presenters.

PROFESSIONAL INVESTMENT MANAGERS

As we've seen, one way to obtain valuable help is to invest in high-quality mutual funds. That puts professional asset managers at work for you. It's a way of having seasoned professionals select and mind investment choices on your behalf.

A lot of people like the idea of selecting and trading individual securities, themselves. But doing that is generally not advantageous. Do-it-yourself trading significantly limits the diversification and risk reduction you could otherwise achieve with funds and indexes. Investing in a fund or index, we saw, will give you more diversification, less risk, and better returns than buying a few securities on your own. Likewise, a fund or index is able to buy huge blocks of stocks or bonds or real estate at a time, normally commanding much better pricing. If you trade in small lots, you are going to pay more. And unless you are an investment professional whose day-to-day business is asset management, it is unlikely that you have the time to do thorough, in-depth research.

Professional asset managers *and funds* can give you better security pricing, broad diversification, and the benefit of sophisticated research. However, asset managers charge for their stewardship. And some of them charge fees that can eat your savings alive. That is also why I urge you to also include index funds and exchange-traded funds (the ETFs we talked about) in your portfolio. Many of these kinds of investments have low management fees.

Before you invest in any fund or index, consult Morningstar.com to ascertain the fund's expense. Go to Morningstar.com, type in the fund's name or symbol, then click "Expense Ratio" in the top right "Key Stats" box. It will give you a breakdown of the management fees and other expenses of any fund.

If a fund has an overall return of 9 percent but its expense ratio is, say, 1.5 percent, then you're really only putting a 7.5 percent return in your pocket.[8] Over time, that difference can actually amount to many months of retirement income. Or as Vanguard, the respected asset-management company, put it, "The lower the expense ratio, the more returns a fund can pass on to its shareholders."[9] And the more compounding and capital growth you will enjoy.

In recent years, the average expense ratio throughout the mutual fund industry has been 1.41 percent for equity funds and not quite 1 percent for fixed income funds.[10] Research confirms that funds with low fees and "no-load" funds—meaning funds that do not charge any up-front fee or commission at the time of your purchase—generate "materially better returns."[11] Consequently, you need to look at fees carefully when you invest. High management fees cause a serious drag on performance. You should generally avoid fees over the averages I cited.

When you invest your retirement savings, get all the professional help you can—*including* professional asset management. Keep good mutual funds in your portfolio! Opt for the professional oversight and diversification of mutual funds, exchange-traded funds, and indexes instead of trying to trade individual securities yourself. And specifically look for indexes or funds that charge low fees.

FINANCIAL ADVISORS

Undoubtedly *the* most important kind of help you can obtain is the advice and counsel of a professional financial planner. A financial advisor—a personal *financial coach*—can help you in powerful ways.

I believe that professional help is no longer "nice to have" or the prerogative of only the wealthy. It is vital for investors of all income sizes. And it is increasingly important on a number of counts.

To invest skillfully, you need to keep abreast of ongoing economic, tax, and investment changes. A professional planner focuses on these changes and opportunities full-time for you.

A professional planner can help you set a detailed, *customized* savings and investment plan—one that pinpoints your retirement income requirement and paces your savings efforts with more rigor than we have attempted here. What is more, a planner can help you draft such a plan *and hold you to it*.

At the same time, a professional wealth manager can help screen investment opportunities for you. There are many thousands of funds, stocks, bonds, REITs, ETFs, and other investments to choose from. A professional advisor can help you distinguish between good choices and bad, saving you hours of research.

You will likewise benefit from the added objectivity and discipline that a professional can bring to investing. To maintain emotional detachment, physicians never perform surgery on their own family members. You need the same kind of detachment when you invest. A professional advisor can help you react to market developments *with* more experience and *without* knee-jerk reflex. A professional planner can help you avoid chasing after bubble gains.

Now you may be saying, "Hey, I can do that stuff all by myself!" Can you? I know from experience that a professional can significantly strengthen your savings resolve and investment performance. A planner can *coach you*, reenforce your saving efforts, and help you attain better results.

Saving for retirement is in many ways like going on a diet. It's easy to set a savings goal, but even easier to fall off the wagon! You need periodic coaching to keep your savings on track and reenforce successful investing behavior. And since you're determined to retire securely with ample capital, you're going to need a good coach to assist, counsel, cajole, and guide you.

As important, you want a professional's help to guide you *before* you begin to actually draw down your savings, to avoid costly tax penalties. Many Americans draw down their retirement savings improperly and trigger mean tax charges. A skilled pro can help you avoid them.

Hiring a professional advisor is an extremely important investment. And I'm hardly preaching anything new. In one poll, 27 percent of the Americans surveyed said that access to a professional financial advisor would be "the single most useful thing in helping them save for retirement."[12] They are absolutely right.

Another nationwide poll found that investors who had professional planning help were substantially more likely to have a written financial plan, have a defined asset-allocation strategy, and have a more broadly diversified portfolio than investors who invested without professional help.[13] Right on!

The important conclusion is this: *a professional financial planner can help you in powerful ways.* If you don't already use the services of a professional planner, it's time to get cracking! As we'll see, you don't have to be wealthy to get professional help. You *do* have to be deadly serious about having adequate cash for retirement. Let's get moving.

THE KINDS OF PROFESSIONAL ADVISORS

There are many different kinds of advisors with different credentials or "certifications." Some advisors have fancy titles on their business cards, but not much experience or financial education. Others are experienced, have to pass rigorous certification tests, take specialized university courses, undertake serious lifetime education, and pledge to uphold a strict code of ethics. You want the latter kind.

Two certifications in particular, I believe, perhaps best distinguish exceptional professionals. They are:

Certification	Supervisory Body
Certified Financial Planner (CFP)	Certified Financial Planner Board of Standards
Certified Investment Management Analyst (CIMA)	Investment Management Consultants Association

These certifications require rigorous testing and lifetime financial education. They are hallmarks of high preparedness and professionalism. Mind you, many excellent financial planners may have other certifications. Don't be afraid of working with them! When you screen planners, ask about their credentials, experience, and their ongoing-education requirement. All good planners and investment advisors—whatever certifications they hold—continue their financial educations to keep abreast of tax, legal, economic, and investment changes.

Because of the many different names for these kinds of specialists, I'm going to use a single term, *financial advisor,* to refer to these professionals going forward. I am also going to help you locate a good financial advisor in just a bit. Before we do that, however, you need to understand how these professionals are compensated. Let's take a look at their charges and remuneration.

THE COST OF AN ADVISOR

When we talk about the cost of a financial advisor, bear in mind two facts. *First, you don't have to be a multimillionaire to enjoy professional help.* The services of a financial advisor are most certainly within your reach, and I urge you—in the strongest possible terms—to tap such expertise. And, two, the *way* these professionals are paid is something just as important as cost. Allow me to explain.

Financial advisors are typically compensated for their services in one of several ways: (1) by an hourly fee, (2) by means of some commission on the funds they sell, (3) by a flat per-service or annual charge, (4) by some fee based on the size of your overall assets, or (5) by working in an organization that earns management and trading income from your portfolio.

Many financial advisors earn their keep by recommending funds that charge front-end fees or "loads." Such fees usually go to the advisor as a kind of sales commission. *There is nothing whatsoever wrong with commission-based compensation.* However, a commission-paid advisor is likely to focus on some funds (the ones that pay the highest commissions) as opposed to others. And that may *not* in your best interest.

Other advisors charge an hourly or per-service or annual fee for their advice. For example, a professional may charge a onetime flat fee to help you prepare a detailed savings and investment allocation plan custom-tailored to your risk tolerance and needs.

When you select a financial advisor, you need to understand that professional's compensation terms. *You want to know whether the advisor can give you access to a broad array of funds—and specifically income-oriented funds.* You also want to be sure that the advisor's compensation mechanics are not going to cloud his or her objectivity.

As a general rule of thumb, I recommend working with a professional advisor paid a flat per-service or annual fee, or affiliated with a reputable group. You will want to know the cost up front, and you want professional objectivity. So a flat fee often makes the most sense. However, talk these points over with an advisor *before* you engage her or him. Even a commission-paid advisor may agree to work on a flat-fee basis or on terms that better suit you.

Most important, don't let concern about costs get in the way of getting good advice! Professional advice is *not* prohibitively expensive. If, however, you cannot afford to retain an advisor to coach you year-round, *at least hire a professional one time* to (1) help you set a rigorous retirement income target, (2) assess your savings progress toward that goal, (3) review your current asset allocation, and (4) guide you when it's time to draw down your savings. At least hire a professional for those services! It will be one of your smartest investments.

SELECTING A FINANCIAL ADVISOR

When you shop for a financial advisor, you want a professional with three main qualifications: (1) good experience; (2) good financial education, as perhaps demonstrated by the CFP or similar certification; and (3) the ability to help you select good income-oriented funds and indexes.

Here are several organizations whose Web sites will guide you to a qualified professional. By visiting these sites and entering your zip code, you can locate an experienced professional near you.

Certified Financial Planning Board of Standards Inc.
www.cfp.net

The National Association of Personal Financial Advisors
www.napfa.org

Financial Planning Association
www.fpanet.org

Alternatively, the financial professionals of several business groups have also impressed me. Their Web sites will put you in touch with skilled professionals.

Wells Fargo
www.wellsfargo.com

Smith Barney
www.smithbarney.com

MassMutual
www.massmutual.com

Once you're in contact with an advisor, be sure to ask these questions:

1. How many years of experience have you had? With which employers?
2. What certification do you have? Specifically, do you have CFP or CIMA certification?
3. Do you take ongoing financial-educational courses? Do you formally subscribe to a code of ethics?
4. How are you compensated for your services? Are you willing to work on a flat-fee basis?
5. Can you help me evaluate and gain access to a large array of funds—particularly funds and indexes with an income orientation like those described in *Cash-Rich Retirement*?

CONCLUSIONS

You don't have to be a multimillionaire to get expert help! There are online resources, educational materials, investment seminars and clubs, as well as professional financial advisors who can help you.

If you have the means, tap the services of a financial advisor long term. Let her or him help you set and *stick to* savings goals, select funds, and check your savings and investment progress every six months. Retain a *financial coach* to heighten your savings and investment success.

If you cannot afford *ongoing* coaching, hire a financial advisor at least *one time* for customized savings, allocation, and drawdown advice. At least one time.

Don't fly a jumbo jet solo! Get all the competent, objective, and expert help you can. Add to the success of your cash-rich retirement funding.

ACTION STEPS

1. Check the Web sites of AARP, MassMutual, Morningstar, and Schwab. Examine their planning tools and educational materials.

2. Go to MeetUp.com and BetterInvesting.com. Use them to identify educational meetings near you that can help you strengthen your investing skills.

3. Use funds and indexes for broad diversification and professional oversight.

4. Check the Web site of the Certified Financial Planner Board of Standards or one of the other groups listed in this chapter. Locate a skilled professional near you.

5. Hire a financial advisor. Ideally, retain an advisor to review your investment progress every six months and be your financial coach long term.

8

BUILD INCOME STREAMS
WITH A LADDER OF ANNUITIES

So far I have recommended a number of ways to protect and enlarge your retirement capital. I have suggested an overriding allocation strategy or Investment Master Plan that broadly diversifies your investments by geography and content. I have specifically urged you to invest so as to generate a variety of different kinds of income. I urged you to invest substantially overseas to capitalize on global demographics. And I urged you to err on the side of conservatism, forsaking speculative gains to avoid harmful correction losses.

These tactics will help mitigate one of the main threats to your retirement—namely, *investment risk* or the risk of sustaining losses due to market volatility or downdraft.

However, you face other kinds of risk as well. You also face *longevity risk*—the risk that you might outlive your savings.

You are, in fact, going to need additional instruments in your portfolio to defuse longevity risk. Annuities are the only financial instruments that can guarantee income for life and offset the risk of outliving your savings. So let's get better acquainted with these instruments. They are excellent retirement investments to consider *after* you have contributed maximum amounts to your 401(k) and IRA.

THE BASICS

An annuity is a financial contract whereby you agree to pay some amount of money to an insurance company in exchange for its giving you (or some other beneficiary) income streams for a specific period or for life. Annuities are a formidable way of generating retirement income *and* offsetting longevity risk. I highly recommend them.

For many Americans, however, the word *annuity* conjures up negative images—pushy salespeople, high sales commissions, hard-to-understand terminology, and fine print that confounds most laymen. Some of this bad press was once well deserved. Most of it, however, is pure fiction today.

IMPORTANT ADVANTAGES

Whatever their former reputation, annuities are powerful investment instruments well worth considering. There are many excellent annuity insurers whose sales tactics, professionalism, financial strength, and ethics are altogether above reproach. What is more, annuities give you important tax and income advantages:

☑ **Deferred taxes.** You can use an annuity to defer taxes on your investment earnings until you actually receive the payout. Annuities give you the power of tax deferrals much like traditional 401(k)s or IRAs. You normally have to pay taxes on the income streams coming *out* of an annuity. But you do *not* have to pay taxes on the investment profits you make until those payouts take place. That's an awesome advantage.

☑ **No size limit.** There is no limit on the amount of money you can put into an annuity. Unlike an IRA and 401(k), which *do* have size limitations, annuities do not have a ceiling or maximum pay-in amount. You can usually put *any amount* of money into annuity investments and defer taxes on the lot! But remember, if you buy an annuity with 401(k) or IRA money, you squelch this no-size-limit advantage. Inside an IRA or 401(k), there are always contribution limits.

It is generally not advantageous to hold an annuity in your 401(k) or IRA. Since an annuity tax-shelters your investment returns, putting a tax-sheltered annuity into a tax-sheltered IRA or 401(k) is counterproductive.

Don't squander the tax advantages! Be sure to check with a financial advisor or tax specialist *before* buying an annuity with 401(k) or IRA funds. You want to be sure that having an annuity inside your 401(k) plan or IRA somehow makes good sense. Generally, it does not.

☑ **Compounding advantage.** Because you can tax-shelter an unlimited amount of savings, annuities give you an important compounding advantage. Taxes are not going to dilute the compounding effect. Let's take an example. Suppose you're in the 25 percent tax bracket and you invest a onetime lump sum of $20,000 that earns 7 percent per annum for the next twenty years. You reinvest the earnings. If you make the investment inside an annuity, your investment will have a cash value of nearly $155,000 by the end of the period. If you make the investment in a normal taxable account, your investment will only be worth $111,000. That's a big difference.

Your investments will always grow to greater heights if you hold them in tax-sheltered accounts. That's why investing in a 401(k), IRA, and annuities is a good tactic for income success.

☑ **Income for Life.** *Finally, annuities are the only financial instrument that can guarantee you income for life. This is a particularly powerful feature of these contracts. Annuities offset longevity risk.*

According to data from the American Society of Actuaries, a man now age thirty-five years who reaches the age of sixty-five has a 78 percent probability of living at least until age eighty. Of a couple both age thirty-five today who both reach age sixty-five, there is a 67 percent probability that one or both of them will be alive twenty-five years later at age ninety.[1] You, most probably, are going to need income for a long time!

Annuities permit you to tax-defer savings of potentially large amounts of money and generate income for life. They defuse longevity risk. They belong in your portfolio.

FOUR MAIN KINDS

Let's become familiar with the main kinds of annuities and some basic annuity jargon. There are four principal kinds: (1) *immediate,* (2) *deferred,* (3) *fixed,* and (4) *variable.* Don't be put off by the terminology. These different

Main Kinds of Annuities

	Immediate	Deferred
Fixed	• Guarantees a *fixed* amount of income. The payments to you are known in advance and always the same. • The income payments commence *immediately* or within one year of purchase. • You make no investment decisions. You are immune from market turbulence. You cannot lose money.	• Guarantees a *fixed* amount of income. The payments to you are known in advance and always the same. • Only begins payouts to you later in time. The payments are *deferred*. • You make no investment decisions. You are immune from market turbulence. You cannot lose money.
Variable	• You invest in a mix of investment funds. Your income payments will *vary* depending on their performance. • The income payments commence *immediately* or within one year of purchase • You can lose money. However, you have the potential for higher returns.	• You investment in a mix of investment funds. Your income payments will *vary* depending on their performance. • Only pays you income later in time. The payments are *deferred*. • You can lose money. However, you have the potential for higher returns.

kinds of annuities are actually quite straightforward. You might want to think of them in this matrix way:

Immediate. With an immediate annuity, you typically turn over a lump sum of money to an insurer and it begins to pay you monthly, quarterly, or annual payments. The payments typically begin within thirteen months of your annuity purchase. Hence, this instrument is called immediate because its payments to you usually begin shortly after or *immediately* after you fix the contract.

When people retire and are ready to begin drawing down their 401(k) and IRA savings, many convert the proceeds into an immediate annuity. They "annuitize" their 401(k) and IRA money to begin income payments right away.

To *annuitize* means to convert cash, an investment account, a 401(k) or IRA, or some other kind of annuity into an *immediate annuity,* kicking off immediate income payments. You yourself may consider buying an immediate annuity one day with the proceeds of your 401(k) or IRA. But whatever you do, get professional advice before drawing down or transfering your 401(k) or IRA money to avoid tax complications.

Deferred. A deferred annuity is different. With a deferred annuity, you pay a lump sum or make periodic payments into the annuity, but only begin receiving income payments at some later time.

For example, suppose you are thirty-five years old today. You might decide to begin funding a deferred annuity and continue doing so for the next fifteen years until you turn fifty. But you might also opt—when you first set the annuity contract—to only have your annuity initiate income payments to you when you turn sixty-five. In other words, a deferred annuity permits you to "defer" the time when the income payments actually commence.

You can also opt for "fixed" or "variable" kinds of annuities.

Fixed. When you buy a fixed annuity, you are buying a preset stream of *fixed* income payments. When you sign the annuity contact, the amount and dates of such fixed payments are locked in. You cannot usually change them. (There are exceptions, but right now it will be easier for you to associate the term *fixed annuity* with locked-in, fixed income.)

As a rule, fixed annuities are low-risk investments that are substantially immune from market turbulence. You do not have to make any investment decisions. The income you receive is preset. However, the returns on a fixed annuity are slim. In recent years, fixed annuities have typically paid annual returns of about 3 to 6 percent per annum after expenses. You can often—but, of course, *not always*—do much better with a stock market investment.

In other words, you have peace of mind with a fixed annuity but often earn smaller returns.

Even so, a fixed annuity is one of few products in the financial industry that guarantees you preset income for a specific period *or for life*. If you buy a fixed annuity, you'll know the specific amount of income you are going to enjoy for the rest of your life or, if you choose, for some shorter period. That is an outstanding feature.

Variable. A variable annuity gives you fluctuating returns and the possibility—but not guarantee—of achieving more income from your investment. It has both upside and downside potential.

With a variable annuity, you can invest in different mutual funds—just as you do in a 401(k) plan—and may achieve higher-than-fixed-annuity results. The income payments you receive will *vary* depending upon the performance of the funds you choose.

Many financial planners like variable annuities because, although the income payouts are not guaranteed, they give you access to stock market returns, have historically surpassed the returns of most other kinds of investments.

With a variable annuity you can usually invest in a mix of different stock, bond, and other funds. These funds are called *subaccounts* in annuity lingo. They are simply kinds of mutual funds. You can change the specific funds you invest in. You can change how much money you allocate to different funds. You can make these investment changes without adverse tax consequences. Your gains grow tax-deferred. And you may, in fact, achieve stronger annuity income depending on the performance of your investments.

But heads up! You also run the risk of investing in funds that may not, *for any number of reasons, perform well. Your variable annuity income could actually produce income streams that are lower than expected because of poor performance.*

So let's recap. A fixed annuity gives you *fixed* income payments, and you will never lose money with one unless the insurance company goes bust. A variable annuity gives you income payments that *vary* according to the performance of your annuity investments, and you could lose money *or* earn stronger returns. A fixed annuity entails less risk; it gives you "sure-thing" preset rates of return. A variable annuity entails more performance or market risk, but—if you're fortunate and invest skillfully—may deliver higher income payments. The trade-off is between sure-thing financial security and larger income potential.

WAYS TO FUND AN ANNUITY

You can put any amount of money into an annuity—often as little as $5,000 to start. And you can fund an annuity in a variety of ways. For example, you can buy an annuity with one lump sum. Or you can make an initial deposit, then add money to your annuity gradually over time.

Many people buy annuities—particularly fixed annuities—with a lump sum. For instance, you might roll over your 401(k) balance into an annuity when you retire. Or you might sell your home and use some of the proceeds to buy an annuity with a lump-sum payment. Or you might have a life insurance policy with a large cash value and decide to convert some of it into an annuity.

You can, as well, fund an annuity by making periodic contributions. Some companies permit contributions of as little as $50 a month. And continual payments will help you build up capital in the annuity (but, of course, dilute some of the compounding effect you would otherwise enjoy if you opt for early-on, lump-sum funding).

Going back to my "automatic pilot" recommendation, I urge you to consider making gradual annuity contributions that are *automatic, habitual*, and *routine. Give your annuity insurer instructions to automatically debit your checking account to add to you annuity investment monthly.* That makes investing in annuities simple and relatively pain-free. Alternatively, use part of your annual bonus to buy an annuity every year and create a "ladder" of income payments for yourself—I'll show you how in just a bit.

WAYS TO INVEST INSIDE AN ANNUITY

Depending on the kind of annuity you choose, your money can be invested in different ways.

With a *fixed annuity,* you lock into a guaranteed rate of return. You do not make any fund choices. You are, in effect, sheltered from market turmoil and investment decision-making.

One particular kind of deferred fixed annuity—an *equity-indexed annuity*—functions a bit differently. Many commentators say it is a distinct kind. So you may see books or insurance companies referring to "the three kinds of annuities," meaning "fixed," "variable," and "equity-indexed" annuities.

But let's keep things simple. An equity-indexed annuity is really a fixed annuity contract with a performance twist. It guarantees you a minimum rate of return. You make no investment decisions. But an equity-indexed annuity gives you the possibility of earning added return depending on the performance of the U.S. stock market.

Equity-indexed annuities are usually linked to a specific stock market index, such as the S&P 500 Index. Depending on how the stated index moves, you are supposed to enjoy some return *in addition to* the return that is guaranteed. So this type of annuity looks like a good choice if you want guaranteed minimum return with upside potential.

While an equity-indexed annuity sounds attractive, it generally is *not*. First, this kind of annuity makes no real stock investments, so you never receive dividends to reinvest. That reduces your upside potential markedly. Second, you do not get any performance "bump up" *each and every year* that will compound. You usually get the greater of the long-term performance of the S&P 500 Index *over some long period* or some low guaranteed return. It is simply not exciting.

And third, you make a single investment with an equity-indexed annuity—usually in a traditional U.S. stock index. You have no international exposure. No dividends or income-orientation. No bonds or real estate exposure. And often mediocre results.

Think twice about investing in equity-indexed annuities! They sound appealing, but usually are not.

With *variable annuities,* you can invest your money in a variety of different stock, bond, and real estate funds. These funds are managed by professional asset managers similar to the funds in a 401(k), 457, or similar plan. And they may, indeed, afford better than "fixed" returns. However, there is no guarantee they will do so.

Each insurance company offers a different menu of funds managed by different asset-management groups. For example, you may be able to choose from funds managed by Fidelity, American Century, T. Rowe Price, OppenheimerFunds, Templeton, Goldman Sachs, Vanguard, and any number of other highly respected asset-management groups. These management groups (called *fund families* in investment lingo) clone their funds for the annuity insurer, so you are often able to invest in funds that are virtually identical to many top-rated offerings.

When you invest in a variable annuity, you can usually select any number of funds and periodically change your selections. Some variable annuities offer the possibility of investing in a "guaranteed return" account as well. Such an account guarantees you some fixed amount of return on a part of your money for, say, one year. So you may be able to split your variable annuity investments between stock funds, bond funds, *and* a placement guaranteeing you some specific fixed rate of return. That is an attractive feature if it is available.

There are, unfortunately, significant limitations when it comes to the funds of most variable annuities. Most annuity funds are the old-fashioned large cap, small cap, growth, and value kinds. Relatively few insurance companies offer (1) market indexes of any kind, (2) dividend-oriented investments of any kind, or (3) much in the way of international funds. You generally get plain vanilla.

Consequently, most fund offerings do *not* match the income-oriented investment strategy that I am championing here. *Even so, you should invest in annuities.* When you do, always look for dividend- and income-focused funds. If they are not available, look for an annuity offering traditional market indexes, value-oriented equity funds, and a good array of international funds. And tell your insurer that you want access to high-quality dividend-oriented funds and indexes if they want to keep your business.

THE INCOME YOU RECEIVE

When you purchase an annuity, you decide when you want it to initiate income payments. You can opt to begin receiving income immediately, when you retire, earlier or later. You can opt for income payments for a fixed number of years or for the rest of your life. You can choose to have payments paid during your lifetime only, until the death of both you and your spouse or partner, or until the death of either you or your partner or spouse (whichever comes first).

To acquaint you with more annuity terminology, here are some of the payout alternatives from which you can choose:

Specified period: The annuity will pay you income for a specific number of years—whatever number you choose.

Individual payout: The annuity pays you for the duration of your life.

Joint survivor: The annuity pays until the death of *both* you and your spouse or designated beneficiary.

Joint life: The annuity pays until the death of *either* you or your spouse, whichever occurs first.

You have a lot of flexibility when it comes to choosing annuity payouts. When making your choice, bear in mind two facts, First, premature withdrawals from an annuity before the age of 59½ normally trigger a 10 percent federal tax penalty—so you want to avoid early withdrawals at all costs. And second, the longer the time span of your income payments and the more people covered, the *lower* the amount of income you'll receive. Ask your financial advisor to guide you.

ANNUITY COSTS

The cost of an annuity depends on a number of factors. The accumulation time, time span of the annuity payments, and the strength and product features of your insurer all impact an annuity's costs.

As a general rule, several layers of annuity expense are standard. You typically pay some annual contract fee, annual fund management fees (just like those charged by any mutual fund), insurance charges to cover the insurance features of your annuity, and sales or administrative fees.

The total annual expense of a variable annuity amounts to approximately 2.3 percent on average. That is a lot of expense.

However, don't let the costs frighten you! Many excellent annuities cost just a fraction of this average. Be sure to investigate the industry's lower-cost products that avoid expensive bells and whistles. Recognize, too, that working with an exceptionally strong insurer is likely to have a higher (and deserved) cost premium.

In addition to annual insurance, administrative, and management costs, many annuities impose "surrender charges" and sometimes "sales loads."

A *"sales load"* or "front-end fee" is a commission deducted from your annuity payments—usually to pay the sales agent who sold you the contract. If you have a 3 percent "load," then every time you contribute toward the annuity, 3 percent of your money actually goes into paying this sales commission instead of going into your annuity. You might contribute $5,000, for example, of which only $4,850 actually funds your contract. Hence, any front fee or load significantly dilutes your savings power. *Avoid such charges whenever possible.*

A *"surrender charge"* is a more common toll meant to discourage your cancellation or early withdrawals from a deferred annuity. Surrender penalties are typically time-tiered. For example, you might be charged a 7 percent penalty on the money you prematurely withdraw in the first year after you buy an annuity, then 6 percent and 5 percent on the money you withdraw in years two and three respectively after your purchase. The surrender penalty usually drops by 1 percent year by year until there is no surrender charge whatsoever. The penalty period is typically seven years.

However, different insurers have different penalty times and surrender charges. Some have no surrender charge whatsoever. Those that charge this penalty often start the "penalty clock" anew on *each payment* you make if you fund an annuity with periodic payments.

When you shop for annuities, always give priority to products with shorter penalty periods.

Annuities come with many different benefits and in a variety cost permutations. You will need to discuss your income targets and benefit requirements with an insurer to ascertain the costs that would apply for you. For the time being, simply bear in mind two facts: (1) annuities are excellent income-producing investments that defuse longevity risk, and (2) annuities are available with a variety of cost structures—you have to comparatively shop for a low-cost product that serves you best.

ANNUITY RISKS

Annuities are available to investors of all sizes with powerful tax and compounding advantages. However, they also have drawbacks and risks.

Inflation risk. You may find that your annuity income stream in the future gives you a lot less purchasing power than you expected. Let's assume that inflation averages 4 percent per annum going forward. If you're fifty years old today and you want to have $10,000 in today's dollars for retirement, you have to factor inflation into your planning. To offset the effect of 4 percent inflation, you will actually need $20,000 by the time you reach sixty-five and $40,000 by the time you're eighty just to maintain the same purchasing power.

Consequently, you need to make provision for a *lot of income*—more and more income the further out your "drawdown time"—to offset inflation.

Default risk. Annuity investments also have default risk. When you entrust money to any annuity insurer, you are relying on that institution's financial strength and continued business longevity to make good on the income payments you are meant to receive. If your insurer stops doing business, your annuity investment could be harmed.

During the accumulation phase of a *variable* annuity, the money you invest in funds is technically kept in subaccounts that are wholly separate from your insurer's other assets. There is less default risk with a variable annuity. That's because, should the insurance company fail, its creditors would not have any claim on your variable annuity capital while it is invested in the subaccounts.

Whatever kind of annuity you choose, only work with an insurer that is financially rock-solid. Always—always!—check the financial ratings of any insurance company before *you do business with it.*

Performance or market risk. Most investments have market risk—the risk of poor performance or losses. You might experience market turmoil and your variable-annuity investment could be harmed.

You do *not* have such risk when you buy a fixed annuity. The return on a fixed annuity is locked in regardless of stock or bond market developments.

You *do* have market risk when you invest in a variable annuity. When you buy a variable annuity, you invest in a variety of different stock, bond, and real estate funds with the advantage of deferring taxes on your earnings. But you run the risk of realizing mediocre returns or even losses. The stock market could turn against you. Or you could experience a bond market turndown. There is performance risk and, specifically, the risk of losing capital with a variable annuity.

You can, however, curtail annuity performance risk in several ways. You can (1) buy a fixed (instead of variable) annuity, (2) broadly diversify the fund investments you make in a variable annuity; (3) periodically change your variable annuity's fund allocations as market conditions change; and/or (4) put some of your variable annuity money into "guaranteed" or "minimum return" placements so you are not 100 percent vulnerable to market downturns.

Expense risk. Most annuities are expensive. Their high costs eat into your income streams. You need to compare costs. You also need to count on holding a deferred variable annuity for at least seven to ten years so that its compounding benefits offset the expense.

Ask different insurers about their lower-cost as well as premium products to compare costs and income.

What to Look for When You Buy

Okay. Now you know what to *avoid*. What, proactively, *should* you look for when you shop for annuities?

You should only consider investing in annuities if (1) you have **first** invested maximum amounts in your 401(k) and IRA, and (2) you have at least seven to ten years before you begin to receive income payments from a variable annuity.

Always invest the maximum you can in a 401(k) and/or IRA *first*. You may qualify for matching 401(k) contributions. And your contributions into a traditional 401(k) are tax-free going in and tax-sheltered until withdrawal. Hence, investments in 401(k)s and IRAs should usually come first. You likewise should count on a long accumulation phase—at least seven years before income payments start—to offset the costs of most variable annuities.

Next, you want these annuity features:

Easy to understand terms. Look for straightforward, easy-to-understand annuity terms and a contract devoid of complicated terminology. If an annuity contract sounds convoluted to you, don't sign it! And however straightforward the language, make sure you talk over any contract with your financial advisor *before* you sign. Always get your advisor's independent views.

Ability to make automatic contributions and periodic fund changes. If you have a lump sum to fund an annuity, go for it! If you're going to make periodic contributions, look for an insurer willing to debit your checking account *automatically*. Make contributions happen painlessly. (Well, almost painlessly.)

You likewise want the ability to phone in or go online to periodically change your variable annuity's fund selections. You can usually change investments throughout the life of your variable annuity. When you select an insurer, look for a company that enables you to make periodic fund changes easily.

Joint survivorship. With joint survivorship the same amount of income (or some reduced amount of income) will be paid to your partner or spouse after your demise. If you're single, the standard "single life" annuity model will probably be satisfactory. If you are part of a couple, consider the *joint survivorship benefit*. You can opt to have 100 percent ongoing payments or some lower payment amount (75 percent or 50 percent) going to the surviving partner. You can opt for the annuity to pay out during one or both of your lifetimes.

Opt for a lower benefit for your partner or no joint-survivor coverage whatsoever if you have ample life insurance in place. And be sure to compare the payouts of annuities *with* and *without* this benefit to see the income effect.

Death benefit. You normally enjoy an automatic death benefit during the accumulation phase of your deferred annuity before payments begin. A death benefit guarantees that should you die before you actually begin receiving any annuity payments (the so-called accumulation phase), your heirs would receive the sum of all the premiums you paid in or the investment value of your annuity contract—whichever is greater.

Some insurance companies give you the option of extending or enhancing this benefit. That is usually costly. What is more, industry statistics show that, if extended, death benefit add-ons are rarely activated. So this is an expensive but seldom-enjoyed benefit. Weigh the costs carefully before you pay anything extra for a longer death benefit or enhancement. You may be better off with a low-cost annuity *without* the added cost.

Low costs. You generally want to avoid annuities with front-end charges, high sales commissions, and a lot of expense. An annuity that charges a front-end fee or load is always less attractive. Likewise avoid products with a long surrender-penalty period. And avoid high management and administrative expenses. Those costs simply whittle away your capital.

As you comparatively shop, ask for a written statement from each insurer that itemizes *all* of its commissions and fees and compares them, one by one, to industry averages.

Look for an annuity with all-in annual costs *at* or *below* the industry's average 2.1 to 2.4 percent expense range. And be sure to consider the bare-bones products offered without a death benefit or other enhancements. The money you save with a low-cost product will compound more powerfully for you long term.

Inflation protection. You have several ways of protecting your income from inflation with annuities. First, set your sights on larger "current dollar" amounts of income for different periods of time in the future to offset inflation's effect. The farther out in time you want income, the larger the amount you need.

Two, consider buying several different annuities that will pay you different amounts of income at different periods. For example, you might want to hold two or three different annuities so that each pays you income for a number of years back-to-back, but with each one structured to have a longer accumulation period and deliver more income than the one before it. I'll show one such strategy in just a bit.

And three, consider adding an "inflation protection rider," which allows your benefit to grow with inflation. Some insurers offer this kind of "escalation" feature. Normally the costs for meaningful protection are high, but check out this option and expense.

High-quality fund array. Insurance companies offer different arrays of mutual funds inside their variable annuities. You want access to a broad mix of funds managed by experienced, high-quality fund managers.

Before buying any annuity, check out the quality of its fund offerings at Morningstar.com. Look, specifically, at the quality and experience of the management teams—not just at the performance numbers.

You also want an annuity insurer offering (1) indexes, (2) multiple kinds of international funds, and (3) dividend-oriented equity funds. Compare the fund offerings of two or three different insurers to size up their offerings.

Anti-loss features. Some variable annuities allow you to invest a part of your money in an account that guarantees a specific twelve-month or twenty-four-month return. *If available, you want this feature.*

Many variable annuities enable you to opt for a number of other anti-loss enhancements as well—such as a "guaranteed withdrawal benefit," "guaranteed minimum income," or "guaranteed minimum accumulation."

These "step-ups" can help you avoid losses, but they are expensive. They can add another ½ or 1 percent or more to your annual costs. And the probability that you will actually benefit from them is low.

Of course, protection insurance is all about shielding yourself from unexpected losses and the "it isn't likely to happen" market turndown. If you want some loss protection, consider the *guaranteed minimum-withdrawal benefit*. It guarantees that you will be able to make minimum annual withdrawals from your variable annuity—typically 5 or 6 percent per annum. It gives you a floor. But it's costly.

If, in fact, you want to avoid losses at all costs, invest in a fixed annuity. You cannot lose money with a fixed annuity. But whatever kind of annuity you chose, a contract with the lowest expense is likely to be the better long-term investment.

Very strong insurer. Most important of all, *only* work with insurance companies having exceptional ratings of financial strength. As one good handbook about annuities succinctly puts it, "Your annuity contract is only as good as the insurance company that wrote it."[2]

ANNUITY INSURERS

When you buy an annuity, you are entrusting your money to a financial institution that is meant to pay you benefits over an extended period of time. You want to make sure that the company is around to meet its obligations! So *only* work with companies that have superior ratings of financial strength.

To size up a company's strength, check the financial ratings by independent rating agencies. I recommend using the ratings of two independent appraisers: Moody's and Standard & Poor's. However, there are a number of different rating groups to choose from.

Here is a comparison of the top-level ratings of Standard & Poor's (or S&P) and Moody's. To learn any insurance company's ratings, visit its Web site, check its annual report, or simply call its toll-free telephone number. Then compare its scores with this top rating list.

Bear in mind that my chart only shows the *very top ratings* of each evaluator out of twenty or more. In addition to the ratings shown here, there are many other ratings from the same evaluators. A rating below A can still be quite good. Likewise, the differences between the top ratings shown here (and rankings in parentheses in following charts) represent only subtle variances.

Top Ratings of Financial Strength

	Rank	S&P Ratings	Moody's Ratings
Highest Grade	1	AAA	Aaa
	2	AA+	Aa1
High Grade	3	AA	Aa2
	4	AA−	Aa3
	5	A+	A1
Upper Grade	6	A	A2
	7	A−	A3

Source: Morgan Stanley, Standard & Poor's, Moody's

All of the ratings shown in the above table are exceptionally strong. Companies with any of these ratings are outstanding.

To assist your search, on page 159 is a short list of some insurance companies that have exceptionally strong ratings and attractive annuity products.

This list is not exhaustive. There are many other excellent insurers that you might consider as well. However, these groups have particularly strong credentials and products.

Also bear in mind that some insurance companies give their *existing clients* better annuity terms than they give new "walk-in" customers. If you already have a business relationship with an insurance group, check its annuity terms and strength ratings, too.

CHARITABLE GIFT TRUSTS

One variation on the annuity concept is to turn some of your assets over to a charity in exchange for its future payments of income to you.

A "charitable gift trust" is a kind of streamlined fixed annuity. In exchange for your contribution or gift, a charity will guarantee fixed payments of income for several years or for the rest of your life. Many nonprofit groups—such as the Sierra Club, United Jewish Appeal, Salvation Army, the Smithsonian, Metropolitan Museum of Art, and a host of relief, medical-research, and education groups—offer such income contracts.

Your income stream is fixed at the time you sign the trust contract. You can, as well, derive an "up-front" tax benefit. For example, you may be able to fund a gift trust by donating stock, a portfolio of bonds, or some other asset and qualify for a tax write-off on your contribution. The tax regulations that govern such programs are complicated and change from time to time, so you will need independent tax advice before signing any trust agreement.

Even so, a charitable gift trust is an attractive way of locking into income streams and, at the same time, helping your favorite charity. You benefit from a fixed stream of income. The charity gets the residual value of your donation. Consequently, give serious thought to this annuity tactic for income as well.

LONGEVITY INSURANCE

Longevity insurance is the latest kind of annuity that can guarantee you lifetime income and peace of mind. It typically begins making income

Annuity Groups to Consider

Group	Insurance Company	Insurance Company Ratings (Rank) S&P	Insurance Company Ratings (Rank) Moody's	Fund Menu Nbr Funds	Fund Menu Families	For Additional Information
Fidelity Income Advantage	Fidelity Investments Life Insurance Company	AA (3rd)	—	51		www.fidelity.com (800) 544-4702
Genworth RetireReady Choice	Genworth Life & Annuity Insurance Company	AA– (4th)	Aa3 (4th)	79		www.genworth.com (888) 436-9678
John Hancock Venture III	John Hancock Life Insurance Company (USA)	AAA (1st)	Aa2 (3rd)	43		www.johnhancock.com 800-334-4437
MassMutual Transitions Select	Massachusetts Life Insurance Company	AAA (1st)	Aa1 (2nd)	48		www.massmutual.com 800-272-2216 (press 2)
Northwestern Select	Northwestern Mutual Life Insurance Co.	AAA (1st)	Aaa (1st)	26		www.nmfn.com
Pacific Life Pacific Odyssey	Pacific Life Insurance Company	AA (3rd)	Aa3 (4th)	33		www.pacificlife.com (800) 722-2333
Schwab OneSource Annuity	Great-West Life & Annuity Insurance Company	AA (3rd)	Aa3 (4th)	50		www.schwab.com (888) 311-4889
Vanguard Vanguard Variable Annuity	Peoples Benefit Life Insurance Company	AA (3rd)	Aa3 (4th)	15		www.vanguard.com (800) 522-5555

Source: Annuity prospectuses and company Web sites

Note: The figures in parentheses in the "Ratings" columns represent the *rank* of each rating in Moody's or Standard & Poor's top rating hierarchy. However, *all* of the above companies enjoy exceptionally strong ratings of financial strength.

payments to you when you turn eighty-five. It is supposedly an insurance policy. In reality, it is a kind of deferred fixed annuity. It is a relatively new kind of financial product—so not every insurance company offers it. Also, many insurance agents are quick to pull out brochures on traditional fixed annuities whenever the term *longevity insurance* is mentioned.

Let's be clear: longevity insurance is a kind of fixed annuity, but one stripped of expenses and basic benefits. Longevity insurance is generally *less* expensive and often pays you a lot *more* than a garden-variety fixed annuity.

Here is how this "insurance" works.

MECHANICS

You can buy longevity insurance when you are in your forties, fifties or older—up to age eighty-four (and sometimes beyond), depending on the insurer. When you buy, you make a lump-sum payment or begin a series of "installment" payments according to a set schedule. Usually people buy it with a lump sum. And the insurance company immediately fixes the amount of income you will receive. However, income payments are deferred until you reach age eighty-five.

Some insurers are willing to begin payments at an earlier age. But for the time being, think of this product as a deferred fixed annuity that begins payments to you late in life beginning at age eighty-five. The amount of income you receive depends on prevailing interest rates when you sign the contract, and how much time you have until payments begin.

Here's an illustration. If a man age sixty paid a lump-sum $100,000 to buy a traditional deferred fixed annuity, he might lock into income payments (as of this writing) of about $5,250 a month beginning at age eighty-five. If, instead, the same man invested the same amount in longevity insurance, he would receive approximately $8,900 a month beginning at age eighty-five.

The payout terms are likely to be quite different by the time you contact an insurer. What I want you to register is the *magnitude of the income difference,* not the payout numbers themselves.

Longevity insurance pays a lot more income. That is fundamentally because longevity insurance is a deferred fixed annuity *without* a death benefit. Your heirs will normally get nothing when you die. You, however, may enjoy larger income payments—assuming you live long enough to enjoy them. But you take the risk of getting no return from this kind of annuity depending on your life span.

Here's the big advantage: You buy longevity insurance today; you lock into a fixed income payment today. You know immediately the exact amount you will receive. And you will normally receive more than you would from a conventional deferred fixed annuity.

RISKS

Obviously, longevity insurance has a big risk. Your contract has no value and there is no "residual" when you die. There is no death benefit. If you enjoy a long life span—great! If you die after receiving only two monthly payments, this annuity self-destructs. Game over. End of capital.

Too, you will lock into sure income streams if you live long enough to enjoy them, but will give up the opportunity to perhaps earn *substantially more* by investing in stocks and other investments.

Here's the paradox: You can buy this insurance or any fixed annuity and lock into a fixed income stream—that gives you sure income, but usually slim, possibly lackluster amounts. Or you can invest in a variable annuity and stock funds *instead of* longevity insurance —that gives you the possibility of earning much better income *or,* of course, earning less! Either can happen.

With longevity insurance and any other fixed annuity, you give up reward opportunity, but lock into "no-surprise" income and peace of mind.

Despite the risks, I urge you to consider longevity insurance or, better yet, a deferred fixed annuity for the later part of your life. If you are far from age eighty-five, you may wish to buy small amounts of longevity insurance or several deferred annuities in staggered doses—one small contract now, another contract in three or four years, and so on. That will give you a "ladder" of fixed annuities and sure-thing income.

FEATURES TO LOOK FOR

Any investment in longevity insurance should be limited to a small amount—no more than 5 percent—of your retirement savings. You will also want to shop for (1) a strong insurer, and possibly (2) the joint-survivor feature if it's of interest.

INSURANCE COMPANIES

Few insurers offer longevity insurance at this time. Here are several highly rated insurers that do:

Longevity Insurance

Group	Insurance Company	Insurance Company Ratings (Rank)		For Additional Information
		S&P	Moody's	
Hartford Hartford Income Security	Hartford Life Insurance and Annuity Company	AA - (4th)	Aa3 (4th)	www.hartfordinvestor.com (800) 862-6668
MetLife Retirement Income Insurance	Metropolitan Life Insurance Company	AA (3rd)	Aa2 (3rd)	www.metlife.com
New York Life Lifetime Income	New York Life Insurance and Annuity Corporation	AA + (2nd)	Aaa (1st)	www.newyorklife.com (800) 598-2019

Source: Annuity prospectuses and company Web sites

Contact these companies for more information about their products. Take your time. Compare terms. And check with other insurance companies as well. They may have a longevity product in the pipeline or a deferred fixed annuity that can be structured to give you similar expense and income terms.

A LIFE-CYCLE ANNUITY STRATEGY

Okay. Let's put all of these good products and advantages together.

To secure your future, you want *sure* income streams—no surprises or maybes. You want financial security. You want to neutralize longevity risk.

And you also want different amounts of income at different periods during your retirement to offset inflation and match your lifestyle.

Here's what I mean. If you retire at age sixty-five or seventy, you are likely to remain active for many years to come. You may want to have extra money available right after you retire for foreign travel, trips to see the grandchildren, adult education, and hobbies. You are likely to be active and want more income.

Over time, your spending patterns and income needs are going to change. You may *not*, after all, want a fifth trip to Kathmandu or new bungee-jumping gear when you're ninety-five. In fact, it's likely that you'll gradually spend more on health care and at-home comforts than for designer clothes, Prada handbags, or solar-powered Segways.

Meanwhile, inflation is a concern. We saw that inflation can erode the purchasing power of your savings as time goes by. By the time you're eighty, $1,000 is going to buy only a fraction of what it did when you were thirty years younger. So you also want to preserve the long-term purchasing power of your savings as well.

All in, you have three fundamental goals: (1) income streams you can count on, (2) different amounts of income for different phases of your retirement life, and (3) some offset to inflation.

To satisfy these needs, I recommend buying three annuities or layers of annuities to build a "life-cycle ladder" of income streams. Consider investing a part of your overall savings in this strategy after you are fully invested in your 401(k) and IRA. It's a unique way of ensuring basic income for your future.

By *ladder,* I mean a series of back-to-back investments that produce different income streams—each annuity investment being a different rung of your financial ladder. Here is the strategy I propose:

BASIC PREMISE

The fundamental idea is to invest in a variety of different annuities geared to produce different amounts of income for different phases of your retirement life. You should *not* use money that is already in a 401(k) or IRA for this strategy. Instead, use funds that you have outside of tax-sheltered accounts. Structure the annuity payout periods so you have different "compounding" times to help build the longer-term income you need.

A Life-Cycle Annuity Strategy

Build a ladder of annuity income

	Annuity #1 +	**Annuity #2** +	**Annuity #3**
Kind of Annuity	Deferred variable annuity	Deferred variable annuity	Deferred variable annuity (later a fixed annuity)
Objective	Income for 9 years (ages 65 thru 74)	Income for 9 years (ages 75 thru 84)	Income for life (age 85 onward)
When to Buy	Buy now. Make monthly payments until you retire (now to age 67).	Buy now. Make monthly payments until you retire (now to age 67).	Buy a deferred *variable* annuity now. Convert to a low-cost *fixed* annuity later.
How to Invest	A diversified mix of USA and international *income-*oriented indexes *or* equity, bond, and real estate funds.	A mix of equity funds, international funds, and annual "guaranteed return" investments.	Invest more conservatively: stock, international, and "guaranteed return" funds. Later, enjoy a fixed return with "longevity" coverage.

ANNUITY #1

Specifically buy a deferred variable annuity (Annuity #1) *now*—whether you are in your forties, fifties, or sixties—with an initial deposit and then monthly additions until the time you retire. Or, buy one such annuity every four years. You can invest in dividend-, rent-, and interest-producing funds along the lines of the diversification strategy I recommended earlier. You can invest more aggressively and may want this annuity to have more "dividend-focused" equity content.

Annuity #1 would begin paying you income from age sixty-five through age seventy-four—for only ten years. You may, of course, opt for a different starting age or different number of payout years, depending on when you decide to retire. You would nevertheless pay into this annuity until you retire, then immediately begin to receive income payments. At the end of ten years (or whatever other number of payout years you choose) this annuity will be depleted.

By limiting the number of years of payouts, you will heighten the income you receive. And by investing more money into this particular annuity at the outset, you can also enhance its income payouts to you for that phase of your retirement life when you will be most active and are likely to need more income.

That gives you basic income for ages sixty-five through seventy-four.

Annuity #2

Buy a second deferred variable annuity (Annuity #2) *now* with an initial starting payment and periodic additions up to your retirement. Or, buy one such annuity every four years. This annuity will have a much longer accumulation phase to beef up returns as an offset to inflation. You will pay in until you retire, but only begin receiving income much later. So this annuity will enjoy longer compounding.

You might invest somewhat more conservatively in Annuity #2. Perhaps consider putting one-fourth into U.S. equity funds, one-fourth into international equity funds, and half into a guaranteed-return account for the time being, making adjustments as time goes by.

Annuity #2 will begin its payouts to you at age seventy-five and continue them for ten years through age eighty-four (or the defined period of your choosing). And, again, the fact that payments are long deferred and the payout period is limited should help to amplify the income you receive.

That gives you income from ages seventy-five through eighty-four.

Annuity #3

For the third leg of the strategy, you can buy a deferred variable annuity *now* and make monthly payments to fund it until you retire. It will continue to be invested in funds until late age—say age seventy-five or eighty. At that time (or earlier depending on market conditions and your tolerance for risk) you can convert this annuity into *longevity insurance* or a *fixed annuity,* locking into fixed income streams for the rest of your life.

Before the "fixed" lock-in, you will be able to invest in different funds in the deferred variable annuity. You might invest very conservatively in this account.

Alternatively, you can put a small amount of money into longevity insurance or a deferred fixed annuity *now,* lock into a fixed amount of income, then purchase additional contracts later in periodic doses—perhaps one contract every several years. This may be the best approach.

The key is to have different annuity pipelines producing different income streams for different phases of your retirement life. This ladder can be structured to deliver the income you need for retirement basics. It must, however, be tailored to your risk tolerance. And instead of buying only three annuities, you can actually buy several more from time to time, always geared to produce income for you in one of the three payout time frames. If you are particularly keen on locking into "sure-thing" income, you can periodically buy deferred fixed annuities to create this same "ladder" effect with only "sure-return" instruments. (See the illustration on page 167.)

PURCHASE TACTICS

Under IRS regulations, multiple annuity contracts purchased within the same calendar year from the same insurer or its affiliates are treated as a single financial instrument for tax purposes. So you have to be cautious. Purchasing all three annuities from one company *in the same year* could result in the more rapid taxation of your income distributions than if the contracts were treated separately.

Don't let tax demonology deter you! This just means that you want to buy one of each kind of annuity in different years or purchase the different annuities from *three different insurance companies.* Buying from different companies may shield you from tax complications. It may lower default risk. And it will allow you to choose from a much larger variety of funds to substantially enhance your overall diversification if you buy variable annuities. Check with your financial advisor and/or tax advisor first, but give thought to separate purchases or—easier yet—avoid buying multiple contracts from one insurer in the same calendar year.

The best approach is to buy one annuity with a lump sum this year (Annuity #1), use *less* money and buy a smaller annuity (Annuity #2) with a lump sum next year, then buy a third annuity with *even less money* (Annuity #3) the year after. You would not make "installment" payments but buy a separate deferred annuity each year and pay for it in full at the time of purchase. You might use annual savings or your annual bonus to buy each one. But here's the twist: you would *continue* buying one annuity

Illustration

Structure annuities back-to-back
so they give you different income payouts

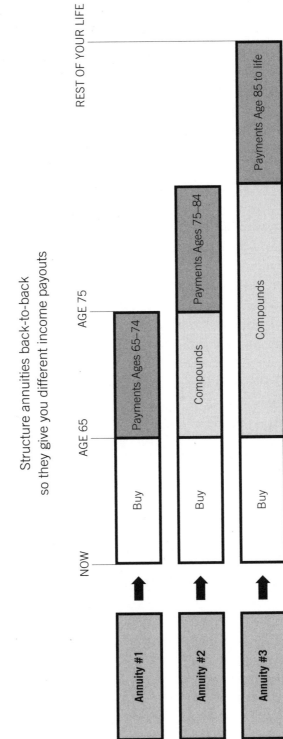

each year in years 4, 5, 6, and so on until you retire, building up *multiple* layers of different annuities to pay you muliple streams of income for each of the three retirement phases. If you cannot afford to buy a new annuity each year, you might buy one every other year until you actually retire. And since the annuities having later payouts (Annuities #2 and #3) will have longer compounding periods, you can put less money into them. This, in fact, is the purchase strategy I recommend. It permits you to build layered, multiple streams of income for yourself.

INVESTMENT TACTICS

When you invest in these annuities, I urge you to consider two features: (1) joint survivorship if you are partnered; and (2) increasing conservatism in the investment content of Annuities #2 and #3, the instruments meant to pay you later in time. I urge more conservatism in the latter annuities as a hedge against demographic risk. You want to adjust your annuities to have more international equity (as opposed to U.S. equity) and more guaranteed-return content during periods when there might be investment turbulence caused by boomer sell-offs.

As I noted, few insurers at the present time offer dividend-oriented funds or indexes. That is unfortunate. It is, however, sure to change over time. Meanwhile, look for traditional indexes, "value" equity funds, and international funds managed by topflight fund managers. You want broad diversification and particularly good international exposure.

Some insurers offer low-cost annuities that put you into "target date" funds—the kind that automatically change your stock and bond allocations as you age. That is *not* my first choice. Such funds generally have little or no income focus and give you little international exposure. They may not perform well when the impact of boomer aging intensifies. However, you may want to consider this kind of annuity *if* you find an annuity product with bare-bones costs and you particularly like the annuity's underlying fund components. You have to check the content of the underlying funds *very* carefully.

Remember, demographics suggest that stronger international exposure is going to be important. Insist on good international exposure even with a low-cost annuity product.

You will, consequently, need to compare the fund alternatives of different insurers. Compare the products of three companies with strong fund arrays. Whenever possible, use indexes, dividend-oriented funds, and "value" funds for the equity investments you make. Put a substantial amount into a variety of international funds for diversification and demographic advantage. And invest in guaranteed-return positions—more so in Annuity #2 and more so yet again in Annuity #3. In fact, you may even opt for fixed annuities when you invest in Annuity #2 and #3.

WHEN SHOULD YOU LOCK INTO A FIXED INCOME STREAM?

This ladder strategy relies on deferred annuities and is meant for long-term implementation. There is no guarantee that the funds in which you invest will deliver attractive or even positive returns. They may not.

Should you lock into fixed returns right now instead and buy fixed annuities? And if not immediately, when *should* you lock into guaranteed income?

Fixing income streams is a "market timing" conundrum. When you lock into a stream of income, you are saying, in effect, "I don't want to speculate or risk losing my savings, so I'll lock into a sure return *now*. I want peace of mind and am willing to forgo results that could be better."

That is perfectly fine. Timing, however, is everything. One study found that a sixty-five-year-old woman who bought an immediate *fixed* annuity in the early 1980s with a lump-sum payment of $100,000 might have received as much as $1,150 a month for life thereafter. If a sixty-five-year-old woman purchased the same contract with the same amount in 2003, she would only have bought $700 of monthly income payments.[3]

Clearly, the *timing* of your "lock-in" can boost or shrivel the income you receive.

On the other hand, studies show that few of us ever make astute or optimal "market timing" decisions. Most folks do not time their investment decisions with any skill or advantage. Trying to pick "the perfect time" to buy or sell an investment—or to lock into income—is a fool's game.

There is no magic formula. However, locking into fixed amounts of income may be prudent if you are near retirement or already retired. It may also make sense if you are concerned about the possibility of investment turbulence in the future.

The choice, however, is not easy—particularly if you buy an annuity but only want income payouts ten or twenty years down the road.

It is fair to say that now is one of the *worst* periods in which to lock into fixed streams of income. Insurance companies fix the annuity income they pay you on the basis of their own ability to generate income from bond investments. There is a direct link, therefore, between your "lock-in" and prevailing interest rates and bond-market performance. Since interest rates continue to hover at historic lows, this is not at all a good time for locking into hearty annuity income. The stock market (at least as of this writing) has been producing attractive (but jumpy) returns as well. Even doomsayers who foresee extreme stock market turbulence because of "boomer shock" expect reasonably good stock performance for some time to come.[4] So most investors might be tempted to enjoy stock market returns and postpone any "income fix" until a later date.

That leaves you with three choices. One, you can buy *variable* annuities, diversify, and hope for positive, better-than-fixed returns. Two, you can opt for *fixed* annuities and simply lock into today's returns with *no* fluctuation risk to worry about. Or three, you can invest in a *mix* of fixed and deferred annuities to diversify your risk/reward prospects.

If you are near or in retirement, you may be better off opting for a lock-in. A fixed annuity probably makes good sense for you.

If you are many years away from retirement but nevertheless fear market turmoil, consider splitting your investments between *both* kinds of annuities. Where my strategy calls for an investment in a deferred *variable* annuity, you might invest half in a variable and half in a fixed annuity. Or, alternatively, buy *only* fixed annuities each year or every two years to stagger your lock-in times—perhaps with overall income benefit.

If, however, you have a long time until retirement and are not haunted by visions of a stock market crash, stick with the three-annuity strategy I just described and postpone your income lock-in until later.

This much is clear: a simple ladder approach to annuity investing can give you mighty tax and income advantages. One size, however, does not fit all. It's up to you to pick suitable income "lock-in" times based on your personal risk tolerance. Talk over your objectives and risk tolerance with a financial advisor to customize this ladder strategy for you.

FOR ADDITIONAL INFORMATION

For additional information about annuities in general, visit AARP's Web site. It has an online educational "workshop" and a number of good articles that will help you better understand how annuities work.

You should also visit the Web sites of different insurance companies to understand their products and view their educational materials. Most companies also have specialists who can answer your questions and provide additional information. They are just a toll-free phone call away.

Learn more about annuities and use them to put lifetime income on the table. They are excellent instruments!

CONCLUSIONS AND NEXT STEPS

A combination of annuities is a powerful way of making income available during retirement. Laddering these instruments can help you defuse longevity and inflation risk. Three layers of annuities can be packaged to deliver different amounts of income at different phases of your retirement life. Take the time to learn more about annuities. Talk over my "life-cycle strategy" with your financial advisor. And make sure annuities are a part of *your* investment portfolio.

ACTION PLAN

1. Visit AARP's Web site to learn more about annuities.
2. Read Ken Little's *The Pocket Idiot's Guide to Annuities* and TheStreet .com's *Consumer Guide to Variable Annuities.*
3. Contact the insurers listed here for more information about specific annuity and longevity products. Compare their costs, income payouts, and funds.
4. Talk over my "life-cycle annuity strategy" with your financial coach.
5. Take steps to lodge some of your retirement capital in a ladder of three annuities to cover basic income needs.
6. Give standing instructions to your insurer to *automatically* debit your checking account to fund these annuities if you purchase them via installments.
7. Make annual adjustments to your variable-annuity-fund allocations as market conditions change.

9

INVEST IN HEALTH
CARE INSURANCE

In addition to building diverse income streams, you need to shield your retirement capital from skyrocketing health-care costs—costs that could wipe out your savings.

In this section you will learn how to protect yourself from medical costs *not* covered by Medicare. To shelter your nest egg from health-care drain, you actually need two different kinds of insurance: so-called Medigap insurance and long-term health care insurance. To understand why, let's start with a simple overview of national health coverage in this country.

MEDICARE AND MEDICAID

In the United States, two basic "national health programs" offset the medical costs of retirees and disabled persons. They are Medicare and Medicaid.

MEDICARE

Medicare is the country's national health insurance system. It was established in 1965. Most people have contact with it via Blue Cross, Blue Shield, or one of several other major insurance companies that have a monopoly on the administration of the program in different parts of the country.

People age sixty-five and over and some people with disabilities—42 million people in total—are currently covered by Medicare.[1] While we often talk about Medicare as a single program, it is really a series of several different programs or "plans." "Part A" is *hospital insurance,* covering inpatient hospital care. "Part B" is *medical insurance,* covering doctors' services, outpatient care, lab tests, and so forth, and you must pay a monthly premium for this coverage. "Part C" is an array of private insurance health plans, such as HMOs or "health maintenance organizations," which provide the same or broader coverage as Parts A and B. (Stay with me!) And "Part D" is the country's new *prescription drug insurance,* which covers many drug costs and for which you must likewise pay a monthly premium.

The coverage and dollar outlays of these programs are huge. About 96 percent of Americans age sixty-five and over have Medicare coverage.[2] In fact, Medicare benefit payouts now total more than $325 billion each year, accounting for a large percentage of the federal budget.[3]

MEDICAID

Medicaid is a federal and state program for individuals with low incomes and resources. Its coverage and eligibility vary from state to state. Generally, you can only qualify for Medicaid if your annual income is less than about $9,800 a year and you have less than $2,000 in assets (or for couples, a bit more).

Some 9 percent of Americans age sixty-five and over have Medicaid coverage.[4] If you qualify for both Medicaid and Medicare, a substantial amount of your health care costs are covered by the two programs. However, the *Medicare-only* coverage enjoyed by the vast majority of Americans is geared to pay only for some—*not all*—of your health care needs. If you are middle-class, affluent, or wealthy, you will probably need deep pockets to pay for health care during retirement.

For details about the monthly premiums and enrollment terms for Medicare and Medicaid, consult these publications:

Medicare's official 2007 handbook: *Medicare & You 2007,* available online at www.medicare.gov.

Joseph L. Matthews and Dorothy Matthews Berman, *Social Security, Medicare & Government Pensions,* 10th ed. (NOLO Publishing, 2005), ISBN: 1-4133-0154-1.

THE NEED FOR SUPPLEMENTAL COVERAGE

What I want to impress upon you here is the need for supplemental health-care insurance. Supplemental insurance is essential because (1) health care costs are skyrocketing; (2) Medicare only plays a fraction of them; (3) Medicare and Medicaid may not be able to continue paying the same level of benefits; and (4) going *without* supplemental insurance puts your savings at enormous risk.

SPIRALING HEALTH CARE COSTS

Americans are deeply unhappy with the country's health care programs and costs. And rightly so. As one author observed, "A recent survey showed that only 17 percent of respondents in the United States were content with their health-care system. . . . Why the discontent? The superficial reasons are simple enough to describe: the system is hugely expensive, very bureaucratic, and extremely patchy. The expenses first: U.S. health care costs a third more, per person, than that of the closest rival, superrich Switzerland, and twice what many European countries spend. The United States government alone spends more per person than the combination of public and private expenditure in Britain, despite the fact that the British government provides free health care for all residents."[5]

The United States pays more for health care per capita than any other industrialized nation—and even then, Medicare is not a comprehensive, pay-for-everything national health program like those of many nations and United States per capita health care costs continue to escalate rapidly.

Here's what you need to know about health care costs as you plan for retirement.

Americans age sixty-five and over spend *four times more* on health care on average than do Americans under the age of sixty-five. At the outset of this decade, the average per capita health-care outlay for a person under the age of sixty-five was about $2,800. For people over the age of sixty-five, it was $11,089. And for Americans ages eighty-five and older it was $20,001.[6] Clearly, health care outlays are likely to get substantially larger as you age. You need to plan for them.

U.S. health care expenses have grown mightily. U.S. health care expenses have dramatically escalated each year as new medications, new treatments, diagnostic tools, and health care innovations have come onto the market.

For example, the median nationwide cost for a hospital stay—*excluding* physicians' charges—was $11,280 in 1997; by 2004 it was almost double at $20,455.[7] The average total cost for treating a heart attack climbed 40 percent in just seven years.[8] All in, health care costs have escalated fast and the increases are gaining momentum.

Health care costs are likely to continue to grow unabated. Unlike in other countries, no laws meaningfully curb the continual climb of health care and drug costs in the United States. For example, many Americans continue to import drugs from Canada because Canadian prices are significantly lower. This is true even though the new Medicare features introduced in 2006 offset the cost of pharmaceuticals for U.S. retirees. To curb the cost of medicines, Canada prohibits drug companies from advertising on its television channels. In the United States, on the other hand, the very legislation that created the new Medicare drug benefit (Part D) expressly prohibits the federal government from attempting to negotiate lower prices with drug companies.[9]

Count on it: medical costs are sky-high *and* likely to keep climbing unless there is a radical overhaul of the system.

More and more corporations are cutting back on health care benefits as medical costs soar. Recent statistics show companies cutting health care benefits and requiring employees and retirees to pay more for them. As one survey of corporate benefit trends concluded, "[Benefit] reductions have become not just common, but expected, with the only question now being of how much more of a reduction in benefits and or an increase in cost will be directly placed on individuals. . . . In the end . . . individuals, either as taxpayers or consumers, will need to pay the bill."[10]

I believe this trend will gain greater momentum over the next decades. It will be part and parcel of the continuing erosion of employment benefits—like the demise of traditional pensions—that is taking place throughout the country. Just like pensions, more and more health-care expense is going to become a do-it-yourself responsibility because heath care insurance costs are simply becoming too great for companies to shoulder competitively.

Taken all together, you can count on: (1) higher and higher health care costs, (2) more health-care-benefit cutbacks by U.S. employers, (3) the need to factor large health-care expenses into your funding plans, and (4) the need to buy supplemental health-care insurance to shield your savings from cost attack.

Of course, these views will not come as a surprise to most folks. Recent polls show that—immediately after the foremost financial concern of having enough money for retirement—the next great concern of most Americans is health care. *More than half of adult Americans are "very worried" or "moderately worried"* about being able to pay for serious illness or catastrophic health-care expense.[11]

MEDICARE WILL ONLY PAY A FRACTION OF YOUR EXPENSES

Most working Americans have no idea for what Medicare will and will not pay. How could they? There are publications the size of phone books explaining "covered" and "not covered" costs, but it's important to understand that Medicare will pay only a portion of your medical costs in retirement and that you are expected to ante up the difference.

On the next page is a partial listing of Medicare's coverage. I offer it simply to illustrate Medicare's piecemeal, convoluted approach to paying benefits.

Before introduction of the new prescription-coverage Plan D, Medicare typically covered about 45 percent of a retiree's health care costs, and American seniors spent about one-fifth of their retirement income on medical costs not covered by Medicare.[12] That's right. About one of out five retirement dollars are routinely spent on health care *not* covered by Medicare.

Since the introduction of the drug benefit, seniors pay about 28 percent less for medicines.[13] Even so, retirees still have to pay for a great deal of medical expense out of their own pockets.

Medicare Coverage

All numbers cited are approximate
because of the system's complexity

Covered	Not Covered
After you pay Part A and Part B deductibles:	• The Part A (hospitalization) deductible for each benefit period ($992 in 2007) that you, yourself, first pay
• 60 days of hospital-only costs (after you co-pay $992 per benefit period)	• Daily co-pay ($248 per day in 2007) for days 61–90 of hospital-only expenses
• 61–90 days of hospital-only costs (you co-pay $248 per day in 2007)	• Daily co-pay ($496 per day in 2007) for days 91–150 of hospital-only charges (the 60 "reserve days")
• 60 "reserve days" of additional hospital-only costs (you co-pay $496 per day in 2007; and once the 60 reserve days are used, this benefit is over)	• All costs incurred for hospital-only care over 150 days (or over 90 days once you use the reserve days)
• 100 days of posthospital nursing care (you co-pay for days 21–100)	• Daily co-pay ($124 per day in 2007) for days 21–100 of nursing-home care
• 80–100% of most lab tests, X-rays, and radiation treatments (if billed by a hospital)	• All costs for nursing-home care over 100 days
• Drugs and medical appliances used in a hospital (splints, casts, shunts, wheelchairs)	• First three pints of blood
• Some (but few) preventive screening exams (prostate, pelvic, diabetes, glaucoma, sundry cancers)	• 20% of the "Medicare-approved" amounts for doctors, outpatient treatment, and equipment *(and all "nonapproved" costs, which can be substantial)*
• 75–100% of prescription drug costs	• Most routine physical exams and preventive testing, routine hearing and eye exams, hearing aids, and glasses
• 80% of "Medicare-approved" doctor charges *(actual fees can be and often are substantially higher)*	• All non-U.S. hospital expenses (with some exceptions)
	• Most long-term-care expenses (e.g., custodial care for patients with Parkinson's, Alzheimer's, etc.)

Source: Joseph L. Matthews, and Dorothy Matthews Berman, *Social Security, Medicare & Government Pensions* 10th ed. (NOLO Publishing, 2005), and Medicare's official handbook, *Medicare & You 2007*

Even with the drug benefit, Medicare will probably cover only about *one-half* of your health care expenses during retirement unless the program is radically over hauled.

As costs rise, moreover, so do Medicare premiums and deductibles. Premiums are the monthly amounts you have to pay for different kinds of Medicare coverage. You typically pay no premium for Part A if you qualify for Social Security, but you do have to pay monthly premiums for Medicare Parts B and D. Deductibles, on the other hand, are the amounts that you must pay before Medicare pays anything at all. Both premiums and deductibles increase each year. For example, the deductible that you had to pay in 2007 for Part A hospitalization was $992 per benefit period, and that amount is expected to increase to about $1,164 in 2010.[14]

Between premiums, deductibles, and the sundry services "not covered" by Medicare, you are going to confront large medical expenses that you must pay—about 50 percent of your total medical outlay. That, of course, is on the assumption that Medicare and Medicaid will continue to pay the same benefits in the future as now. They may not be able to do so.

MEDICARE AND MEDICAID
MAY HAVE TO REDUCE BENEFITS

Like Social Security, Medicare and Medicaid were designed for short life spans, for cost *assistance* (*not* full coverage), and for a limited number of beneficiaries. The country's health insurance programs are already financially strained. The boomer surge will strain them to near breaking.

We saw that baby boomers will begin reaching age sixty-five in 2011 and begin going on Medicare. In the words of one commentator, "Of all of the nation's fiscal problems, this is by far the biggest."[15] In fact, the sheer numbers of people about to enter Medicare could cause the program's payouts to reach the size of today's *entire federal budget* in several decades' time.

The situation is serious. One expert group sizes it up this way: "Over the long-term, Medicare will face the fiscal challenges of an aging baby-boom generation and a declining number of workers per beneficiary. Assets in the Part A (Medicare) Health Insurance trust fund are projected to exceed income beginning in 2012 and trust fund reserves are projected to be exhausted in 2020."[16]

These facts lead me to several conclusions. Some of our national health programs will begin to operate in the red by 2020. The government may have no choice but to "redesign"—meaning *cut back*—health care benefits or require more public funding. So you and I are going to need ample savings to pay for medical care or taxes. There is simply not enough money in the government's coffers for these kinds of benefits in the long term unless sweeping funding changes *or* benefit cuts are made.

There is no cause for panic. But you should be saving hard.

SUPPLEMENTAL INSURANCE IS *IMPERATIVE*, NOT "NICE TO HAVE"

Even without taking *future* cost hikes or possible benefit changes into account, the need to supplement Medicare coverage *already* puts a formidable strain on the finances of many retirees.

Studies by the Employee Benefit Research Institute conclude that individuals now age fifty-five who live to age ninety would need to accumulate over $210,000 by age sixty-five just to pay for insurance to supplement Medicare and to cover out-of-pocket medical expenses in retirement.[17]

Other research groups say that we need even *more* savings because of Medicare's shortfalls. In fact, one group estimates that a retiring couple will need at least $200,000 in retirement savings just to pay for "the most basic medical coverage" in retirement—but $300,000 if you look forward to "ample" medical care.[18]

These numbers are sobering. They hammer home a vital fact: *your* need for personal savings and supplemental medical insurance is very real and very large. You need to offset the threat of uncovered health-care expense. And that's why you need supplemental Medigap coverage as well as long-term-care insurance.

MEDIGAP INSURANCE

To encourage the public to buy private insurance as a supplement to Medicare, the government has actually defined twelve Standard Supplemental Plans. They are collectively called Medigap insurance because they offset the "gaps" of Medicare's coverage. These twelve plans—named Plan A through L—are basically the same across the country. (There are variances in several states, but the plans are otherwise standard nationwide.) The coverage you get in Plan A is the same no matter which insurer you buy it from. Plan B pays somewhat larger benefits, but all Plan B benefits are likewise the same. Plan C pays even higher benefits, and so on. However, while the benefits of any one standard plan (say Plan A) are the same no matter which insurer you choose, the cost for that same plan may vary substantially from one insurer to the next. You have to shop around.

TWELVE STANDARD PLANS

For an easy comparison of the different plans, visit these Web sites:

The Henry J. Kaiser Family Foundation
www.kff.org/medicare/7067/med_supplement.cfm

Medicare
www.medicare.gov/Publications/Pubs/pdf/02110.pdf

You can no longer buy several of the plans covering prescription drugs since that benefit is now provided by Medicare. However, Medigap insurance nevertheless covers more—*but still not all!*—of the expenses otherwise not covered by Medicare insurance. So count on buying a Medigap policy to enlarge your protective shield.

WHEN TO BUY

The time to buy Medigap is when you turn sixty-five and first qualify for Medicare. When you turn sixty-five, you have a six-month "open enrollment period" during which you can sign up for Medigap insurance. During that period, insurance companies are obligated to insure you regardless of your health status. And as long as you pay the premiums for this insurance, the insurance company is obligated to renew your policy each year.[19]

Be sure to sign up for Medigap when you turn sixty-five unless you have access to some kind of supplemental coverage.

FINDING A GOOD INSURER

As we noted in the previous chapter, you always want to work with insurance companies having exceptionally strong ratings of financial strength. That gives you the assurance that you will be dealing with a company whose finances and balance sheet are certifiably powerful.

To spare you some research time, on page 182 is a short list of some insurance companies having particularly strong ratings.

As you make retirement plans, select a standard Medigap plan of interest to you (using the plan descriptions from the online sites I cited on page 180), then obtain quotes from at least three different insurance companies to compare each one's pricing. Be sure to check with AARP as well. AARP helps the public obtain Medigap insurance on preferential terms. You can call AARP's "product telephone number" to obtain straightforward answers to all your questions about supplemental insurance.

If you cannot afford Medigap insurance, Medicaid may be an alternative. Go online or call your state Medicaid agency to ascertain its eligibility terms. However, you may not qualify for Medicaid because of its income and net-worth limitations. Most folks will have to rely on Medicare as well as supplemental insurance—and then some.

MEDIGAP INSURANCE IS NOT ENOUGH

Even a supplemental Medigap policy will not cover all of the medical expenses you are likely to confront. You need a second kind of insurance as well. Specifically, Medicare and Medigap do not cover extended stays in nursing homes or extended home care.

If, for example, you develop a neurological or cognitive disorder such as Parkinson's or Alzheimer's disease, you will incur substantial costs that are *not* covered by Medicare or Medigap. You need additional insurance. And in the words of the government's own Medicare handbook, "It's important to think about how to get and pay for long-term care before you need it."[20]

LONG-TERM HEALTH CARE INSURANCE

Few people planning for retirement focus on the possibility of needing long-term health care. According to one poll, 65 percent of adult Ameri-

Medigap Insurance Companies

Insurer	Ratings		For More Information
	S&P	Moody's	
AARP (United Healthcare Insurance Company)	A (6th)	A2 (6th)	www.aarphealthcare.com (800) 317-8626
Anthem Blue Cross Blue Shiled	State specific	State specific	www.anthem.com State specific
Blue Cross Blue Shield	State specific	State specific	www.bcbs.com (800) 624-1723
Golden Rule Insurance Company	A+ (5th)	n/a	www.goldenrule.com (800) 444-8990
Mutual of Omaha Insurance Company	AA– (4th)	Aa3 (4th)	www.mutualofomaha.com (800) 775-6000
State Farm Mutual Automobile Insurance Company	AA (3rd)	Aa1 (2nd)	www.statefarm.com agents contacts provided online
United American Insurance Company	AA (3rd)	n/a	www.unitedamerican.com (800) 331-2512

Note: Figures in parentheses in the "Ratings" columns represent the *rank* of each rating in Moody's or Standard & Poor's respective rating hierarchy. The ranking "(1st)" means the highest rating by that rating group; "(2nd)," the second-highest rating of that rater; etc. However, all of the above companies enjoy exceptionally strong ratings of financial strength.

cans said they had made no provision for long-term health care for themselves or their spouses.[21] *But the probability of needing long-term care not covered by Medicare is high and the expense for such care is extremely high.*

THE NEED FOR LONG-TERM CARE

A comprehensive study recently conducted by health specialists Peter Kemper, Harriet Komisar, and Lisa Alecxih drew the following conclusions regarding people who had turned sixty-five in 2005:[22]

- People who had reached age sixty-five would, on average, need *three years* of long-term care—meaning nursing-home, assisted-living, or facility care, and/or formal or informal home care.
- An estimated 32 percent of all adults age sixty-five and over will need *one to five years* of long-term care.
- Twenty percent of those age sixty-five and over will need *more than five years* of long-term care.
- Women have a higher risk of needing such care. A woman age sixty-five today has more than a 30 percent probability of living past ninety.[23] In fact, 79 percent of all women reaching age sixty-five will need some amount of long-term care. And 28 percent of all women—more than one out of four—will need long-term care for *more than five years*.
- *More than one out of three people*—35 percent—will need some amount of nursing-home care.
- An estimated 18 percent—almost *one out of every five seniors—will need two years or more* of nursing-home or assisted-living care.
- However, needing long-term care is not at all a certainty. Three out of ten people will never need any long-term care at all. On the other hand, two out of ten will need some kind of long-term care for five or more years.[24]

Medicare will not offset the full brunt of long-term-care costs. And Medicaid requires that you have a low income or exhaust your financial resources. In the words of the Henry J. Kaiser Family Foundation, a respected specialist in health information and policy:

"The price tag for long-term care can be astronomical, beyond the resources of most families. At best, Medicare pays only a fraction of these costs. Extended nursing home stays for an individual requiring skilled care can easily cost in excess of $5,000 a month, although fees vary widely. . . . You should consider very carefully how to pay for it: through Medicaid, if you qualify, with private long-term care insurance, or out-of-pocket."[25]

As you plan for retirement, you must factor in the need for long-term care. You may be lucky and not require it. I hope that is the case. On the other hand, you may find your savings sabotaged by unexpected, huge, out-of-pocket care expenses that Medicare and Medigap do not cover.

The probability of needing some kind of long-term care is high. So are the costs.

THE EXPENSE DILEMMA

Long-term care is expensive. The average cost for a private room in a nursing home is now just over $70,900 a year nationwide.[26] The cost of assisted-living care averages about $29,000 a year, but can reach as much as $80,000 annually.[27] And these expenses are growing. Here is the dilemma:

> Looking to the future, an estimated one-half of people who had turned age sixty-five in 2005 will have *no* personal out-of-pocket outlay for long-term care. However, one in twenty people will incur out-of-pocket expenses amounting to *$100,000 or more.*[28]
>
> And many people in between those extremes will confront a substantial amount of out-of-pocket expense *and financial hardship* because of long-term-care needs.

It is also helpful to remember that women have an even great need for long-term care or LTC: "The current cohort of sixty-five-year-olds will need, on average, LTC (facility care, formal home care services, or informal care at home) for a total of three years, according to . . . model simulations. . . . Dramatic differences, although not surprising, exist between women and men. Women will need LTC for a longer time—for an average of 3.7 years, compared with 2.2 years for men."[29]

The odds are reasonable that *you* will need long-term health care at some time. Odds are also strong that health care expenses will continue to climb as will the cost of health insurance. Indeed, health insurance premiums have necessarily grown as life spans have pushed out longer.

I draw two conclusions: One, you cannot afford the risk of *not* having private insurance to cover long-term-care needs; you simply cannot play Russian roulette with your savings. And, two, you may be better off locking into health insurance premiums early on before insurance costs grow larger still.

There are compelling reasons for buying long-term health care insurance—insurance that pays for formal and informal home care, adult day care, and care in assisted-living facilities as well as nursing homes. And there's substantial advantage in doing so *in advance* of your actual retirement.

WHO SHOULD BUY

Ideally, *every person* should buy long-term health care coverage. However, many people may not be able to afford the premiums or may have family or employers to count on for care or financial aid.

You should *not* buy this kind of insurance if (1) you have limited assets; (2) are on Medicaid; (3) Social Security will be your primary source of retirement income; (4) you cannot afford to pay for the insurance premiums and escalations of those premiums over time; and/or (5) you work for a company that gives its retirees broad health-care coverage.

Otherwise, you need to consider long-term health care insurance to protect your retirement capital. I have it. You should as well.

WHEN TO BUY

The best time to buy long-term health care insurance is between the ages of fifty-seven and sixty-five. In fact, you may do best buying it in your late fifties. Here's why.

More applicants are declined access to long-term-care insurance when they are older because of poor health. A recent study shows that *one out of ten* people between the ages of fifty and fifty-nine were denied long-term-care coverage. Of applicants at or over the age of eighty, almost *six out of ten* were declined coverage.[30] So you want to lock into insurance when you're still in good health.

Buying at an early age may also help contain the expense. You may lock into a decidedly lower cost base if you buy this insurance before you turn 59½ years of age. You will still have periodic premium increases, but they will start on a lower cost base.

For example, the average premium for a person who buys in at age sixty-five to sixty-nine is approximately $2,340 per year. The average cost for people ages fifty to fifty-nine is approximately $1,857—or *26 percent less.*[31]

Please note that these average costs are somewhat misleading since they represent a mix of different kinds of coverage. There are lower-cost policies. My examples simply illustrate that it costs a lot less to buy into this insurance when you are younger and in good health. The actual premiums depend on the specific kinds of benefits you buy. So let me tell you which kinds of benefits to look for. And let me explain, as well, the drawbacks associated with this kind of insurance.

THE DOWNSIDE

Long-term-care insurance is an excellent investment. However, it has drawbacks or risks that you need to understand as well.

Long expense. The average age of people admitted to a nursing home is about eighty-three.[32] Consequently, if you buy a long-term health care policy when you're in your fifties or sixties, you may pay premiums for many years before you ever derive benefits—if you derive them at all.

Continual premium escalations. Although some policies theoretically "limit" premium escalations over time, virtually all policies permit them. And the increases can become quite hefty as you age. For example, one survey found that a plan that costs $1,625 annually for a man age fifty may cost $3,100 a year at age sixty-five and $7,500 a year at age seventy.[33] My own survey suggests that strongly rated insurers and "upper end" policies tend *not* to hike up premiums out of orbit. Premium increases are much more prevalent among "discount" insurers. So stick with reputable insurers and avoid "bargain basement" pricing. And remember that the alternative—having no long-term-care coverage at all—is even more fearsome. Bite the bullet.

Benefit qualification. To actually receive long-term-care benefits one day, you usually have to demonstrate an inability to perform basic "activities of daily living" such as bathing, dressing, eating, and hygiene. Some insurers may also require you to see their own physicians. Not surprisingly, data from the National Association of Insurance Commissioners shows that long-term health care policies paid out benefits amounting to only 35 percent of the premiums they collected in prior years.[34] Critics cite this as a reason why you should *not* buy long-term-care insurance. I believe it is precisely why you *do* need this coverage—to offset the "off chance" of needing long-term care that might otherwise irreparably harm your finances.

Benefit erosion. Over time, the "dollar power" of your insurance benefits may diminish as well. That is because health care costs are likely to continue to climb, and inflation is also likely to erode the benefit coverage you enjoy. The daily benefit you buy today might only pay a *fraction* of the nursing-home expense you incur in ten years' time. You have to factor in that possibility.

There are drawbacks. Nevertheless, I *strongly* recommend long-term health care insurance. You should give such coverage serious thought. It is an important investment that belongs in your overall portfolio.

Long-term-care insurance is every bit as important as an IRA or 401(k). Add this insurance to your arsenal of protective investments. But only do so if you understand the product, understand the costs, and appreciate the significant protection that such coverage can afford.

WHAT TO LOOK FOR

Long-term health care policies can be set up with a great number of different features and benefits. Of course, the more benefits you enjoy, the higher the cost. So let's take a streamlined "tour" of some of the basic benefit alternatives that are available. Specifically, here are the features I urge you to look for when you shop for long-term-care coverage.

Strong financial ratings. First, let me restate the principle we established earlier: whenever you entrust money to any financial services group or insurer, you want to be sure that it enjoys the highest ratings of financial strength. *You want to avoid, at all costs, the possibility of that company or bank being unable to pay you or serve you because of financial weakness.*

Consequently, check into the Standard & Poor's and Moody's ratings for any insurance group you consider. You can call the insurance company's toll-free number and ask for its (1) Moody's and (2) Standard and Poor's ratings directly. As I suggested earlier, you should be looking for *A level* or *exceptionally strong* ratings when you shop. So use the table in the prior annuity chapter to compare company ratings.

Benefit amount. The average cost for nursing-home care varies substantially state by state. When you talk to an insurance representative, ascertain the average cost of care per day *in your state*. In your policy, you should consider fixing the benefit amount as your state's *average cost plus at least 15 percent*—a markup for added protection against inflation. Remember, inflation is a real threat. So are rising medical costs. Consequently, you want to lock into an initial benefit amount that is *higher* than today's prevailing costs.

Benefit time limit. Most policies typically set a time limit or maximum period for payment benefits of one year, two years, four years, six years, or your lifetime. The longer the benefit period, the higher the insurance cost. On average, people reaching sixty-five require *three years* of some kind of care, but one out of five people will need some kind of care for *more than five years*.[35] So consider a *four- or six-year benefit period*—four years if you are a man and six years if you are a woman—instead of the much more expensive lifetime option.

The longer the benefit period you can afford, the better. Lifetime coverage, of course, is the most expensive. But four to six years of coverage should be satisfactory for most people.

Home care. Long-term-care insurance is also available with different amounts of benefit that can be spent for "home care"—meaning care provided inside your own home such as professional nursing care, physical therapy, home health aides, and the like. The average amount of any kind of care *at home* is approximately 1.9 years. By comparison, the average amount of care needed in a nursing home *or* assisted-living facility is only about 1.1 years. (But don't let these averages mislead you. An estimated 30 percent of retirees will need care at home for *more than two years*. More than one out of ten people—11 percent—will need more than *five years of home care*.[36]

My point is that home care is important. When you buy long-term-care insurance, you will be asked to fix the percent of benefits that can be used for home care. The higher the home care percentage, the higher the insurance premium or cost.

Because home care is the *more likely* kind of care you may need and also the *longer* kind of care you may need, I recommend that you *opt for the 100 percent home care benefit*. That means that the full amount of your insurance benefit can be used to pay for home care costs or, alternatively, the costs of nursing-home care.

Elimination period. Most insurance companies require you to pay for the first twenty, thirty, sixty, or ninety days of care *before* their own payments kick in. You must opt for this specific number of days (or "elimination period") when you first buy the policy. The shorter the elimination period, the higher the insurance cost. To spare you premium expense, I recommend looking at a *ninety-day* period. Medicare may, in many instances, at least cover some of the first days of expense. And your annual premiums will be a lot less. However, a longer elimination period means that you will have to pay several months of care costs out of your own pocket—and that expense can be substantial. When you comparatively shop for a policy, compare the premiums for a sixty- and ninety-day elimination period.

Inflation protection. Inflation protection is an important feature to add to your coverage. Because health care costs are escalating sharply and inflation is a perennial threat, you want to be sure that the amount of benefit coverage you buy today will give you adequate benefit in the future.

Here's what I mean. If the average nursing-home rate today is $175 to $200 per day, it could very well increase to a multiple of that amount by the time you need long-term care. Unless your policy *automatically* keeps pace with cost escalations, your benefits may not be very helpful to you in the future.

Many insurance companies allow you to add inflation protection. It costs more, and there are two kinds: simple and compound. If the inflation protection is *simple,* then your benefit increases by the same dollar amount each year. For example, a daily benefit of $100 with a 5 percent *simple protection* feature will go up by $5 a year and become a $105 daily benefit next year and a $200 daily benefit in twenty years.

If the benefit is *compound,* then the dollar amount of the benefit increases by incremental, cumulative amounts. A $100 daily benefit with a 5 percent *compounded protection* feature would increase by $5 after one year, by $10.25 in the second, and so on. After twenty years on a compounded basis, a $100 daily benefit would increase to $265. That's a substantial difference.

If you can afford it, *buy automatic 5 percent compounded inflation adjustments.* Costs are likely to rise. Consequently, you want *automatic* and *compounded* inflation adjustments, meaning that your coverage will increase each year without you needing to buy additional coverage.

You do *not* want "simple" inflation adjustments. You do *not* want the right (at great expense) to buy additional insurance later in time. You *do* want automatic, *compounded* 3 to 5 percent inflation increases. This may be the most important feature of all—but be sure to compare insurers and costs.

Nonforfeiture. Should you cancel your policy or let it lapse, this benefit assures you of getting back something for the premiums you've paid. This would normally be repaid as a kind of health care "credit," not cash. For example, you might be entitled to a "shortened benefit period" that you can draw upon. Without this benefit, you get nothing back— even if you paid premiums for ten or fifteen years. If available, *you do want this feature.*

Return of premium or return of contribution. With this advantage, your insurer is supposed to pay some or all of the premiums you have paid in—less the benefit payments you have received—to your heirs or estate. Many policies make such "returns" difficult if not downright impossible. The cost for it is also high. So you will keep costs down and probably not sacrifice much real benefit if you *decline this option.*

Waiver of premium. With this benefit, you will not be required to continue paying insurance premiums when you begin receiving benefit payments for certain services. *You do want this option.*

Shared care or joint benefit. Some insurers will establish a policy so that spouses or partners can share each other's total benefit amount. If one of the covered individuals collects benefits, those amounts are deducted from the total benefit of the overall coverage for *both* parties. This can be useful if you select a benefit period other than lifetime. With a four- or six-year benefit period, *the "shared care" benefit is advantageous.* At the same time, some insurance companies offer discounts if *both* spouses buy long-term-care policies. *Inquire about a "joint policy discount" that can knock as much as 30 percent off of each spouse's insurance premium.*

Tax-qualified contract. With a tax-qualified plan, you may be able to deduct some of the premiums in your tax declarations (provided you itemize deductions). If you are asked to choose between a qualified and nonqualified plan, *choose tax-qualified.* However, get guidance from a tax specialist or accountant before you make any tax deductions or count on any tax advantage. A "tax-qualified contract" may not, after all, give you tax benefit.

These different benefit alternatives sound complicated, but they are not. Most insurers have specialists on hand who can explain these alternatives in more detail to you by telephone. They will make it easy to decide on the specific benefits that are suitable for you. But remember, you want an exceptionally strong, financially solid insurer foremost of all.

FINDING A GOOD INSURER

Many companies offer long-term-care insurance, but you need to screen them carefully for financial soundness, for the product features I have just highlighted, as well as for good pricing.

You specifically want an insurer that has exceptionally strong, independently certified ratings of financial strength. I cannot overemphasize the importance of that qualification.

To give you a head start, on page 192 is a list of some insurance companies that offer long-term health care insurance and have exceptional ratings. You need to contact several and compare their policy features and pricing.

Of course, this list is not exhaustive. There are many good insurance companies offering long-term health care coverage. Whichever insurers you consider, call for their most recent ratings and speak with their representatives about their pricing and benefit terms. You need to comparatively shop.

Long-Term Health Care Insurance Companies

Insurer	Ratings		For More Information
	S&P	**Moody's**	
AARP (Met Life)	AA (3rd)	Aa2 (3rd)	www.aarphealthcare.com (800) 828-7472
John Hancock Life Insurance Company	AA+ (2nd)	Aa2 (3rd)	www.johnhancock.com (800) 334-4437
Mass Mutual (Massachusetts Mutual Life Insurance Company)	AAA (1st)	Aa1 (2nd)	www.massmutual.com e-mail online
Mutual of Omaha Insurance Company	AA– (4th)	Aa3 (4th)	www.mutualofomaha.com e-mail online
New York Life Insurance Company	AA+ (2nd)	Aaa (1st)	www.newyorklife.com (800) 710-7945
Northwestern Long Term Care Insurance Company	AAA (1st)	Aaa (1st)	www.nmfn.com (800) 890-6700

Note: The Figures in parentheses in the "Ratings" columns represent the *rank* of each rating in Moody's or Standard & Poor's respective rating hierarchy. The ranking "(1st)" means it is the rater's highest rating; "(2nd)," the rater's second-highest rating; etc. However, all of the above companies enjoy exceptionally strong ratings of financial strength.

CONCLUSIONS

When you plan and save for retirement, you must factor in (1) the need to pay substantial health care expenses out of your own pocket; (2) the likelihood that health care costs will continue to climb; and (3) the need to prevent harm to your savings due to health care outlays that are not covered by national programs or employer benefits.

You want to amass retirement capital, protect it from financial drain, and enjoy good health during retirement! Buy Medigap and long-term health care insurance. Both are important. Lock into Medigap insurance when you turn sixty-five. And if you are over the age of fifty-eight, the time to look into long-term health care insurance is *right now*.

ACTION PLAN

1. Visit the Kaiser Family Foundation Web site. Compare the twelve standard Medigap plans. Pick a plan that is suitable for you.

2. Determine whether you will have access to supplemental or Medigap insurance during your retirement via your employer. If so, what costs would you incur after retirement if you sign on for your employer's supplemental coverage?

3. If your employer does not give you access to Medigap insurance in retirement, call the insurance department in your state for a list of insurance companies offering such coverage. Contact them. Compare costs.

4. Contact two of the companies listed on page 192 for cost estimates for long-term health care insurance. Compare terms and premiums.

5. Next, determine whether you will have sufficient resources in retirement to pay for long-term-heath-care-insurance premiums.

6. Factor these premiums into your financial planning.

7. Make note of two key enrollment periods: (1) enroll for Medigap during the six months immediately following your sixty-fifth birthday *without fail;* and (2) invest in a long-term health care policy when you are in your late fifties.

PART III

THE CARE
AND FEEDING
OF YOUR
NEST EGG

L et's pause for a moment and take stock of your progress.

Before we proceed, I would like you to test your savings habits and investment defenses. Go to this book's companion Web site, www.cashrich
retirement.com. Click on "Readiness Test" and enter the code word *income*. Take this five-minute test to determine whether you need to
strengthen your investment defenses and retirement preparations. How
do you rate?

You should now have an Investment Master Plan, a new "automatic
pilot" that has you *automatically* saving and investing, insurance coverage, an annuity strategy that you will continue to fund, and a new approach to successful investing that is rooted in income fundamentals.
You are operating in "success mode." You're unswerving in your intent to
amass all the capital you need for retirement. You're off the speculation
fix. You have a healthy "Show me the money!" insistence on interest income, dividend income, and rent income. You are automatically rein-

vesting that income. And you're saving the maximum in your 401(k) and IRA.

Where do you go from here? In this section I explain how to take care of your investments going forward, how to tap your home for retirement income, and when to exit from investments to help you avoid losses.

10

THE IMPORTANCE OF
PERIODIC TUNE-UPS

Periodic quality checks on your investments are important. Of course, checking into the performance of your funds day in and day out is the stuff of day traders. It will drive you crazy! And if it doesn't, it will surely seduce you into frantic buying, manic selling, and frequent changes of investments in the quest for red-hot returns. That is simply not a recipe for success with your retirement money.

On the other hand, *not* checking your investments from time to time can lead to haphazard performance. Without periodic checks, you may miss clear warning signals that a fund is undergoing unsafe management or content changes.

The bottom line is that you need to make periodic—but not daily—surveys of your investments. In this chapter we will highlight several quality-control techniques that will help you.

THE TWENTY-MINUTE TUNE-UP

I recommend investing just *twenty minutes each quarter* to check into the "health attributes" of your investments.

Here's the basic premise: you're better off spending time studying and picking superior stock, bond, and real estate funds *before you invest* in them as opposed to monitoring your investments continually, frantically, and daily *after* you buy them. So use the steps I describe below to screen funds carefully and in greater depth before you buy in.

Once you select good funds, you only need to spend twenty minutes each quarter checking on the (1) management, (2) content, (3) pricing, and (4) performance of your holdings.

Here's what to do in easy steps:

Keep a quarterly log of your funds, recording each one's key characteristics. The data you register will vary somewhat depending on whether the fund is fundamentally a stock, bond, or real estate fund. Even so, write down the following data and compare it quarter by quarter.

Go to Morningstar.com for free, objective research. Enter the call letters of each fund (or the fund's name if you do not know its call letters) in the "Quotes" box at the top left of Morningstar's home page. For example, you can obtain details about Vanguard's Emerging Market Stock Index by entering that name or the fund's call letters VEIEX. A fund summary page called "Snapshot" will open. Try the site as you read the next steps.

Note the "Morningstar Category" or content classification in your log from the top right of the Morningstar opening page for the fund. Go to (1) the fund's opening page called "Snapshot," (2) look for "Key Statistics" at the top right, then (3) make note of the "Morningstar Category" in that section. This is the content category of the fund according to Morningstar's breakdown. Should that classification change for any reason, it means that your fund has undergone substantive content change and should be flagged for closer investigation.

Next, scroll down the gray column at the far left and click on "Management." Note the manager's name and her or his start date. What experience and expertise does this manager or team of managers have? Management talent and stability are extremely important characteristics of any actively managed fund. A change of managers can adversely impact the performance of a fund. So check each quarter to make sure the same expert managers are in place.

Remember, however, that index funds and exchange-traded funds or ETFs invest in entire markets. They do not require managers picking one kind of stock or bond over another. Consequently, management changes are not important with indexes or ETFs. With actively managed funds, however, stable and expert management is vital. If management changes have recently taken place with one of your actively managed funds, add it to your Caution List.

Go to the gray column at the far left and click on "Portfolio." For stock and real estate funds, you want to make note of two fund characteristics located in "Style Box Details" as you scroll down the "Portfolio" section:

"Price/Prospective Earnings": Morningstar gives you a crude price-to-earnings ratio for most funds. This ratio compares the prices of all the stocks in the fund with their *projected*—but not actual—earnings. Don't fret the mathematics. Just remember that this ratio, in the words of Yale's Robert Shiller, is "a measure of how expensive the market is relative to . . . the ability of corporations to earn profits."[1] In other words, a price-earnings ratio tells you how much investors are willing to spend to buy company earnings. And as investment author John Mauldin tells us, *"The most significant driver of stock market returns is the valuation embedded in the P/E ratio"* (italics compliments of Mr. Mauldin).[2]

Price-earnings ratios are important because they help us judge whether an investment is overvalued. They tell us how much corporate revenue or earnings we are buying.

We noted earlier that the historical price-earnings ratio for stocks has been about fifteen.[3] That means that investors have typically been willing to pay about $15 on average to buy $1 of corporate earnings. A ratio substantially above this average—say twenty-five or thirty—tells you that investors in the fund are paying a great deal more to buy a dollar's worth of earnings. A high ratio is a signal that a fund is holding securities that are highly priced or speculatively inflated. You want to be cautious with stock funds having an exceptionally high P/E ratio.

Admittedly, Morningstar's number is only "directionally" helpful. Morningstar computes its P/E ratio using "projected" or estimated future earnings instead of the earnings that actually took place in the prior year. As with any projected data, the estimates of future earnings may be overly optimistic if not outright wrong. Nevertheless, I urge you to use Morningstar's ratio as a crude way of sizing up whether the stocks in your fund are overpriced relative to the corporate earnings you are buying.

You want stock investments with *low* P/E ratios. High P/E stocks and funds are overvalued and invariably lead to lower returns. Solid research is clear on this point. In his study of the entire history of the S&P 500 stock index, for example, Wharton's Jeremy Siegel found that portfolios invested in the lowest-P/E stocks in the index returned almost 3 *percent more* per year than the index itself, while investments in its high-P/E stocks lagged 2 *percent behind* the index.[4]

Be attentive to the P/E ratio of your equity funds. A ratio below ten is low, ten to twenty is moderate, greater than twenty is expensive[5]—*and over twenty-seven, outright dangerous.*

Of course, selecting stocks or equity funds *solely* on the basis of their price-earnings ratio would be simplistic. Many other factors make a stock or fund attractive long term. And a more sophisticated approach would take interest rates into account as well. For example, some economists divide one hundred by the prevailing Treasury-bill rate.[6] If the Treasury bill rate is 5 percent, then a sound P/E ratio, they say, might be twenty. The higher the T-bill rate, the lower the "ideal" P/E ratio. That adjustment perhaps better reflects the trade-off that you have to make when deciding whether to buy stocks or bonds.

For simplicity's sake, however, don't worry about more calculations and stay focused on funds with low price-earnings ratios. Use the Morningstar number. Even with "projected" data and simplistic application, a P/E ratio of twenty-seven or higher is grounds for caution.

"Dividend Yield": Next, make a note of each fund's dividend yield. It is a ratio showing the dividend return you get from a fund. It is simply the result you get when you divide the total dividends of all the stocks in your fund by the aggregate of the stock prices. A dividend yield of 3 means that you are getting a dividend return of 3 percent—or, put another way, it means that your fund is paying you $3 of dividends each year for every $100 you have in the fund.

Historical dividend yields for U.S. stocks have averaged 4.9 percent over a two-hundred-year span,[7] but recent yields are in the much lower 1 to 2 percent range. *Despite today's low dividend numbers, you nevertheless want stock funds giving you high dividend yields from companies that are financially healthy.*

Since Morningstar also computes this ratio using estimates of expected *future* dividends rather than *past* actual numbers, its version of any fund's dividend yield is also somewhat of a guesstimate. Even so, a yield below 2 percent or a declining ratio for a stock fund suggests you may not be obtaining adequate dividend income or may be experiencing inflated stock prices.

A low dividend yield ratio is grounds for caution. Less than 2 is poor. A ratio below 1.2 for a stock fund is dangerous. Look for a yield of 3.5 or better—particularly as more investors regain their senses and return to income fundamentals.

On the other hand, dividend yields on real estate funds are often higher.[8] As I write this, real estate investment trusts or REITs have a dividend yield of mid-3 percent, down from more than double that level and trading at a high multiple of earnings.[9] Such investments have become expensive. And both price-earnings and dividend-yield yardsticks point to the expense.

Many other kinds of ratios and performance data can be helpful. However, these two simple ratios—the price-earnings ratio and dividend-yield ratio—give you a good start. Make a note of these ratios for each fund in your log. Red-flag any stock or real estate fund with a high P/E ratio or particularly low dividend yield.

For interest-income funds, click on "Portfolio" in the far left-hand, gray column of Morningstar's site and make note of the "% of AAA" securities. Go to (1) "Portfolio," (2) "Bond Quality," and (3) "% of AAA" and "% of AA." These numbers tell you the percentages of your bond portfolio that are invested in highest-quality securities. If an interest-income fund has most of its holdings in bonds with low BB ratings or below, that may be cause for concern. You may have a lot of junk-bond content. Instead, look for high-quality content or make sure your exposure in a higher-risk fund is limited.

Next, go to the far-left, gray column and click "Total Returns." Scroll down to the "Trailing Total Return" section. Make note in your log of the "3-Month Total Return." That is the return of your fund over the last three months. Is your fund beginning to show losses or exceptionally "hot" returns? Is short-term performance any cause for closer monitoring?

Also make note of the "% Rank in Category" at the far right of the three-month number. That is the ranking of your fund's performance relative to the performance of other funds in the same content category. The highest rank—1—means that your fund was the top performer. Ideally, your fund should be operating somewhere in the top 25 percent of the category. If your fund consistently has a lower ranking, check into its performance for other periods. It may simply be having a short performance slump right now. Alternatively, you may be able to do better by investing elsewhere.

In the same section, scroll down and make note of the "1-Year Total Return" and "% Rank in Category." This is the fund's performance for the prior twelve months. Is it problematic? Does it show a loss? Or is it showing an annual return of more than 30 percent? If so, red-flag this fund.

Checking on performance is important. But choosing funds on the basis of "the biggest one-year returns" is foolhardy. It doesn't work! As Dr. Shiller confirms, "People appear to believe that it is smart to pore over rankings of mutual fund performance and constantly shift their investments to the current top performers, but in fact they gain relatively little doing so."[10]

Note your funds' performance as a part of your risk-control tune-ups. But do not chase high performance or invest solely in "top-performing" funds. More often than not, that tactic will actually impede your investment success.

Click on "Analyst Research" in the far-left, gray column if you are a Morningstar premium subscriber. In addition to obtaining extensive research free of charge from Morningstar, we noted that you can pay Morningstar an annual fee to become a "premium" service member. That gives you access to commentary from Morningstar's independent analysts about many funds and managers. If you subscribe to this service, click on "Analyst Research" in the far-left gray column and read the analyst's views.

I find this premium service extremely helpful. The views of Morningstar's analysts are independent and insightful. The "Analyst Research" section often has a great deal of good advice. Not all funds or ETFs are covered. Nevertheless, consider a premium subscription and take the time to read over the analysts' views carefully.

If any fund shows significant management, content, or performance change, put that fund on a Caution List. As you do your quarterly checks, look specifically for the following: (1) a change of managers, (2) any significant change of content, (3) evidence of losses, (4) high price-earnings or low dividend-yield ratios, and (5) exceptionally high returns. These developments—including exceptionally high returns, believe it or not—are grounds for caution. Monitor any funds with these characteristics more closely until the investment comes off your Caution List.

If a fund has incured large losses since you bought it, sell it. We will formulate a clear exit strategy in a subsequent chapter. If a fund has a high price-earnings ratio, exercise caution as well. And if a fund delivers exceptionally high performance, you may be headed for a correction. We'll discuss how to handle that good news in just a bit, too.

Fundamentally, use quarterly tune-ups to capture fresh data about your investments' management, content, and performance. If you have a financial advisor working with you, ask for his or her views. Use this information to decide whether any investment you hold should be closed outright or sold by half. If a fund has taken on risky content, lost a key manager, or developed a high P/E ratio, it may be prudent to dilute your holding.

REBALANCE ANNUALLY

Your asset allocation strategy—that is, your Investment Master Plan—does not have to substantially change from one year to the next. Barring major upheavals in the economy, the financial markets, or your personal life, the diversification wisdom of your master plan will probably stand pat.

You do not need to make substantial allocation changes as you age. Instead, you are going to invest in prudent investments with a continual *fixation on income fundamentals and strong adversity to speculation.*

Regardless of your birth date, you are *always* going to mitigate risks and try to avoid irreparable harm. You are continually going to invest to achieve hard income—dividend income, interest income, and rent income—instead of chasing speculative gains.

On the other hand, the allocation of your money across investments *will* change over time because of performance. Let's say that your dividend-producing investments fare exceptionally well and gain a lot of value. Because of good performance, you may find that your allocation in dividend-producing investments three years from now is much higher than the allocation target called for in your master plan. Suppose your master plan tells you to have 15 percent of your total holdings in dividend-paying U.S. stocks, and those investments now amount to 23 percent instead. Congratulations! You're achieving good results. But you're no longer honoring your diversification blueprint. Good performance is making you a tad top-heavy in one income category. And that actually represents more *risk*.

Rebalancing your portfolio is the way to get back to your blueprint's basic diversification, risk-spreading targets. By rebalancing I mean selling some of your top-performing funds to buy more of the poorer performers! It's a way of rigorously sticking to your diversification plan and avoiding risk. And it is, of course, completely counterintuitive.

Just as most folks are hardwired to chase "top performance," most of us are so delighted when one of our funds performs exceptionally well that we want to plow more money into it! Damn any blueprint! We want those big returns!

But wandering off your diversification road map is neither skillful nor prudent. As the chairman of one of the country's largest asset-management organizations made clear, "Investors often have an excessive affection for their winning investments, and they find that the hardest thing to do is to sell that winner to buy an under-performing investment. But that is the very essence of rebalancing. In fact, diversification among non-correlated assets means, by definition and design, that something in your portfolio will lag. . . . The reality is that today's laggard is often tomorrow's winner."[11]

How often should you rebalance? Here's what I recommend: examine the management, content, and performance of your investments quarterly, but rebalance annually. Rebalancing should not entail a lot of work. Once a year you will recalibrate your holdings to get back to your master plan's original allocation targets. *Sell down* the funds that have higher-than-planned allocations. *Buy* funds that have less-than-planned allocations. And while you're at it, check on the need to either exit from some funds or reduce your holdings in some because of overheating, management changes, or the concerns voiced by your financial advisor or neutral analysts.

Are you incurring losses that should be stopped? Are any of your investments delivering exceptionally high, perhaps excessively risky returns? In the final chapter I will show you how to react to losses and high-performance risk. In the meantime, register the need to recalibrate your investments once a year—across different 401(k), IRA, and other accounts—to revert back to the planned risk-diversification of your holdings.

NEVER SIPHON OFF RETIREMENT SAVINGS!

Of course, most retirement portfolios are more severely harmed by owner drawdowns than by market crashes or corrections. The facts are disquieting. According to a number of academic surveys and government reports, the *majority* of Americans who change jobs cash out their 401(k) plans and spend the proceeds.[12] Almost six out of ten people changing jobs do *not* roll over their tax-sheltered savings or keep them intact.

That is retirement suicide! It demolishes your nest egg and derails your compounding push. What's more, it's usually comes with a hefty 10 percent tax penalty. Nevertheless, that doesn't stop most Americans from spending their 401(k) money on clothes, electronic gear, and home improvements instead of allowing their investments to keep growing when they change jobs.

Don't sabotage your retirement savings! You do yourself grave harm when you drain off your savings prematurely. *The care and feeding of your nest egg starts first with absolute insistence on keeping your savings intact.*

When you change jobs, compare the advantages of moving your 401(k) money into your new employer's plan or moving it into a new and separate IRA at a broker such as Schwab or Fidelity. Do not draw down or attempt to transfer these monies yourself. *I repeat, Do not attempt to draw down or move this money yourself when you change jobs.* Doing so can trigger tax penalties. Instead, give instructions to your new employer *or* to your broker to transfer the funds for you.

Never draw down retirement savings prematurely. Never dismantle your nest egg! Stay on course. Save continually. Invest prudently. And avoid the premature depletion of your savings at all costs.

ACTION PLAN

1. Check the management, content, and performance of your investments each quarter using free Morningstar data. Keep a log of quarterly performance.

2. Red-flag funds that sustain management changes, show atypical ratios, or underperform relative to other funds in the same category. Talk over such funds with your financial advisor.

3. Exercise particular caution with funds showing losses, content changes, or exceptionally high returns. You may want to reduce your stake in such funds to avoid harm.

4. Rebalance your portfolio once a year. Go back to the original allocation percentages of your Investment Master Plan as an key way of curbing risk.

11

TAPPING YOUR HOME
FOR RETIREMENT INCOME

Many Americans have most of their retirement nest egg invested primarily in real estate—in the value of their own home! Many are counting on selling their home or borrowing against it for a substantial chunk of retirement capital. In fact, a lot of folks are counting on borrowing against their homes or downsizing and using the proceeds as a *principal* source of retirement income.

In this chapter, I want to communicate four pieces of advice: (1) your residence may, indeed, be a good source of retirement capital; (2) if you intend to downsize for retirement income, it may be advantageous do so in advance of any boomer sell-off; (3) exercise caution with "reverse mortgages"—they are an excellent way of raising cash, but are exceedingly expensive; and (4) *don't* fall into the trap of believing that "homestead appreciation" is the only retirement capital you'll ever need.

Overconfidence in "homestead wealth" or your ability to raise large amounts of retirement capital from your primary residence is going to prove unrealistic for a great many people. Let's see why.

SELL NEST—ENLARGE EGG

Your home *can* be an important source of retirement capital. If you sell your residence, up to $250,000 of homestead profit is tax-exempt if you are single ($500,000 if you are married). You do not have to pay taxes on this profit. So it's an important way of generating cash.

To qualify for the tax exemption, the property you sell must be your primary residence. You must have lived in it for at least two of the last five years—not necessarily sequentially—prior to its sale. You need not reside in it at the time of sale. In other words, you have substantial flexibility qualifying for the tax exemption. However, check with a specialist regarding your individual tax status.

If you sell your home and claim this exemption, you are not obligated to invest the proceeds in another house. You can, as well, use this tax exemption repeatedly.[1] Selling your residence to realize profit may be an excellent way to fund the annuities I've recommended. Or, alternatively, you might buy health insurance *and* annuities with the sale proceeds of your residence.

Tax exemption makes home ownership an attractive investment. But for many people it is the *only* investment they hold. And that is serious problem. Many folks are counting on a large amount of "homestead income" that may simply never materialize.

THE ADVANTAGE OF DOWNSIZING EARLY

A great many Americans are counting on selling their homes to help fund their retirement. They intend to "downsize"—meaning sell their primary residence and move to lower-cost digs,while pocketing capital for retirement.

According to recent polls, many Americans expect home equity to be an important source of retirement income. In one Gallup Poll, about *one out of four* working adults said that home equity will be a "major source of income" in retirement. Among those earning an annual income of $75,000 or more, the percentage—33 percent—is even higher.[2]

Interestingly, Americans who have already retired look upon their homes in a different way. More than half of Americans already retired say that home equity has *not* been a significant source of retirement capital for them,[3] perhaps reflecting their standing in the shift from traditional pensions to do-it-yourself retirement funding.

For many Americans yet to retire, however, home equity is looked upon as an extremely important source of eventual capital. The view is so pervasive that some economists have begun to warn the public that expecting huge amounts of cash from one's primary residence may be wishful thinking. I agree. In fact, I believe that home prices may weaken and that overreliance on "homestead capital" will be increasingly dangerous. That is because (1) post-2005 real estate corrections are likely to continue, (2) the prevalence of adjustable-rate mortgages and the possibility of higher interest rates will adversely impact home prices, (3) the likelihood of higher property taxes in many communities will add to the effect, and (4) a radical demographic shift is about to take place that will significantly alter sale dynamics.

On one hand, a surge of speculative investing in real estate has pushed home prices in many locations to unprecedented heights. As the speculative stock gains of the 1990s deflated, investors moved into real estate with fever. Home prices spiked. But red-hot "gains" inevitably fade. As I write this, home prices in numerous locations are on the decline. That effect is likely to become wider-spread as more of the market's speculative excess burns off. Meaning that if you decide to downsize in the future, the value of your residence might actually be a lot *less* than the price your neighbor got for his house when he sold not long ago.

Low interest rates also helped to fuel the surge of real estate prices. It's important to remember that homeownership for most Americans is heavily dependent on debt. Today, two in three homeowners have a mortgage.[4] One in five has a home equity loan. And nearly one in three have borrowed against their home to make improvements and, they hope, enhance the value of their property.

What is more, one-quarter of all outstanding mortgages are adjustable rate.[5] If and when interest rates rise, such mortgages will become more costly, and some borrowers may not be able to service their debt.

Many recent mortgages—about one out of four of all mortgages originated in the second half of 2005 and first half of 2006—are, in fact, "interest only" loans.[6] These mortgages allow buyers to really "stretch" on home prices since they only require payments of interest, not principal, for some period. They are a variety of "hybrid loans," which often start with low interest rates, then reset the rate higher after two or three years. Many of those loans are now moving into a higher-rate phase, and we can expect to see an uptick in the number of borrowers defaulting around the country.

Altogether, the prevalence of floating-rate mortgages and hybrid interest-only loans suggests that an increase in interest costs is likely to adversely affect housing prices. In the words of Alan Greenspan, *"These products could be cause for some concern both because they expose borrowers to more interest-rate and house-price risk than the standard thirty-year, fixed-rate mortgage and because they are seen as vehicles that enable marginally qualified, highly leveraged borrowers to purchase homes at inflated prices."*[7]

The good news is that interest rates continue to remain at historic lows. Nevertheless, trillions of dollars of adjustable-rate and hybrid mortgages will have their payments reset in 2008 and subsequent years.[8] And higher interest rates and higher reset rates will surely have a restraining effect on home prices. As a study by the Center for Economic and Policy Research concluded, "If interest rates rise, as virtually all economists expect, homebuyers with adjustable rate mortgages will find themselves paying much more on their monthly mortgages. Many homeowners will be unable to make these higher payments."[9]

What we can expect are more foreclosures and more downward pressure on home prices. In fact, one study is now projecting 1.1 million home mortgage foreclosures over the next six years as adjustable-rate mortgages reset to higher levels of interest.[10] Such numbers do not at all bode well for home prices.

Higher property taxes may also cause home prices to buckle. Many municipalities, counties, and states have promised their employees pension and retirement health care benefits for which they lack adequate funding. We saw that 77 percent of reporting municipal and county pension plans were *underfunded* according to Wilshire Associates[11]—meaning that many municipalities and counties have greater pension and benefit liabilities than they actually have money in the till.

Of *state* retirement systems that provided actuarial data to Wilshire Associates, about 80 percent were underfunded.[12] Commenting on an earlier version of these same reports, investment author John Mauldin noted, "Of the 123 state retirement systems covered in the '2003 Wilshire Report'...at least nine states have pension fund liabilities that exceed their annual budgets. Nevada would have to devote 267 percent of its annual state budget to make up the current shortfall."[13]

These pension statistics are actually improving in some measure at this time. Nevertheless, they suggest that many state, county, and municipal governments will have to increase taxes—in particular, property taxes—to fund their retirement liabilities. As bestselling author Harry Dent put it, pervasive pension underfunding "will drive states and local governments to raise taxes in an effort to pay what they have promised."[14] This is already beginning to take place in a number of locations. Over time, we will see more municipalities resorting to higher property taxes, putting pressure on home prices as well.

But that's only part of the story. A radical shift in the number of "prime sellers" relative to "prime buyers" is about to take place. That demographic shift will buffet real estate prices resoundingly.

Boomers account for nearly one of every four households in the United States, and own *more than half* of all vacation homes, seasonal homes, and rental properties.[15] Not surprisingly, boomers in particular are counting on selling real estate to raise cash for retirement. In fact, polls show that between 17 and 20 percent of that age cohort expects home equity will be a "primary source of income during retirement."[16] According to the chief economist of the National Association of Realtors:

"As a group, boomers are in their peak earning years and continue to wield great influence in the U.S. economy, but they are not homogenous . . . On one hand [they have] an almost insatiable desire for real estate, with some owning multiple properties, and on the other, many have not adequately planned for retirement."[17]

Let's also recall the statistics I provided earlier. In 2005, there were 8.5 "prime buyers"—Americans between the ages of thirty-five and fifty-four in their peak spending and investing years—for every one "prime seller" or person aged sixty-five to sixty-nine about to enter retirement and poised to sell assets to raise cash. By 2025, there will be only *4.4 prime buyers to each prime seller.*[18] Demographics will change supply-and-demand dynamics markedly.

The possibility of a large number of boomers selling off real estate to *relatively fewer* buyers—even over fifteen or twenty years—may well cause home prices to weaken. We do not know that this will happen with certainty. It may not. However, it is likely that a larger inventory of homes coming onto the market—even if it comes in staggered doses over several decades—could depress prices. (And don't count on Indian or Chinese nationals buying up homes in Peoria anytime soon.)

Here's what the chief economist of the Gallup Organization had to say several years ago when the housing market was still escalating by leaps and bounds, "The problem is that supply and demand can significantly affect real estate prices. Baby boomers planning on retirement could be contributing to the current surge in real estate prices. Some may be buying second homes they plan to live in when they retire. Others may be investing for the great rates of return. The question is, what happens as these investors begin retiring? Will the supply of housing for sale by retirees reverse current market conditions and flood the market? What would this mean for future real estate prices?"[19]

Given the possibility of higher interest rates, the exceptional and unsustainable escalation in home prices that has already taken place, and the prospect of some exceptional selling momentum just ahead, you should *not* count on your primary residence being your foremost source of retirement capital.

Don't count on realizing huge profits from your house to the exclusion of achieving other savings!

If you *are* planning to downsize over the next ten years, it may be advantageous to make the move *now*—in advance of any interest-rate changes or boomer sales. *And if you have held off investing for retirement in assets other than your residence, it is most definitely time to save more and diversify your wealth.*

REVERSE MORTGAGES

Another way of generating cash from your house is via a *reverse mortgage.* Such loans can be helpful. They are innovative products with extremely attractive tax benefits. However, they also require close scrutiny and a clear understanding of their high-expense mechanics.

A reverse mortgage is a home equity loan that enables owners over the age of sixty-two to convert some of their home equity into cash. It is a loan. You borrow money against your home. You do not make interest payments. And you only have to repay the loan after a fixed, long-term date or—much more typically—when the property ceases to be your principal residence.

Reverse mortgages are a recent financial product. Only 167 of them were issued in 1990.[20] By 2007, thousands were being issued each month.[21] And despite periodic articles about these new mortgages, there is little comprehensive advice. So let me help you understand this kind of mortgage a bit better.

THREE BASIC KINDS

There are three basic kinds of reverse mortgages—some "guaranteed" or insured by the federal government, and some not.

Generally speaking, federally insured "home equity conversion mort-

Kinds of Reverse Mortgages

	1. Federally Insured	2. Single Purpose	3. Private Loans
Other Names	HECM (Home Equity Conversion Mortgages) or FHA (Federal Housing Administration) loans	Home Keeper or Fannie Mae loans	Loans without government insurance backing from private financial institutions
Loan Amount General	Varies by age, interest rate, location, and home value	Varies by age, interest rate, location, and home value	Varies by age, interest rate, location, and home value. No limit
Maximum at any age	$362,790 in 2007 (varies by state and county)	$417,000 in 2007 (varies by state & county)	No maximum amount
Key Features	For any purpose. About 90% of all reverse mortgages are this type	Generally granted for a specific purpose (e.g., paying taxes or making repairs) to help a homeowner to remain in his/her residence	For any purpose
Fees and Expenses	Normally the least expensive with the lowest interest rate	Low expense	Typically the most expensive with the highest rates of interest

Source: AARP and FinancialFreedom

gages" or HECM loans are the most common kind of reverse mortgage. The vast majority of all reverse mortgages—about nine out of ten—are this kind. The banks granting them enjoy a federal government guarantee of repayment. Hence, such loans are less risky for lenders and less expensive for you. In fact, federally insured reverse mortgages significantly limit the interest expense and fees you pay, but also limit the maximum loan amount you can obtain. The government sets those limits.

"Single purpose" loans are reverse mortgages that are usually backed by a state government agency or a nonprofit organization. They are typically granted for a particular purpose—such as to fix a roof or pay property taxes—to borrowers having modest incomes. They expressly limit how you may use the loan proceeds. More often than not, these loans help homeowners of limited means retain ownership of their homes or continue residence in them when an emergency strikes.

"Private" reverse mortgages are loans that do not have government or nonprofit backing. They usually give you much more money for your house, and you can use the money for any purpose. However, such loans charge the highest interest and high fees. They are significantly more expensive.

As boomers move into retirement, we are sure to see more consumer interest in all three kinds—particularly in private reverse mortgages because they make much more loan money available. But the price tag, as we will see, can be prohibitive.

ELIGIBILITY

For a reverse mortgage, you must meet the following eligibility criteria:

- You must be sixty-two years old (sometimes sixty).
- The property must be in your name, not your children's or another party's, and must be your primary residence.[22]
- The property must usually be a single-family, one-to-four-unit dwelling. Reverse mortgages are generally not granted for mobile homes or co-ops.[23]
- All debts on the property must be paid off first or the reverse mortgage will make these payments for you and reduce your payout.
- A formal counseling session with an independent, government-approved financial advisor is also mandatory before you can finalize a federally insured reverse mortgage, the most common kind.

THE AMOUNT OF MONEY YOU CAN OBTAIN

The amount of money you obtain from a reverse mortgagee primarily depends on your age and the value of your house. The more expensive the house and the older you are, the more you can derive.

As a general rule of thumb, you can usually obtain 40 percent to 70 percent of the value of your home. Age is a significant factor. A sixty-two year-old might only receive 30 percent, while a seventy-five-year-old would more typically receive 40 to 50 percent and a ninety-five-year-old perhaps 80 percent of the appraised value of his or her property.[24]

Federally insured and specific purpose mortgages limit the amount of money you can draw. In the case of federally insured loans, the home value used in calculating the loan amount is capped by the Federal Housing Administration. That limit periodically changes and varies by location. The cap was recently in the range of $200,160 to $362,760,[25] with the specific limit within the range dependent on the median home value of the community. As one report noted, this kind of limit means that "a $1 million home and a $400,000 home might be eligible for exactly the same loan amount. . . . The lower limit of $200,160 is applicable in about 80 percent of the counties in the United States."[26]

To get some idea how much money you might obtain from a reverse mortgage, use these online calculators:

AARP: www.rmaarp.com
Financial Freedom: www.financialfreedom.com/calculator

Bear in mind, however, that the actual payout you receive will depend on the median home values of the community in which you reside, and that taking out a reverse mortgage at an early age will significantly *reduce* your cash takeout. You also have to shop around. A seventy-five-year-old person with a house valued at $150,000 might find the payouts offered by different banks to vary by as much as $30,000.[27]

THE INTEREST YOU PAY

A reverse mortgage can have a fixed or adjustable rate of interest. The interest rate on a federally insured or HECM loan, the most common kind, is usually adjustable. It is set by the federal government and tied to the one-year U.S. Treasury bill. Of course, the "floating" nature of this expense is chancy. Since interest rates are at historic lows and may eventually rise, this is a good time to lock into *fixed*—not adjustable—rates of interest. On the other hand, HECM mortgages have a cap on the amount of annual interest escalation, as well as a limit on the total interest increase that can take place over the life of your loan. These limits give you reasonable expense protection if you have a federally insured reverse mortgage.

Reverse mortgages that are private or not government-insured do not have interest limits. Their interest charges are substantially higher. In fact, such loans carry some of the highest rates of interest of all mortgages.

Interest rates on reverse mortgages are substantially higher than the rates on conventional mortgages. You need to shop for a low—ideally *fixed* or *capped*—rate.

Fees and Other Costs

If interest charges for reverse mortgages are high, the fees for most reverse mortgage are even more of a detraction. The costs can be astronomical. Reverse mortgage lenders usually charge a host of fees, closing costs, and other charges. Here is a list of some of them.

Typical Reverse Mortgage Fees

- Appraisal or survey fee
- Title and tax search fee
- Credit report charge
- Flood zone search fee
- Inspection fee
- Repairs at or before the loan's closing
- Loan orgination fee
- Document preparation fee
- Attorney's fee upon closing the loan
- Tax reporting fee
- Mortgage insurance
- Monthly servicing fees (maximum $30)
- Mortgage brokerage service fee
- Termination or maturity fees
- Fees for the sale or foreclosure of the property

Source: State of New York Banking Department

A number of these charges are the same kinds that you pay with a conventional mortgage. With a reverse mortgage, however, you incur higher charges and pay compound interest on them. That is one of the reasons why the federal government requires that you have a counseling session with a government-approved independent financial advisor before you commit to any federally insured reverse mortgage. Or as one commentator put it, "Caution is required because reverse mortgages can be prohibitively expensive unless the homeowner has a substantial amount of home equity, plans to convert all or most of the equity into retirement funding and lives in the home and benefits from the reverse mortgage for the long term."[28]

The fees of most reverse mortgages are high, multilayered, and very expensive—particularly in the early years of the mortgage.

The good news is that you don't have to bring your checkbook with you for a lot of payments when you close on a reverse mortgage. You do not have to pay any costs when you first obtain the loan. You do not have to pay interest or fees each month. There are no up-front or periodic payments whatsoever. All charges simply become part of your loan or are deducted from the money that is paid to you.

The bad news is that you end up paying for layers of fees and compound, high interest on them. Reverse mortgages are particularly expensive in the first years of the loan, so you want to be sure that you will remain in the house long term. Federally insured reverse mortgages are always the least expensive—which is why you should look into that kind of reverse mortgage first. And you must, in any event, eventually pay for this growing ball of debt when you finally vacate your home and have to repay the layers of borrowings.

THE COMPOUNDING EFFECT

Reverse mortgages are expensive "rising debt" loans. They are entirely different from conventional mortgages. With a traditional mortgage, you make periodic payments and gradually *reduce* your debt. With a reverse mortgage, you do *not* make periodic payments and your debt *increases* over time.

This is an important distinction. With a reverse mortgage, you only pay fees and interest when your property is finally sold or you vacate it. You pay nothing until then. Consequently, a mighty compounding effect takes place, continually enlarging your debt.

Since you do not make interim payments from your own pocket, a reverse mortgage actually advances *more money* to you each month and uses it to offset your fee and interest expenses. Your debt grows at an accelerating rate. You end up paying layers of fees, layers of interest on the fee advances, and then layers of interest on the interest! You take on more and more debt. And a large part if not all of your home equity may end up paying the compound interest.

As one government publication alerts consumers, "The amount you owe on a reverse mortgage generally grows over time. Interest is charged on the outstanding balance and added to the amount you owe each month. That means your total debt increases over time as loan funds are advanced to you and interest accrues on the loan."[29]

How You Draw Cash

You can obtain the proceeds of a reverse mortgage in a number of ways: (1) an immediate lump sum; (2) a credit line against which you can draw down funds until the line is exhausted; (3) monthly payments; (4) some combination of a lump sum plus monthly payments; or (5) payments for the rest of your life by using the mortgage proceeds to buy an annuity. You can select the payment mechanism that works best for you. Using the funds to buy annuities would be particularly useful. I strongly urge you to invest in annuities if you do, in fact, take out a reverse mortgage.

Tax Advantages

A reverse mortgage also gives you significant tax advantages. On one hand, the funds you derive from a reverse mortgage are "loan proceeds," not "income." Hence, they are not taxable. You can also deduct interest expenses from your tax declarations when you actually vacate your residence and repay the loan. So there is a double tax advantage. You pay no tax on the money when you get it, *and* you eventually (but not immediately) get a tax concession for the interest. However, be sure to check with a tax specialist to make sure these tax advantages apply to you.

WHEN YOU REPAY

A reverse mortgage must be repaid when you die, sell your house, or no longer live in it as your primary residence. Repayment also becomes due if you declare bankruptcy or do not keep up tax or house insurance payments.

In the federally insured program, you can live in a nursing home or other medical facility for up to twelve months before the loan becomes due. As long as your home is otherwise your primary residence and your tax and insurance payments are up-to-date, no payment of any kind is due.

Over time, a reverse mortgage uses up some or all of your home equity. When your property is eventually sold, the proceeds are used to repay the mortgage. Any money left over will go to you or your heirs. If the money from the sale is *insufficient* to fully repay the loan, you or your estate owe nothing more. That is because most reverse mortgages have a "nonrecourse" clause that expressly prevents you from ever owing more than the value of your home.

OWNERSHIP

With a reverse mortgage, you continue to own the property. Consequently, you are responsible for property taxes, utilities, home insurance, and maintenance. You do *not* give up ownership or the obligations that go with it.

BENEFITS

A reverse mortgage can be an innovative way for house-rich, cash-shy retirees to obtain cash. You can stay in your house. You aren't forced to relocate. You continue to be the owner (and have all the responsibilities that go with ownership). Your loan proceeds are not taxed as income. There is usually no penalty if you decide to prepay the loan for any reason. You make no payments of any kind until you leave the house. And you won't owe more than what your house is worth, *at most,* no matter when you leave. These are all excellent features.

DRAWBACKS AND RISKS

However, you should keep in mind these negative aspects. You may not obtain much money from such a loan. You normally pay many fees—

charges that can substantially add to your debt and eat up your home equity. You incur multiple layers of interest expense that will greatly snowball over time. There may be little or nothing left over for you or your estate when you finally leave or sell the property. And such a loan can be financially risky if you are forced to leave your home early into the loan, reducing the time you have to defray the heavy initial expenses and actually enjoy the cash benefits.

One accounting group put it this way: "Reverse mortgages use up the equity in your home, leaving fewer assets for you and your heirs. If you are forced to move soon after taking the reverse mortgage (e.g., because of illness) you will almost certainly end up with a great deal less equity to live on than if you had simply sold the house. This is particularly true in the case of loans terminated in five years or less."[30]

All in, a reverse mortgage is usually a very expensive proposition. It can put money in your pocket—but you pay through the nose for it.

Would *You* Benefit?

A reverse mortgage is a good funding technique for some people, but not all. Here is how you might benefit:

A Reverse Mortgage *May* Be Helpful If:

- **You are "house rich" but "cash poor."** A reverse mortgage can help you tap the value of your home without forcing you to leave it.
- **You are past the age of seventy-five.** At a later age, you will have fewer remaining years for mortgage advances, substantially less accumulation of interest and loan expense, and larger proceeds from the loan.
- **You already have substantial equity in your home.** If you are debt-free or have little remaining on your existing mortgages, you will receive larger advances from the reverse mortgage.
- **You have no reason to leave your residence anytime soon.** Staying in your home long term helps to justify the high expenses you will incur with a reverse mortgage—particularly in the early years of the loan.
- **You obtain tax and benefit advice *before* you sign for the mortgage.** Be sure that the income you receive from a reverse mortgage will not disqualify you from Medicaid, Supplemental Security Income (SSI), or other benefits.

A Reverse Mortgage Will *Not* Be Helpful If:

- **You are at or near age sixty-two.** At a younger age, your life expectancy will translate into large layers of fees and compound interest, and the amount of cash you derive from the mortgage will be low.
- **You have little equity in your home.** A reverse mortgage will pay off any debt you have on the property first, leaving you with large expense and little drawdown. A traditional mortgage is likely to be far less expensive and flexible.
- **You might move elsewhere in the next five years.** High closing costs and fees make a reverse mortgage unsatisfactory for a short stay. If you might move elsewhere or enter a nursing home during the first five years of the loan, the high costs of a reverse mortgage would not be attractive.

Source: AARP, *Journal of Accountancy*

HELPFUL TIPS

If you consider a reverse mortgage, the following guidelines may also help you:

Take out the mortgage in your late seventies. Since reverse mortgages give more money to homeowners the more advanced they are in years, consider taking out this kind of mortgage when you are in your late seventies *or later*. That will boost the amount of cash you will enjoy.

Require a "nonrecourse clause." Make sure your mortgage contract has nonrecourse language, meaning that you will never owe anything more to the lender than your home itself.

Shop for low fees. Consider a federally insured mortgage *first* and compare costs. Banks are obligated to give you full disclosure of a loan's "total annual loan cost." Ask for a complete itemization of all expenses footing to this total when you compare the loan terms of different banks. You need to shop around. And you need to understand the immense costs of such mortgages before you sign any loan papers.

Lock into a fixed rate of interest. Look for a *fixed-rate mortgage* if it is available or, next best, a mortgage with an adjustable interest rate provided it can only be modified once a year and has a maximum 5 percent loan-lifetime cap. You want to curtail interest expense so that it does not eat up your home equity.

Avoid "equity-sharing" provisions. Some reverse mortgages give the bank a cut of any profit you or your estate derive when your home is finally sold on top of the interest and fees that are charged. That is a superfluous drain on your home equity. Always shop for a reverse mortgage that does *not* have equity-sharing provisions.

Only work with reputable institutions. As with annuities and insurance, insist on knowing the financial ratings of any financial group or lender with which you work. Only deal with institutions having superior ratings of financial strength.

Never pay for advice. Ignore people who contact you offering to sell you reverse-mortgage advice. You can get all the advice you need about reverse mortgages free of charge. I'll tell you how in just a bit.

Seek independent counsel. In addition to any government-approved advisor, you also want your personal financial advisor to explain the small print before you commit to any loan. You want to thoroughly understand the terms. You likewise want to make sure that a reverse mortgage will not disqualify you from Medicare, Social Security, or other related benefits. Normally it will not. However, double-check just the same.

WHERE TO GO FOR MORE INFORMATION

A reverse mortgage may help you fund the annuities and insurance I have recommended. As a first step, learn more about these mortgages and how they function. Remember that a counseling session with an independent, government-approved advisor is mandatory for all federally insured reverse mortgages. You can also obtain helpful information from the following organizations:

AARP Reverse Mortgage Education Program
(800) 209-8085
www.aarp.org/money/revmort

U.S. Department of Housing and Urban Development
(800) 569-4287
www.hud.gov (type *"reverse mortgage"* in the search window)

National Foundation for Credit Counseling
Reverse Mortgage Hotline: (866) 698-6322

AARP has particularly helpful materials on the topic. Be sure to visit its
Web site for more detail.

DON'T MISTAKE "HOMESTEAD APPRECIATION" FOR BROAD RETIREMENT PREPAREDNESS

Tapping home equity can be an advantageous way of raising retirement
capital. But there is an important caveat. If you believe that all you have to
do to prepare for retirement is take out a reverse mortgage or perhaps mod-
ernize your kitchen, downsize, and enjoy fat profits to the exclusion of doing anything else—you are badly mistaken! Counting on your home as the
foremost source of retirement income is simply not realistic. Instead, you
need a diverse, prudent, low-risk array of income-producing investments,
annuities, and insurance.

*Let's get the facts straight about real estate appreciation. As we've seen, re-
search by Yale University's Dr. Robert Shiller confirms that U.S. home values
have historically showed a modest 3.4 percent average annual increase over a
hundred year–plus span—and this* includes *the 1998–2005 bubble as well as
the price run-up that took place right after World War II.*[31]

That is fact. However, many people persist in believing that real estate's
recent price increases are normal and perennial. They believe that hyper
real-estate appreciation is something they can count on long term. That is
not realistic. In the words of Dr. Shiller, "The notion that home prices always go up is very strong, and very wrong."[32]

In fact, demographics have contributed mightily to the escalation of
home prices, but may soon begin pushing prices *down* in a similarly forceful fashion.

Clearly some of the price escalations we have seen recently have been
due to boomer demographics. For example, sales data show that two out of
every five homes sold in 2005 were a second or third home sold to boomers
for investment purposes or as the advance part of their downsizing plans.[33]
Second-home sales—"driven by the baby boom generation," according to
the National Association of Realtors[34]—set records in 2005, and one out

of five buyers said they intended to make their purchase their primary residence in retirement.[35]

As one real estate commentator observed, "What's driving this second-home buying boom? The primary driver is demographics—in a phrase, it's the baby boom generation. Baby boomers are at the optimum point in life when people become interested in second homes. In addition, they are at the peak of their earnings cycle, want to take advantage of still-historically low interest rates, and want to diversify their investments in order to plan for their future retirement."[36]

In 2006 and 2007, boomers continued to be prime movers in the real estate market, and one poll found that 39 percent of the people in this age block who reported they were "very likely" or "extremely likely" to purchase a second home in the future said they planned to convert it to their primary residence one day.[37]

Indisputably, the number of boomers active in the country's real estate markets is large and historically unprecedented. This cohort has pushed up sales and prices. However, we cannot count on boomers to continue to fuel home purchases and stoke market demand ad infinitum. Many boomers will soon begin *selling*—not buying—real estate as part of their "downsizing" strategy and quest for cash. And just as boomers massively stimulated home sales and prices when they moved *into* the real estate market, so their eventual *exits* from real estate may well depress prices in the decades ahead.

The core message to you is this: not every home on the block is going to skyrocket in value as it did in years past! Demographics will change real estate demand, sales, and pricing in profound ways. That is already happening.

The real restate industry is sure to disagree with these views. However, ample research from highly respected experts and analysts—including Robert Shiller, Alan Greenspan, John Commarianos, David Rosenberg, Gary Shilling, Dean Baker, and a host of others—backs this judgment.

This much is crystal clear: you *cannot* count on your residence giving you windfall income. You *should not* count on selling your residence tomorrow for yesterday's price. *Don't* expect "homestead appreciation" to be your primary source of retirement income. *Do* make sure you have savings lodged in a variety of different asset classes and different income-producing investments so you are not hostage to the fortunes of any single market—the real estate market or any other.

ACTION STEPS

1. Take demographics into account if you are planning to sell your residence for retirement capital. If you are planning to sell over the next ten years, consider doing so early on.

2. If you downsize, use some of the proceeds to buy annuities and long-term-care insurance.

3. Exercise caution with reverse mortgages. Consider such a loan at a late age. Study the costs carefully. Compare the terms of different banks.

4. Do *not* expect homestead gains to be your sole source of retirement capital. Be sure to save and invest in *nonhomestead* assets to generate a variety of different income streams for retirement.

12

WHEN TO GET DEFENSIVE

Losses are the bane of retirement investing. They can derail your financial plans and stunt your capital accumulation for years. Like the wealthy, you want to be *defensive* with your capital to protect what you've amassed. You want to avoid correction losses. You want to keep your holdings intact and growing strong.

One of the priorities I learned serving mega-wealthy clients is the need to *protect* your nest egg as well as enlarge it. That is why I have encouraged you to be wary of speculation and unrealistic returns as the precursors of price corrections. It's why I have suggested ways to offset risk and losses.

In this section we will reiterate some of those key defense tactics and articulate several new ones. I want to encourage you to employ five defenses: (1) an adamant income focus; (2) extrastrength diversification; (3) caution when you make interest-income investments; (4) a "stop loss"; and (5) "circuit breakers" to cut off investments when they overheat and could cause trouble.

DEFENSE #1: MAINTAIN AN INCOME FIXATION

Of all the advice contained in this book, one piece is by far the most important, so I'll repeat it here:

> **Defense #1:** Set your sights on achieving real income—interest *income,* dividend *income,* and rent *income*—that you can re-invest.

Stay focused on income fundamentals! Forget about windfall gains and becoming a zillionaire by speculating. That's poppycock! Instead, put your money into income-producing investments that deliver real returns at good prices that you can reinvest.

The one elemental investment behavior I want you to adopt after reading this book is an antispeculative approach to investing. I want you to invest your retirement capital like a multimillionaire, always thinking, "*Show me real income!*"

Develop an income-demanding mind-set! It's the most powerful defense mechanism of all. Remember, investments that produce real income tend to appreciate *more* in value when a market rises and sustain *smaller* losses when a market corrects. You want to invest with a continual income fixation.

DEFENSE #2: DIVERSIFY COMPREHENSIVELY

I have also encouraged you to reduce risk and enhance your returns by diversifying your investments as thoroughly as possible. I have specifically urged you to diversify your holdings (1) by income stream, (2) by geography, and (3) by content—meaning that you should use broad, income-oriented indexes and high-quality actively managed funds, diversifying across different investment categories and holding a broad mix of different investments in each one.

> **Defense #2:** Diversity your investments—by *income type,* by *geography,* and by *broad fund content*—so that no single investment can cause you insurmountable harm.

We have already talked about the advantages of investing in *mutual funds, exchange-traded funds,* and income-focused *index funds*. When you invest in a mutual fund, you are investing in twenty or thirty or fifty different securities. Investing in a fund reduces your risk that any one stock or bond or real estate holding can cause insurmountable harm. When you invest in an index, you are investing in an entire investment market or a subsegment of an entire market—in one hundred or two hundred or even a thousand underlying holdings. An index investment reduces risk even more powerfully. And we have seen expert findings that investing in "alternative indexes"—such as an index of low-priced, high-dividend-yield equities—may be the most powerful investment proposition of all.

I have also recommended enlarging your holdings in international or non-U.S. investments. That's not for a lack of patriotism. It simply makes good diversification and demographic sense. As noted, more than half of the world's equity capital is in non-U.S. stocks. So you can *more than double* your access to potentially exciting equity investments when you look at non-U.S. as well as U.S. investment alternatives. It's a major diversification and income opportunity.

With strong international exposure, you achieve broad geographic diversification. That, in turn, should mean less risk. And demographics, we saw, should also heighten the attractiveness of international diversification. Over the coming decades, the U.S. population will age and consumer spending of many kinds in the United States will slow. By comparison, countries such as India, China, Brazil, and Indonesia will have many millions of people moving into peak consumer and investment years.

Consequently, demographics encourage you to consider larger international investment exposure because there is sure to be exciting economic growth and great investment foment offshore. Gurus such as Professor Jeremy Siegel recommend holding "up to 40 percent" of your portfolio in non-U.S. stocks.[1] I go further. I urge you to hold *50 percent of all your investments* in international placements. Since there could be turmoil in some investment markets because of aging demographics, you want the broadest geographic diversification possible.

Finally, I have urged you to diversify your holdings so that no single investment represents more than 10 percent of your total. I specifically suggested that you avoid being top-heavy in your employer's or any one company's stock.

The important takeaways are these: Defend your capital like wealthy people who shelter their money in Swiss private banks! Diversify your holdings *extensively* so that no single investment can cause you irreparable harm.

DEFENSE #3: EXERCISE CAUTION WHEN YOU MAKE INTEREST-INCOME INVESTMENTS

Many investors are top-heavy in stocks. That's not risk-wise. And when they do invest in interest-income investments, many believe that any bank deposit, bond, or bond fund is virtually "risk-free." That is also not savvy.

Defense #3: Hold cautious interest-income positions that diversify your portfolio and avoid inflation, opportunity-loss, and default risks.

Interest-income investments have risks, too. Here's how you can defend against them.

BANK DEPOSITS

When you invest in bank deposits, do so in ways that protect your savings from inflation, the risk of default, and the risk of opportunity loss.

Make short-term placements for a maximum tenor of one year with institutions that have FDIC insurance and high ratings. You want "short duration" or short-maturity deposits—meaning deposits that mature in one year or less—so you can capitalize on the possibility of rising interest rates. Unless rates are high, you don't want to lock into long-maturity deposits or bonds. You also want to be sure that your deposits are FDIC insured. *FDIC* stands for the Federal Deposit Insurance Corporation. It is the government entity that guarantees bank deposits for up to $100,000. If you make a deposit with an institution that does *not* enjoy this kind of insurance, you open yourself up to default risk.

To find banks that participate in this insurance program, go to www.fdic.gov. Then check their financial ratings. There are many rock-solid institutions to choose from.

U.S. TREASURIES

When it comes to government bonds, be mindful of their risks as well. Many investors mistakenly believe that all government bonds are completely harmless. That is not so.

U.S. Treasuries are, indeed, called "risk-free" by many economists. As Yale University's David Swensen put it, "Of all risky investments, investors expect the lowest returns from U.S. Treasury bonds, due to the high degree of security intrinsic in obligations of the U.S. government."[2]

But in fact, all bonds—including U.S. Treasuries—have some risk. If you lock into bonds with long-term maturities, their value can be eroded by inflation over time. That is why I have urged you to include Treasury Inflation-Protected Securities, or TIPS, in your holdings.

TIPS have a low correlation with stocks and other bonds, meaning that they tend to go up in value when other investments go down.[3] The principal of these bonds is periodically increased when there is inflation. They are important kinds of investments to hold—*provided* that you buy and hold them in a tax-sheltered account such as a 401(k) or IRA.

GOVERNMENT AGENCY BONDS

Many investors also believe that government agency bonds are risk-free. That is another fallacy. Agency bonds are issued by a number of different entities—some of them true appendages of the U.S. government and some of them not really government bodies at all. These groups buy mortgages, bundle them, then sell the packaged debt as bonds to funds and investors.

Among such bonds, three main kinds are perhaps best known. *Fannie Mae* bonds (named after the Federal National Mortgage Association or FNMA) and *Freddie Mac* bonds (named after the Federal Home Loan Mortgage Corporation or FHLMC) are mortgaged-backed bonds that have no government guarantee or protection. They are *not* risk-free.

Ginnie Mae bonds (named after the Government National Mortgage Association or GNMA) are the securities of a government-owned corporation within the U.S. Department of Housing and Urban Development. *They are the only mortgage-backed "government agency" securities that are actually guaranteed by the U.S. government.*

Altogether, the bonds of these agencies are said to be "as strong as Plymouth Rock."[4] Many bond funds have a good deal of agency bond content, but only one kind (Ginnie Mae) has a government guarantee. All three kinds tend to pay interest rates slightly above those paid by U.S. Treasury bills—precisely because they have somewhat higher risk—and that is a key point to remember.

Agency bonds have risk. They are backed by mortgages. Homeowners may decide to prepay their mortgages if interest rates change or if home prices fall. That could impact the value of your bond fund.

When you invest in any bond fund, use Morningstar.com to investigate the underlying bond content. Concentrate on funds that predominantly hold U.S. Treasury, TIPS, Ginnie Mae, and blue-chip corporate bonds. Don't take on a lot of bond risk, and don't fall into the trap of believing that all government bonds are risk-free.

STATE BONDS

The bonds of many state governments are, I believe, risky. As we noted before, many states and state agencies have serious pension-funding problems. They have pension liabilities they cannot pay. Their bonds could lose value. Consequently, stay clear of state bonds unless you know that a particular state has good financials.

MUNICIPAL BONDS

The same holds true for municipal bonds. At first glance, "munis" look quite attractive. After all, they pay good rates of interest, and you usually do not have to pay any city, state, or federal tax on the interest from them. Because of pension and fiscal mismanagement, however, many municipalities also have extremely weak financials. Some municipalities are near bankruptcy. So I would urge you to steer clear of municipal bonds as well unless you are certain of the borrower's financial strength. Avoid taking unnecessary risk with your retirement capital.

HIGH-GRADE CORPORATE BONDS:

Corporate bonds are the debt obligations of companies. When you own corporate bonds or corporate-bond funds, you are lending money to companies to finance their business activities and growth. The risk of this debt is reflected in each institution's bond rating.

"Blue-chip" corporate bonds are bonds with "investment grade" ratings such as AA or better. They pay more interest than U.S. Treasuries. They are generally less risky than stocks, and the high ratings of these bonds mean that they have a low risk of default.

However, even high-quality corporate bonds have credit, illiquidity, and callability risks.[5] A company can decide to prepay its debt to you or post-pone repayment. Since many blue-chip companies have inadequate funding for their huge pension liabilities, their bonds beg vigilance, too. Invest in corporate bonds cautiously. Funds containing the bonds of companies with pension-funding issues are not, in my view, conservative investments whatsoever.

High-Yield Bonds

Most 401(k) plans also offer one or more high-yield bond funds. And, again, investors often misunderstand the risks of such investments.

High-yield bonds are corporate debt obligations that have "below investment grade" ratings. Sometimes called junk bonds, they are rated BB and lower.[6] In other words, they have substantially more risk than U.S. Treasuries and more risk than A-rated or high-grade corporate bonds. And because of their higher risk, they pay higher returns. We're talking about the debt of financially weak companies.

Remember this rule of thumb: higher returns—whether from bonds, stocks, or real estate—invariably imply higher risk. There is a direct correlation between risk and reward. And you want to broadly diversify and contain the risks of your investments rather than become top-heavy in "high-return" kinds of investments.

Also bear in mind that high-yield bonds are often included in target date funds. It's important to carefully check the bond content of any target date fund *before you buy in* to make sure it has only limited exposure in higher-risk kinds of investments. Many target date funds have strong allocations into high-yield bonds but little international exposure.

Exercise caution. High-yield bond funds can be good holdings in limited doses. But your retirement portfolio should not be top-heavy in them. You likewise want to make sure that any target date or balanced fund in which you invest is not top-heavy in higher-risk content either.

The bottom line is this: When you invest for interest income, you want to be sure the bonds, bond funds, and bank deposits you hold are issued by high-quality institutions having *strong* financials. You want to avoid inflation risk, default risk, and the risk of losses. Consequently, avoid bank time deposits with banks lacking FDIC insurance. Avoid large positions in municipal, state agency, Freddie Mac, Fannie Mae, and junk bonds (having ratings of BBB or below). You do not need large doses of those kinds of securities in your portfolio. And when you invest in any bond or balanced or target date fund, use Morningstar.com to carefully check into each fund's bond content. You primarily want interest-income funds having (1) short-term (maximum one-year) bond maturities as well as (2) substantial U.S. Treasury, TIPS, and high-quality (AA or better) corporate content. If a fund you hold begins to take on content with substantially more risk, dilute your position in it.

DEFENSE #4: SET A "STOP LOSS"

You also want to defend your savings from knee-jerk investment decisions. Let's face it. Most of us are often self-defeating when we invest. We see stock prices climbing, and we want to buy in! And then we end up "buying high," catching the correction end of the cycle. When we see prices dropping, we scramble to sell! Over and over, most of us buy high and sell low. But that's the antithesis of successful investing.

Wealthy people often avoid this problem because, more often than not, they have the world's best professional managers minding their money for them. You, however, may not. I have therefore urged you to set a clear Investment Master Plan to bring discipline, cold objectivity, and forward vision to your investment activities. In addition to a good allocation plan, however, other guidelines will help you make skillful risk decisions when a market is correcting, booming, or just plain standing still.

At times, in fact, you need to ditch poor-performing investments. However, all the financial commentary on television is usually *not* going to give you a suitable sell signal, and emotional reactions to losses are often unskillful and harmful as well. How many times have you sold off a perfectly good investment because you stopped thinking objectively and moved into high anxiety? Many times, I bet. So how can you prevent knee-jerk selloffs in the future?

To interject discipline into exiting, I recommend setting an advance "stop loss."

Defense #4: Set a stop loss. Exit from any investment when it produces a loss of 10 percent or more.

You don't have react to every up and down wobble of an investment's performance. You don't have to follow ticker-tape feeds describing a particular stock's minute-by-minute trading moves. If, however, the market moves against you, and one of your investments hits your preset, 10 percent loss limit, then—yes—it's time to exit.

Of course, you may have a greater tolerance for risk. You may be willing to set a higher stop loss—say 12 or even 15 percent. That's fine. Whatever your cutoff, it's important for you to set a clear stop loss in advance and then honor it as part of your investment plan.

Step one, set a stop loss. I recommend 10 percent, but make it higher if that's suitable. Step two, look for ways to activate your cutoff automatically. Let me give you an example. If you purchase income-focused exchange-traded funds or ETFs such as the ones I cited in chapter 6, you can give Schwab or your broker an advance "sell order" for that position if the price drops by 10 percent. Remember, exchange-traded funds trade like stocks, so you can give your broker a standing sell order that will stay in effect for months before you have to renew it.

Set a clear loss limit. Take emotion and procrastination out of exit decisions. That will heighten your portfolio's defense as well.

DEFENSE #5: SET "CIRCUIT BREAKERS" TO AVOID PAINFUL CORRECTIONS

Overvalued investments always deflate. *Always.* So do hyperinflated markets. Like the mega-wealthy, you want to avoid a "two steps forward, three steps back" approach to investing your capital. You want to avoid corrections that might impair the compounding and steady growth of your savings. You want to avoid hard-to-repair losses.

Let's remember what happened in the stock market in the late 1990s. As more and more investors pumped money into tech stocks and the stock market as a whole, share prices soared. The S&P 500 Index climbed a whopping 346 percent from 1990 through 1999.[7] Companies that hadn't produced one iota of income saw their shares trading at sky-high prices. Alan Greenspan and Robert Shiller warned of "irrational exuberance," and debates broke out about whether the market had become a bubble or not—and then the bubble burst.

Writing in 1999 just before the market plummeted 30 percent, economist

Richard Thaler noted, "The consensus on Wall Street (and on similar streets around the world) is that the U.S. stock market is 20–30 percent overvalued; yet, prices can continue to increase. . . . First, in the U.S. market, the largest investors—pension funds, endowments, and wealthy individuals—typically use some rule of thumb for asset allocation, such as 60 percent in equities, and are thus relatively insensitive to the level of asset prices. Second, such insensitivity is even more characteristic of individual investors in 401(k) plans, who rarely rebalance their portfolios."[8]

Regrettably, most investors ignored the warning signs, and many suffered large losses. Yet, ample research shows again and again that whenever a market or investment overheats and produces abnormally high returns, it invariably corrects, dropping back to more realistic values. In investment lingo, that's called "reverting to the mean." It means that investments eventually adjust back to income fundamentals and burn off hypervaluation gains. If the historical average return of the stock market has been 10.1 percent each year, then returns of 50 percent per annum are telling you that a price correction is coming! It may take months or years, but red-hot, abnormally performing investments always correct. *Always.*

These facts lead me to draw another "defense" conclusion: *At times it is best to reduce your stake in certain investments or to exit from them altogether. When a market or investment poses strong correction risk, move to the sidelines.*

I call this "setting a circuit breaker." It's simply turning off the juice when the voltage becomes dangerously high. With investments, it means staying clear of bubble or overvalued investments and moving to safer ground.

Defense #5: Set a circuit breaker. Get out of any investment or market as a whole when it exhibits abnormally high pricing and may be poised for a harmful correction.

I want you to keep away from unrealistic pricing and here-today-gone-tomorrow "gains." I want you to invest knowing that red-hot investments of every kind always come down. Always. And it could take you years to repair the damage.

There are metrics you can use as crude warning signals that it may be prudent to reduce your position in an investment or exit from it. Mind you, there is no magic exit formula. And most experts would rightly insist that you cannot, after all, successfully "time the market"—meaning move in and out of investments to lock into the highest returns and always avoid losses.

There are no magic timing formulas and no miracle ways of avoiding losses.

There are, however, alarm signals that may nevertheless help you recognize when defensive action might be appropriate. And I would argue that you will fare best adopting a defensive investment posture, avoiding investments when they emit these signals. I argue that it's best to keep your retirement savings intact. Let's see how.

STOCK METRIC

We already noted several clear measures—such as dividends and price-earnings ratios—that are crude but helpful ways of calibrating the ballpark fair valuation of stock investments.

The stock market, we saw, has operated for over one hundred years with an average price-to-earnings ratio of approximately fifteen.[9] A price-earnings ratio, we said, is the price of a share of stock divided by the amount of company earnings that one share of stock buys. So when we say that the historical average P/E ratio has been fifteen, we simply mean that investors have historically been willing to pay about $15 to buy $1 of a company's earnings. In other words, investors have historically expected a return of about 6.7 percent on stocks (that's the $1 divided by $15). It's an important "stake in the ground."

Obviously, a stock investment with a price-earnings ratio substantially *over* fifteen has a high price and gives you a lower return. If a stock has a P/E ratio of twenty-eight, for example, it means that you have to pay $28 to acquire $1 of corporate earnings and are willing to accept a return of only 3.6 percent ($1 divided by $28). With that kind of return, you might be better off investing in lower-risk Treasury bills.

Given the historical average price-earnings ratio of fifteen, experts such as Benjamin Graham have suggested that a ratio *below fifteen* is attractive and signals "low" stock pricing while a ratio *above twenty* is less attractive and signals "high" pricing.[10]

Other experts believe that these guidelines have lost some relevance. They argue that a somewhat higher P/E ratio may be a more realistic measure of a stock's "price reasonableness" today, given modern company performance.[11] And I agree that a P/E ratio of, say, nineteen or twenty-one today may be a more appropriate measure. Let's put it to practical use.

The U.S. stock market has sustained four painful corrections when "irrational exuberance" or herd panic caused stock prices to tumble. In two of the four instances, exceptionally high P/E ratios heralded sharp corrections.

- **Crash of 1929:** Between 1920 and 1929, stocks more than quadrupled in value. By the end of September 1929, the stock market registered an overall P/E ratio of thirty-four,[12] then crashed. *The New York Times* voiced scorn for those who had participated in the "orgy of speculation."[13] The pain for investors was intense: the S&P 500 Index dropped 80 percent by June 1932. It did not return to its September 1929 level until 1958.[14]

- **Correction of 1972–74:** Between 1969 and 1972, the stock market climbed 40 percent then took a 46 percent nosedive.[15] At its high point before the plunge, the marketwide P/E ratio was not quite twenty.[16] There was no disturbing news or unusual financial data to which we can attribute the fall—but it caused many investors to lose a great deal of capital.

- **Correction of October 1987:** At the outset of September 1987, the stock market had a modest 19.4 P/E ratio.[17] In the next month, however, the Dow Jones Industrial Average, an index of blue-chip stocks, plummeted almost 23 percent.[18] By the end of November 1987, the S&P 500 index had lost 28 percent.

- **Correction of 2000–2002:** Fast-forward to the late 1990s. Between 1990 and the close of 1999, the S&P 500 Index skyrocketed 346 percent.[19] At the peak of the euphoria in January 2000, the U.S. stock market had a whopping 46.8 P/E ratio according to some estimates.[20] In the words of one commentator, "By 2000, investors were willing to pay $4,500 for shares that brought $100 of profits throughout the 1990s. . . . Investors . . . were betting . . . that tomorrow's profits would be much, much larger than today's profits—in a way that had never been seen in the history of the stock markets, not when the railroads came, nor when America was electrified, nor in the great expansion of the 1950s and 1960s."[21]

Not surprisingly, the 1990s stock market bubble—like all bubbles—eventually burst. Between December 1999 and September 2001, investors in the S&P 500 Index lost 29 percent of their money.[22]

What does all of this tell us? It suggests that two of the country's most powerful stock market corrections—those of 1929 and 2000—where preceded by periods in which marketwide P/E ratios surpassed thirty and were signaling danger. The ratios told investors that stock prices had reached unrealistic levels—levels well above those warranted by income fundamentals. In two of the four corrections, there were clear signals that investors needed to exercise caution and take a defensive stand. In fact, throughout the history of the U.S stock market, the P/E ratio has only spiked over thirty in these two instances,[23] heralding strong corrections.

In the case of the corrections of 1972–4 and 1987, however, there were no "warning signals." No alarm bells. No unusual ratios.

Here, then, is my take: We cannot predict each and every correction. Too many economic, psychological, and "herd behavior" factors come into play. However, stock investments are clearly risky, and investors periodically go on abnormal speculative binges. We can use P/E ratios as well as dividend payouts to help judge the income attractiveness of stock investments. I believe it is prudent to concentrate on equity investments that pay dividends *and* have a low P/E ratio—certainly a P/E ratio below thirty. When the P/E ratio for any stock, stock fund, or the stock market as a whole reaches thirty, it's time to take defensive action.

I specifically recommend cutting any stock or stock fund position by at least half when the P/E ratio surpasses twenty-seven and exiting from the investment altogether when the ratio is thirty or higher.

Now let me be clear. This is admittedly a crude "alarm system." It has many faults. Professional asset managers would also insist upon taking many other financial metrics into account. In fact, we saw in chapter 10 that a P/E ratio should take prevailing interest rates into account, and that P/E ratios are, indeed, likely to be higher in a low-interest-rate environment.

In other words, saying that a stock investment with a high P/E ratio is "dangerously expensive" and should be sold off is outright simplistic, I know. Ratios alone do not provide foolproof entry and exit signals. Reducing your holdings solely on the basis of a high ratio will *not* guarantee that you will avoid stock losses. You may, after all, incur losses even when a much *lower* P/E ratio prevails—as happened in 1987 when the P/E ratio was a very acceptable nineteen, thank you! And if you do cut back on your stock holdings on the basis of a high ratio, you may well miss out on the opportunity to earn a lot more money. Expensive stocks can get even more expensive. A stock fund or stock market with a P/E ratio of twenty-eight or thirty may *continue* to climb.

Acting defensively when P/E ratios are high is not fail-safe or magical. Even so, I urge you to err on the side of caution. I urge you to set cutoff points or circuit breakers. *Deciding in advance on cutoff benchmarks will protect you from losing a lot of money in bubble markets.* And the tactic dovetails, I believe, with the findings of leading investment experts and commentators.

> "High-P/E stocks are, on average, overvalued by the market and lead to lower returns." . . . "If you invested $1,000 in 1957 in the 100 stocks in the S&P 500 with the highest price-to-earnings ratios, and rebalanced annually, you'd have had $56,700 by 2003; if you bought the 100 stocks with the lowest P/Es, you'd have had $425,700."
>
> Wharton professor Jeremy Siegel[24]

> "We can look for some answers in two important chapters in Yale professor Robert Shiller's must-read book, *Irrational Exuberance.* Shiller clearly demonstrates that when broad market indexes go above P/E ratios of twenty-three or so, investors essentially get no return over the next ten years. The markets return to trend."
>
> John Mauldin, *"Bull's Eye Investing: Targeting Real Returns in a Smoke and Mirrors Market"*[25]

> "Look back over history . . . and you'll see that buying high P/Es is almost always a recipe for lousy returns, regardless where interest rates are."
>
> Cliff Asness, AQR Capital Management[26]

Pay attention to the P/E ratios of the stock market as a whole and to the P/E ratios of your mutual funds, exchange-traded funds, and indexes! Funds and indexes also have a price-to-earnings ratio—the composite of the ratios of all the securities they hold. So when you invest in funds or indexes, check out each one's P/E as well. In the spirit of avoiding losses, dilute your holdings or outright exit from stocks or equity funds or stock indexes when they have an exceptionally high ratio. That's good defense.

You can check on prevailing P/E ratios during your quarterly tune-ups by using these online resources:

STOCK MARKET AS A WHOLE

1. Go to Standard & Poor's Web site: www.marketattributes.standardandpoors.com.

   Click "S&P 500 Earnings and Estimates." This will give you the ratio for the country's largest five hundred companies.

   Or click on "United States" and in the search box (top right) enter "P/E ratio." Then click "Indices S&P Composite 1500." That will give you ratios for the top fifteen hundred U.S. stocks.

2. Alternatively, consult Dr. Robert Shiller's database at www.econ.yale.edu/~shiller/data/ie_data.htm. It has both historical data and recent updates. Dr. Shiller explains these numbers in his book *Irrational Exuberance*. Use this data.

INDIVIDUAL FUNDS AND INDEXES

1. Subscribe to Value Line's *Mutual Fund Survey*. Try a trial subscription first. Then check its "Fund Reports." These reports show the P/E ratios for many but not all funds.
2. You can also use Morningstar's free data. Go to www.morningstar.com, enter the name of the fund, then click "Portfolio." But be cautious. Morningstar usually provides a "price-to-prospective earnings" ratio. It is computed using *estimated,* not actual, earnings. And those kinds of guesstimates have led many investors astray. So use Morningstar's ratios cautiously.

3. Perhaps the best way of obtaining individual fund ratios is to visit the Web site of each fund. For Vanguard's funds, for example, go to www.vanguard.com, key in the name or ticker symbol for a fund, then click "Holdings."

REAL ESTATE METRIC

There are ways of sizing up the reasonableness of real estate investments as well. To keep things simple, let's focus on one of them—the price-rent ratio.

According to one Federal Reserve study, there is "most conclusive evidence that house prices correct back to rents."[27] Other Fed commentators went further, "One common way of thinking about housing's fundamental value is to consider the ratio of housing prices to rents. . . . Historically, the ratio for the nation as a whole has had many ups and downs, but over time has tended to return to its long-run average. Thus, when the price-to-rent ratio is high, housing prices tend to grow more slowly or fall for a time, and when the ratio is low, prices tend to rise more rapidly. I want to emphasize, though, that this is a loose relationship that can be counted on only for rough guidance rather than a precise reading."[28]

The rent return of any real estate investment is a crude measure of whether it is reasonably priced. The "price-to-rent ratio" is the price of a property divided by its rent income net of insurance, property taxes, and maintenance costs. It measures how much a buyer is willing to pay for each $1 of net rent income.

Generally speaking, reasonable price-to-rent multiples in the United States have ranged from a low of nine to a high of about twenty-three, depending on mortgage rates and investor optimism.[29] Of course, price-rent ratios are not computed taking mortgage rates into account—and they should be. When mortgage rates are low, we can expect higher property prices and higher ratios.

Even without adjusting for interest, however, price-rent ratios can help you identify—if only crudely—bubble markets and speculative overpricing. Here's what I mean.

Apartment prices in New York City jumped from twelve times rent income in the mid-1990s to *twenty-four times* rent income at the height of the real estate boom in 2005. The ratio for homes in San Diego climbed from thirteen to *twenty-seven times* over the same period. In Los Angeles it jumped from *ten to twenty*.[30] By July 2005, the nationwide ratio was 25 percent higher than its long-term average—higher, in fact, than it had been at any time since the data first became available.[31] These ratios signaled the need for caution.

Once again, price-rent ratios are only rough valuation measurements. They are not, in the words of one government report, precise indicators of "if, when, and how much house prices will change direction."[32] However, they may help you avoid catching the correction end of a price surge. And they directionally signal when it may be time to exit from or reduce your stake in real estate investments that are likely to correct.

Here are three rules of thumb: (1) avoid real estate investments in high-appreciation locations—you may be buying high and setting yourself up for correction losses; (2) reduce your position in real estate investments having a price-to-rent ratio of more than seventeen; and (3) expect a return on a real estate investment to be at least 2 percent more *than the return of a U.S. Treasury bill.*[33] *If the rent-income return (real or hypothetical) is less, it is probably not an attractive investment.*

Real estate investments have more risk than Treasury bonds. You should therefore expect a larger return for the additional risk. If a real estate investment cannot give you better-than-Treasury-bond returns, you're better off investing in Treasuries.

There is no central database for price-to-rent information. You have to tabulate the ratios yourself. However, you can obtain good "appreciation" or "overvaluation" information at these Web sites:

1. **National City**
   Go to www.nationalcity.com/corporate
   Click "Economics"
   Scroll to "Housing Valuation Analysis"
2. **Office of Federal Housing Enterprise Oversight**
   Go to www.ofheo.gov
   Click "House Price Index" (far left in blue section)
   Click "Metropolitan Statistical Areas (MSAs)" (center, white)
   Scroll to the three boxes at the bottom of this page

These sites identify pricing trends for residential properties in metropolitan locations. Commercial properties and hotels are not factored in and may, of course, have very different pricing and risk characteristics.

Even if the information is strictly "residential," however, it is nevertheless insightful. You want to avoid real estate investments in locations that have recently experienced sky-high appreciation, such as California, Florida, and Arizona. You want to avoid buying high and then suffering a correction or getting stuck in a valuation holding pattern for years and years.

You can also use Morningstar.com and the Web sites of individual real estate funds and REITs to ascertain each one's geographic focus and content.

Be defensive when you invest in real estate—as defensive as when you invest in stocks. Forget about "flipping" houses! Invest in real estate via funds or REITs so you diversify your exposure across many different properties. Focus specifically on funds or REITs having content that is *not* located in bubble or high-appreciation markets. Look for real estate funds with good rent-income characteristics. Look for experienced property managers. Look for international content, because demographics are sure to open excellent real estate investment opportunities offshore. And check Morningstar as well as each fund's Web site to ascertain exactly what kinds of property content, leases, and geographic concentration it has.

CONCLUSIONS

There is no defense magic. You cannot "time the market" or rely on one or two ratios to defend your investments from harm. And research shows that if you pull out of a red-hot investment market, you may, indeed, give up a great deal of additional profit.

Even so, don't put your hard-earned retirement savings in the path of correction losses! *Protect* as well as enlarge what you've earned. Remain defensive. Be satisfied with more conservative results. Set "circuit breakers" to reduce your exposure or altogether stop exposure in overvalued investments or markets. Step back from stock investments when their P/E ratio surpasses twenty-seven or from real estate investments that pay the same or less income than a Treasury bill. Use the crude metrics of price-earnings ratios and price-rent ratios to identify bubble markets and defend your retirement capital from harm. Be vigilant against holding speculative froth. Focus instead on well-priced investments that produce *real income*!

ACTION PLAN

1. Set a "stop loss." Exit from any investment once it results in a 10 percent loss (or a loss threshold of your choosing).
2. Make your loss limit "automatic" whenever possible. Give standing instructions to your broker to sell any exchange-traded funds when they reach your loss limit to help avoid losses and speculative oversurge.
3. Set "circuit breakers." Reduce your stock exposure by at least half when the marketwide P/E ratio surpasses twenty-seven. Exit from real estate investments when their rent return is the same as or *less than* the return of a Treasury bill or bank deposit.
4. Maintain an income focus. Adopt a defensive, antispeculation approach to investing. Remember that insistence on real returns—*"Show me real income!"*—is your strongest defense and best offense.

CONCLUSIONS

We have seen that retirement is a strictly modern concept—a social and economic experiment increasingly beset by funding shortfalls and risks. In this book, we have identified ways to offset these risks. We have looked at a number of strategies and tactics that can help you protect and enlarge your retirement capital as summarized on the next page.

Foremost of all, we have seen the importance of investing for *real income* instead of speculative, here-today-gone-tomorrow "gains." We have explored ways to capitalize on—rather than be punished by—the demographic tumult ahead. And we have also looked at a unique annuity strategy—a way of compounding your investment growth on a tax-advantageous basis to create *life-cycle* and *lifetime* income streams.

Now it's up to you to change your "automatic pilot" about saving and investing. It's up to you to step up your savings and invest differently beginning right *now*.

I hope this book has goaded you into thinking soberly and with determination about preparing for retirement. I hope it makes you decide to save more, to invest more skillfully, and to use income investments, insurance, and annuities to safeguard your financial future. At the same time, I hope this book has added to your confidence about the good future you have ahead.

Now some of you are probably saying, "Hold on! This is way too much.

	Accumulation Risk	Market and Demographic Risk	Longevity Risk	Inflation Risk
The Issues	You Don't Save Enough!	Your Investments Could Lose Value	You Could Outlive Y Savings	Your Capital Will Lose Purchasing Power Over Time
What to Do About It	• Participate in your 401(k) and IRA *to the max*	• Invest in *income*-focused funds and indexes	• Buy Medigap insurance	• Increase estimates of the income you'll need later in life
	• Set up an *automatic* savings and transfer plan	• Enlarge your international exposure	• Buy long-term health care insurance	• Buy different annuities for different income streams. Add "inflation riders"
	• Give standing investment instructions	• Hold "insurance" investments	• Build a life-cycle ladder of annuities	• Invest in TIPS (Treasury inflation-protected securities) inside tax-sheltered accounts
	• Retain a financial planner to coach and help you	• Set a "stop loss" and "circuit breaker"	• Consider a reverse mortgage after age 75 as a fallback strategy	• Invest in a variety of asset classes for *rent, dividend,* and *interest income*
		• Limit any holding to a max 10% of your total (excepting indexes)	• Get professional guidance to pace your drawdowns	
		• Capitalize on demographics: health care, natural resources, emerging . markets, etc		

I don't have enough money to buy a lot of different annuities. I don't have enough money to even invest in three mutual funds!"

If so, don't worry! Let me offer you a distilled version of my advice:

Whatever amount you have to invest, make these your priorities:

Put the maximum in your 401(k) or IRA—always invest in a tax-deferred or tax-sheltered way. Invest for income, not "gains." Increase international exposure. Hold dividend-oriented indexes and funds. Invest in a ladder of annuities for different "life-cycle" income streams. Prepare for big economic changes and new investment opportunities as the population ages. Get all the professional help you can. Itemize and quantify your benefits. And save! Save! Save!

Over time, the government may modify our health-care and retirement-savings programs. Your own investment priorities may shift. But don't stand on the sidelines waiting for these changes. Get cracking! Save more! And invest prudently and defensively with a steadfast income fixation.

I also hope you won't focus on the "toothpicks" of this book and lose sight of the forest. Let's not quibble about how much should be invested in actively managed funds versus market indexes. And let's not debate whether you should invest in one kind of annuity or another.

Instead, I want you to stay focused on the important issues.

Issue #1. Have you quantified your postretirement income needs? Have you confirmed the amount of Social Security money and the amount of defined benefit money you can expect to supplement your savings? (The key word here is *supplement*—because you will most certainly need to have *ample savings* of your own for retirement in our era's new do-it-yourself retirement model.)

Issue #2. Are your savings and investments on target to meet your retirement income needs? Have you factored in inflation? The possibility of a long life span? *If not, what are you going to do about it beginning right now?*

Issue #3. Is your knowledge about stocks, bonds, real estate, and taxes adequate to enable you to make skillful investment choices and prudent drawdowns? If not, do you know where to turn for objective research, guidance, and advice? Have you contacted a financial advisor?

Issue #4. Do you recognize the dangers of chasing after speculative, get-rich-quick stock "gains" or real estate "gains" that have nothing to do with income fundamentals? *Has the rationale for real income sunk in? If so, how are you going to invest differently?*

Issue #5. Have you made provisions for the *possibility* of economic turmoil because of the boomer retirement wave? Are you addressing that potential risk in your investment plans? Are you holding "safe haven" investments to protect your savings from possible commotion? And are you prepared to capitalize on the coming demographic shifts and great investment opportunities—in health care, energy, international equities, and emerging markets?

This book has presented a number of ideas to help you answer these questions. It urges you to recognize that grave dangers loom ahead and to anticipate them in your retirement plans right now. It entreats you to build a life raft and prepare for the coming storm.

But let me make a confession. I believe in and practice every word of advice contained in this book. But I nevertheless find fault with the imagery of "life rafts" and the philosophy of "every man and woman for him- or herself." They are, after all, rather selfish ways of thinking about retirement, aren't they? Is this the way we should go about retirement planning? Does it all come down to amassing as much money as each of us possibly can?

I do not believe so.

First, retirement entails other, *nonfinancial* concerns and opportunities. How will you use your retirement time and resources? Will you teach underprivileged children? Be a mentor? Become a charity volunteer? Or perhaps establish a new university scholarship to help talented young people complete their educations?

There are important *nonfinancial* adventures that you and I have to look forward to as well. Those important opportunities are not within the scope of this book, but are features of retirement every bit as important as money.

Second, the economics of do-it-yourself retirement funding are also troublesome. We have seen that when you and I prepare for retirement *individually,* we are forced to amass capital for a *maximum* possible life span.

That's right—you may live to be 95 or 103! And I certainly hope you *do* enjoy a long life with good health, zip, and gusto!

Consequently, each of us needs to make income provisions for the possibility of a long and ripe *maximum* life span. We need money and insurance for a long span of time. If there is any chance of living until age ninety-five, we have to have funding for it! That's part and parcel of the do-it-yourself American approach to retirement.

If, however, we prepare for the future *collectively,* then we only need to make provision for the *average* life span of the group. Some people will live to be 99 or 110. Others will live into their seventies. So as a collective, we would only need to save and invest for the group's average life span. Ask any economist. The collective approach is far less costly.

The way I see it, our increasing emphasis on do-it-yourself retirement preparedness is *not* economically smart and is not helping most people. It is not cost-effective. Many people are left out of key savings programs. We can do better.

Three, not every man and woman has the time, skill, or inclination to do the necessary research, study the many tax angles, and make feast-or-famine investment decisions. Not every individual wants to be a self-schooled financial brain surgeon! That is why I strongly urge you to seek the advice of a professional financial advisor. The economic issues are too complex. The tax considerations are too convoluted. And the investment alternatives are too bewildering for a do-it-yourself approach to ever succeed without professional help.

And, four, there is clearly not much *compassion* in the "life raft" strategy that we're saddled with. Are the haves of this country meant to triumphantly enjoy golf games and the finest of assisted-living care while the have-nots languish just above poverty? Are people suffering from dementia going to be left in low-grade facilities as "retirement survivors" drive on by in hybrid SUVs? Are we going to be Ayn Rand smug about it and say, "Sorry! You had plenty of time to build your *own* financial raft!"

Is *that* the best we can do? I do not believe so.

I believe we need to forge a new vision about retirement that is economically functional, demographically savvy, and—yes—compassionate. We need to redesign our "social security" programs so they do not bankrupt generations to come. We need to legally acknowledge the right of Americans to work *past* the age of 65. We need, as a priority, to overhaul our medical programs as well. If we do not, large numbers of Americans will be pushed into poverty during our very lifetimes, and future generations will be saddled with outlandish debt.

We need to use our talents, ethics, and forward thinking to design a better approach. And surely we can do so.

In the meantime, will most of us have to work until we drop? Is retirement in the United States a dying experiment?

Anything but! I am confident that a combination of steadfast savings, income-fixated investments, annuity income streams, and insurance can—most assuredly—give you a long and financially secure retirement.

It's time to step up your preparations for a secure and active retirement! Contribute to the overhaul of our retirement systems. Save more! Invest for income. And take action now to enjoy the fruits of saving and income-oriented investing!

Notes

1: Is Retirement a Dying Experiment?

1. Stephen Alsford, "Charitable Provision for the Aged," *Florilegium Urbanum,* August 18, 2001. Original source: Public Record Office, Chancery Miscellanea, Gild Certificates, transcribed in *English Gilds,* Early English Text Society, old series, vol. 40 (1870), http://www.trytell.com/~tristan/towns/lifecycle/lcret01.html.

2. Karl H. E. Kroemer, *"Extra-Ordinary" Ergonomics* (CRC Press, 2006), 128.

3. Joanna Short, "Economic History of Retirement in the United States," Economic History Web site, EH.Net Encyclopedia, ed. Robert Whaples, October 1, 2002, www.eh.net/encyclopedia/article/short.retirement.history.us.

4. Kroemer, *"Extra-Ordinary" Ergonomics,* 128.

5. Short, "Economic History," with attribution to Moen (1987) and Costa (1998).

6. Ibid.

7. Employee Benefit Research Institute, "The U.S. Retirement Income System," Facts from EBRI, April 2005, http://www.ebri.com/pdf/publications/facts/0405fact.pdf.

8. Standard & Poor's Index Analysis and Management Group, "S&P 500: Pensions and Other Post-Employment Benefits," June 6, 2006, 3, http://www2.standardandpoors.com/spf/pdf/index/060606_5OPEB-rpt.pdf.

9. Social Security Administration, "Historical Background of Social Security," Social Security Online, updated March 2003, http://www.ssa.gov/history/briefhistory3.html.

10. AIG SunAmerica, "The History of Retirement," AIG SunAmerican Re-Visioning Retirement Survey, no date, www.re-visioningretirement.com/History/history.html.

11. Employee Benefit Research Institute, "The Retirement System in Transition: The 2007 Retirement Confidence Survey," Issue Brief 304, April 2007, 12, http://www.ebri.org/pdf/briefspd/EBRI_IB_04a-20075.pdf.

12. Bryandt R. Dickerson, Bureau of Labor Statistics, U.S. Department of Labor, "Employee Participation in Defined Benefit and Defined Contribution Plans, 1985–2000," Bureau of Labor Statistics Web site, data originally posted March 26, 2003, and revised June 16, 2004, http://www.bls.gov/opub/cwc/cm20030325tb01.htm.

13. Bureau of Labor Statistics, U.S. Department of Labor, "National Compensation Survey: Employee Benefits in Private Industry in the United States, March 2006," Summary 06-05, August 2006, 6, table 1, http://www.bls.gov/ncs/ebs/ep/ebsm0004.pdf.

14. Centers for Disease Control and Prevention, National Center for Health Statistics, U.S. Department of Health and Human Services, *Health, United States, 2006 with Chartbook Trends in the Health of Americans* (Hyattsville, MD: 2006), 176, table 27, http://www.cdc.gov/nchs/data/hus/hus06.pdf#027.

15. Employee Benefit Research Institute, "Retirement System in Transition," 13.

16. Ibid.

17. Administration on Aging, U.S. Department of Health and Human Services, "A Statistical Profile of Older Americans Aged 65+" (Washington, D.C.: November, 2006), 2, http://www.aoa.gov/press/fact/pdf/ss_stat_profile.pdf.

18. Bureau of Labor Statistics, "National Compensation Survey," 6, table 1.

19. Dennis Cauchon, "Pension Gap Divides Public and Private Workers," *USA Today*, February 20, 2007, http://www.usatoday.com/news/nation/2007-02-20-pensions-cover_x.htm.

20. Patrick J. Purcell, *Pensions and Retirement Savings Plans: Sponsorship and Participation,* Congressional Research Service, Library of Congress, report to Congress, code RL30122; updated October 22, 2003, with attribution to the Pension and Welfare Administration of the U.S. Department of Labor.

21. Bureau of Labor Statistics, "National Compensation Survey," 8, table 3.

22. Employee Benefit Research Institute, *"Retirement System in Transition,"* 4.

23. Poor's Index Analysis and Management Group, "S&P 500," 1, 8.

24. Ibid.

25. Congressional Budget Office, *Defined-Benefit Pension Plans: Current Problems and Future Challenges,* testimony of the Congressional Budget Office before the U.S. Senate Committee on Finance, June 7, 2005, http://finance.senate.gov/hearings/testimony/2005test060705.pdf; and Douglas Holtz-Eakin, *Defined-Benefit Pension Plans: Current Problems and Future Challenges,* testimony of the director of the Congressional Budget Office before the Senate Committee on Finance, June 7, 2005, http://www.senate.gov/~finance/hearings/testimony/2005test/dhetest060705.pdf.

26. Wilshire Associates Incorporated, *2007 Wilshire Report on State Retirement Systems: Funding Levels and Asset Allocation,* March 5, 2007, 1, http://www.wilshire.com/BusinessUnits/Consulting/Investment/2007_State_Retirement_Funding_Report.pdf.

27. John Mauldin, *Bull's Eye Investing: Targeting Real Returns in a Smoke and Mirrors Market* (Hoboken, NJ: John Wiley & Sons, 2004), 129.

28. Wilshire Associates Incorporated, *2007 Wilshire Report,* 1.

29. Robert D. Arnott, "DB and DC Plans Face Trillion-Dollar Time Bomb," *Pensions & Investments,* March 18, 2002, http://www.findarticles.com/p/articles/mi_go1518/is_200203/ai_n6776755.

30. Harry S. Dent Jr. and Michael A. Burns & Associates, Public Relations Agency of Record, "HS Dent Publishing Issues 'Death of Pensions,'" press release, HS Dent Foundation, December 5, 2006, http://www.hsdent.com/newsreleases.php.

31. Bureau of Labor Statistics, "National Compensation Survey," 8, table 3, and 6, table 1.

32. Ibid., 7, table 2.

33. Ibid., 2; Joint Economic Committee/Democrats, *Improving Defined Contribution Pension Plans,* Economic Policy Brief, October 2005, http://jec.senate.gov/democrats/Documents/Reports/dcpensionplans06oct2005.pdf; and Profit Sharing /401k Council of America, "Overview of Survey Results," *48th Annual Survey of Profit Sharing and 401(k) Plans,* 2004, http://www.psca.org/DATA/48th.html.

34. Joint Economic Committee/Democrats, *Improving Defined Contribution Pension Plans;* and Alice Munnell, "Pension Expert Advocates Reform of Flawed 401(k)," interview, *Employee Benefit News,* June 1, 2004, http://www.benefitnews.com/retire/detail.cfm?id=6021&arch=1.

35. Joint Economic Committee/Democrats, *Improving Defined Contribution Pension Plans;* and Leslie A. Muller, "Does Retirement Education Teach People to Save Pension Distributions? Perspectives," *Social Security Bulletin* 64, no. 4 (June 2003).

36. Employee Benefit Research Institute, "401(k) Plan Asset Allocation, Account Balances, and Loan Activity in 2005," Issue Brief 296, August 2006, 5, http://www.ebri.org/pdf/briefspdf/EBRI_IB_08-20061.pdf.

37. Ibid., 3.

38. Ibid., 3, 5.

39. Employee Benefit Research Institute, "Encouraging Workers to Save: The 2005 Retirement Confidence Survey," Issue Brief 280, April 2005, 10, http://www.ebri.org/pdf/briefspdf/0405ib.pdf; and Employee Benefit Research Institute, "Will More of Us Be Working Forever? The 2006 Retirement Confidence Survey," Issue Brief 292, April 2006, 22, http://www.ebri.org/pdf/briefspdf/EBRI_IB_04-020061.pdf.

40. Jesus Garcia, Donna M. Ogle, C. Frederick Risinger, and Joyce Stevos, *Creating America: A History of the United States* (McDougal Littell, 2005), S33.

41. Office of Policy, U.S. Social Security Administration, "Monthly Statistical Snapshot, March 2007," table 1, http://www.ssa.gov/policy/docs/quickfacts/stat_snapshot/index.html.

42. Ibid., table 2.

43. Social Security Administration, "Social Security Basic Facts," July 20, 2006, http://www.ssa.gov/pressoffice/basicfact.htm.

44. Howard Ruff, *Safely Prosperous or Really Rich?* (Hoboken, NJ: John Wiley & Sons, 2004), 106–7.

45. Robert D. Arnott and Anne Casscells, "Will We Retire Later and Poorer?" *Journal of Investing,* Summer 2004, no. 10257, 32.

46. Employee Benefit Research Institute, "Facts from EBRI: The Basics of Social Security," May 2006, http://www.ebri.org/pdf/publications/facts/FS-195_May06_SocSecBasics.pdf.

47. Social Security Trustees, *The 2006 Annual Report of the Board of Trustees of the Federal Old-Age and Survivors Insurance and Disability Insurance Trust Funds,* May 1, 2006, table IV.B2, http://www.ssa.gov/OACT/TR/TR06/index.html.

48. Ibid.

49. Social Security Administration, "Social Security's Future—Frequently Asked Questions," http://www.ssa.gov/qa.htm.

50. Ibid.

51. Social Security Administration, "The Distribution Consequences of a 'No-Action' Scenario: Updated Results," Policy Brief No. 2005-01, July 2005, 1, http://www.ssa.gov/policy/docs/policybriefs/pb2005-01.pdf; Congressional Budget Office, *The Role of the Economy in the Outlook for Social Security,* CBO testimony before

the Subcommittee on Social Security, Committee on Ways and Means, U.S. House of Representatives, June 21, 2005, 2, figure 1, http://www.cbo.gov/ftpdocs/64xx/doc6492/06-21-Prefunding.pdf; and Jeremy J. Siegel, *The Future for Investors* (New York: Crown Business, 2005), 191.

52. Social Security Administration, "Social Security's Future."

53. Joseph L. Matthews and Dorothy Matthews Berman, *Social Security, Medicare & Government Pensions,* 10th ed. (NOLO Publishing, 2005), 11/3.

54. "Social Security Still the Third Rail," *Economist* 382, no. 8517 (February 24, 2007): 38.

55. Employee Benefit Research Institute, "Retirement Income Security: A Look at Social Security, Employment-Based Retirement Plans, and Health Savings Accounts," *EBRI Notes* 26, no. 8 (August 2005), http://www.ebri.org/pdf/notespdf/EBRI_Notes_08-20051.pdf.

56. Office of the Assistant Secretary for Planning and Evaluation, U.S. Department of Health and Human Services, "Long-Term Growth of Medical Expenditures—Public and Private," ASPE Issue Brief, May 2005, http://aspe.hhs.gov/health/MedicalExpenditures/ib.pdf.

57. Employee Benefit Research Institute, "Retirement System in Transition," 8, figure 5.

58. Ibid., 8, figure 6.

59. Ibid., 9.

60. Ibid., 10, figure 7.

61. Ibid., 10.

62. Dickerson, "Employee Participation."

63. Bureau of Labor Statistics, "National Compensation Survey," 7, table 2.

64. Bradley D. Belt, transcript of remarks made by the executive director of the Pension Benefit Guaranty Corporation to the Federal Reserve Bank of Chicago's 2005 Bank Structure Conference, May 6, 2005, http://www.pbgc.gov/media/news-archive/speeches/sp15332.html.

2: *Your Core Investment Beliefs* Are Wrong—*Dead Wrong!*

1. Moody's Investors Services, *Default and Recovery Rates of Corporate Bond Issuers, 1920–2005* (New York: Moody's, released January 2006 and revised March 2006), 22, "Exhibit 20: Moody's-Rated Sovereign Bond Defaults, 1998–2005," http://www.moodys.com/moodys/cust/research/MDCdocs/01/2005200000425952.pdf?search=6&searchQuery=default+history&click=1.

2. Moody's Investor Services, *The U.S. Municipal Bond Rating Scale: Mapping to the Global Rating Scale and Assigning Global Scale Ratings to Municipal Obligations* (New York: Moody's, March 2007), 5, figure 2, http://www.moodys.com/moodys/cust/research/MDCdocs/28/2006500000424630.pdf?search=6&searchQuery-municipal%2c+default&click=1.

3. Elroy Dimson, Paul Marsh, and Mike Staunton, *Triumph of the Optimists: 101 Years of Global Investment Returns* (Princeton: Princeton University Press, 2002), 46.

4. Ibid, 47.

5. Ibid, 55.

6. John Mauldin, *Bull's Eye Investing: Targeting Real Returns in a Smoke and Mirrors Market* (Hoboken, NJ: John Wiley & Sons, 2004), 11.

7. Dimson, Marsh, and Staunton, *Triumph of the Optimists*, 9.

8. Jason Zweig, commentary on Benjamin Graham's *The Intelligent Investor*, 4th rev. ed., 1973; new material and commentary by Jason Zweig, 2003 (New York: HarperBusiness Essentials, 2004), 84, http://www.myone1.com/book/the.intelligent.invetor.pdf.

9. Robert J. Shiller, "Irrational Exuberance—Again," CNN Money Web site, Cable News Network LP, LLP, January 25, 2005, http://money.cnn.com/2005/01/13/real _estate/realestate_shiller1_0502/index.htm; and Dr. Shiller's letter to the author, dated September 12, 2007.

10. Ibid.

11. Ibid.

12. Ibid.

13. Mauldin, *Bull's Eye Investing*, 96–97.

14. Robert D. Arnott, "Dividends and the Three Dwarfs," *Financial Analysts Journal*, 2003, 4, http://www.researchaffiliates.com/pubs/pdf/dividendreturns1095916170 .pdf.

15. American Century Investments, "Dividend-Paying Investments Can Provide Benefits," American Century Web site, no date, http://www.americancentury.com/ workshop/articles/dividend_paying.jsp.

16. John C. Bogle in Liz Claman's *The Best Investment Advice I've Ever Received* (New York: Warner Business Books, 2006), 29.

3: *The Coming Demographic Storm*

1. Ron Gebhardtsbauer, Senior Pensions Fellow, American Academy of Actuaries; and data from the fully projected UP94 mortality table, which is based on pensioner and group annuitant data.

2. Public Information Office, U.S. Census Bureau, "Oldest Baby Boomers Turn 60!" Facts for Features, CB06-FFSE.01-2, January 3, 2006, http://www.census.gov/ PressRelease/www/releases/archives/facts_for_features_special_editions/006105.html.

3. Ibid.

4. Yuval Rosenberg, "The Boomer Bust: Will aging boomers pull their money out of the market and cause an asset meltdown on their way to retirement," *Fortune*, June 19, 2006, http://money.cnn.com/2006/06/13/magazines/fortune/boomers_retirementguide _fortune/index.htm.

5. Ibid.

6. Bill Gross, "No Cuts, No Butts, No Coconuts," PIMCO Investment Outlook Series (Newport Beach, CA: Pacific Investment Management Company, LLC, September 2006), http://www2.pimco.com/pdf/IO%20September%202006%20WEB.pdf.

7. United States Government Accountability Office, Report to Congressional Committees, GAO Report 06-718, *Baby Boom Generation: Retirement of Baby Boomers Is Unlikely to Precipitate Dramatic Decline in Market Returns, but Broader Risks Threaten Retirement Security* (Washington, D.C.: July 2006), 8, http://www.gao.gov/new.items/ d06718.pdf.

8. Ibid., 9.

9. John C. Bogle, "The Amazing Disappearance of the Individual Stockholder," *The Wall Street Journal*, October 3, 2005, http://johncbogle.com/wordpress/2006/03/15/the -amazing-disappearance-of-the-individual-stockholder-the-wall-street-journal-october -32005/.

10. National Association of Realtors, "Baby Boomer Survey Shows Big Appetite for Real Estate," NAR's Web site (Washington, D.C.: May 18, 2006), http://www.realtor.org/press_room/news_releases/2006/babyboomerstudy06.html.

11. Ibid.

12. Robert Arnott, transcript of his interview by *Wall Street Week* cohost Karen Gibbs, Maryland Public Television, November 15, 2002, http://www.pbs.org/wsw/tvprogram/arnottinterview.html.

13. John Mauldin, *Bull's Eye Investing: Targeting Real Returns in a Smoke and Mirrors Market* (Hoboken, NJ: John Wiley & Sons, 2004), 140–41.

14. Jeremy J. Siegel, *The Future for Investors* (New York: Crown Business, 2005), two separate quotes, 14–15, 3.

15. Gross, "No Cuts."

16. Peter G. Peterson, *Running on Empty: How the Democratic and Republican Parties Are Bankrupting Our Future and What Americans Can Do About It* (New York: Farrar, Straus and Giroux, 2004) 49–50

17. Jeremy J. Siegel, quoted in Rosenberg, "Boomer Bust."

18. Siegel, *Future for Investors,* 222.

19. Population Division, International Programs Center, U.S. Census Bureau, "IDB Summary Demographic Data," August 24, 2006, http://www.census.gov/ipc/www/idbsum.html.

20. Ibid.

21. United States Government Accountability Office, *Baby Boom Generation,* 2.

22. Population Division, "IDB Summary Demographic Data."

23. Ibid.

24. Wall Street Journal Online/Harris Interactive Personal Finance Poll, *Harris Interactive Newsletter* 3, no. 2 (February 22, 2007), http://www.harrisinteractive.com/news/newsletters/WSJfinance/HI_WSJ_PersFinPoll_2007_vol3_iss02.pdf.

25. National Association of Realtors, "Baby Boomer Survey."

26. Annamaria Lusardi and Olivia S. Mitchell, "Baby Boomer Security: The Roles of Planning, Financial Literacy, and Housing Wealth" (paper presented at annual meeting of American Economic Association, November 2006), 8, http://www.aeaweb.org/annual_mtg_papers/2007/0106_0800_0303.pdf.

27. United States Government Accountability Office, *Baby Boom Generation,* 8.

28. BBC News, "China Tops India on Average Pay," November 14, 2005, http://news.bbc.co.uk/2/low/business/4436692.stm.

29. Robert Arnott, transcript of his comments in Ira Carnahan's "Should You Still Be a Bull?" Forbes.com, April 19, 2004, http://www.forbes.com/forbes/2004/0419/096-print.html.

30. Fidelity Registered Investment Advisor Group, "Retirement Solutions," Fidelity Investments Web site, no date, http://ria.fidelity.com/ria_invest_retirement.html.

4: Change Your "Automatic Pilot"

1. Selena Maranjian, "All About Compounding," Motley Fool Web site, September 12, 2001, http://www.fool.com/portfolios/rulebreaker/2001/rulebreaker010912.htm.

2. Moshe A. Milevsky, "What Is a Sustainable Spending Rate? A Simple Answer," IFID Centre, Version 28, December 2004, 5, www.ifid.ca/pdf_workingpapers/WP2004DEC29.pdf.

3. National Center for Health Sciences, *Health, United States, 2005, with Chartbook on Trends in the Health of Americans* (Hyattsville, MD: 2005), 3, http:cdc.gov/nchs/hus.htm.

4. Employee Benefit Research Institute, "EBRI Issue Brief no. 292" (Washington, D.C.: April 2, 2006), figure 11, http://www.ebri.org/pdf/briefspdf/EBRI_IB_04-20061.pdf.

5. Raksha Arora, "Investors May Underestimate Retirement Needs," Gallup Poll Web site, December 7, 2004, and 2004 UBS/Gallup Retirement Survey, http://www.galluppoll.com/content/?ci=14266&pg=1.

6. Employee Benefit Research Institute, "Issue Brief No. 292," figure 4.

7. This same view is shared by Charles Schwab & Company's Center for Investment Research. Investigate Schwab's excellent "retirement help" materials and check this article for more information on retirement income: Rande Spiegelman, "How Much Should You Save for Retirement? Play the Percentages," Charles Schwab & Co. Web site, March 15, 2005.

8. Employee Benefit Research Institute, "Issue Brief No. 292."

9. Alicia H. Munnell, Francesca Golub-Sass, Pamela Perun, and Anthony Webb, "Households 'At Risk': A Closer Look at the Bottom Third," commentary on the National Retirement Risk Index (NRRI), Center for Retirement Research at Boston College, Issue Brief Number 2007–2, January 2007, http://www.bc.edu/centers/crr/issues/ib_2007-2.pdf.

10. Bureau of Labor Statistics, U.S. Department of Labor, "National Compensation Survey: Employee Benefits in Private Industry in the United States, March 2005," August 2005, 2, http://www.bls.gov/ncs/ebs/sp/ebsm0003. pdf.

11. Alice Munnell, "Pension Expert Advocates Reform of Flawed 401(k)," interview published in *Employee Benefit News,* June 1, 2004, http://www.benefitnews.com/retire/detail.cfm?id=6021&arch=1; and Joint Economic Committee/Democrats, "Improving Defined Contribution Pension Plans," Economic Policy Brief, October 2005, http://jec.senate.gov/democrats/Documents/Reports/dcpensionplans06oct2005.pdf.

12. John C. Bogle, "In Investing, You Get What You Don't Pay For," (remarks at World Money Show, Orlando, Florida, February 2, 2005), http://www.vanguard.com/bogle_site/sp20050202.htm.

13. Ken Ziesenheim, "On the Importance of the Dividend," Thornburg Investment Management Web site, August 2005, http://www.thornburginvestments.com/research/articles/pdfs/TH737_Dividend_KenZ.pdf.

14. Robert J. Shiller, "Irrational Exuberance—Again," excerpts from the latest edition of Shiller's book *Irrational Exuberance,* CNNMoney.com, January 25, 2005, http://money.cnn.com/2005/01/13/real_estate/realestate_shiller1_0502/index.htm.

15. Jeremy J. Siegel, *The Future for Investors* (New York: Crown Business, 2005), 127.

16. Ari Weinberg, "Dividend All-Stars," Forbes.com, January 7, 2003, http://www.forbes.com/2003/01/07/cx_aw_0107dividend.html.

17. Burton G. Malkiel, *A Random Walk down Wall Street* (New York: W. W. Norton, 2003), 106.

18. Don Durfee, "Learning to Love Dividends: Why an Old-Fashioned Financial Tool Is Worth a Second Look," *CFO,* August 1, 2006, http://www.cfo.com/article.cfm/7239589/c_7242823?f=singlepage.

19. John Zbesko, "The Power of Dividends," Charles Schwab & Co. Web site, January 25, 2007, http:schwabinsights.com/2007_01/income.html.

20. Ziesenheim, "Importance of the Dividend."

21. Wilson/Bennett Capital Management, "What Can Dividends Do?" Wilson/Bennett Web site, no date, http://www.finance-insights.com/report.asp?id=737.

22. Jeremy Siegel, interviewed in Pablo Galarza, "Siegel: How to Invest Now," *Money,* November 30, 2004, http://money.cnn.com/2004/11/30/markets/siegel_0412/index.htm.

5: *Diversify Your Holdings in Radically Different Ways*

1. AllianceBernstein, "When It Comes to Asset Allocation, Many Investors Talk the Talk, but May Overstate Knowledge, Behave Badly or, Worse Yet, Do Nothing," AllianceBernstein's educational Web site, November 2, 2005, 2, https://therightmix.alliancebernstein.com/CmsObjectTRM/PDF/PressRelease_051102_INV.pdf.

2. Shlomo Benartzi and Richard H. Thaler, "Naïve Diversification Strategies in Defined Contribution Savings Plans," *American Economic Review* 91, no. 1 (March 2001): 79, http://faculty.chicagogsb/richard.thaler/research/91010079.pdfior.

3. Roger G. Ibbotson, "The True Impact of Asset Allocation on Returns," IbbotsonAssociates' Web site, originally printed in *Financial Analysts Journal,* January/February 2000, http://www.ifa.com/Media/Images/PDF%20files/Does_Asset_Allocation_Explain_Performance.pdf.

4. Ibid.

5. AllianceBernstein, "Investors Paying a Heavy Price," Morningstar.com, November 2, 2005, http://news.morningstar.com/PR/M11/D02/113090663758.html.

6. Thomas J. Fontaine, "Target-Date Retirement Funds: A Blueprint for Effective Portfolio Construction," AllianceBernstein Investment Research and Management, October 2005; and AllianceBernstein, "When It Comes to Asset Allocation."

7. AllianceBernstein, "When It Comes to Asset Allocation."

8. Ibid., 1.

9. Benartzi and Thaler, "Naïve Diversification Strategies," 89–90, table 5.

10. Ibid.

11. Ibid., 79.

12. Richard H. Thaler, "The End of Behavioral Finance," Association for Investment Management and Research, November/December 1999, 15, http://faculty.chicagogsb.edu/richard.thaler/research/end.pdf.

13. Shlomo Benartzi and Richard H. Thaler, "Risk Aversion or Myopia? Choices in Repeated Gambles and Retirement Investments," *Management Science* 45, no. 3 (March 1999): 364, http://faculty.chicagogsb.edu/richard.thaler/research/RiskAversionOr.pdf.

14. Hewitt Associates LLC, "Hewitt 401(k) Index," Hewitt's Web site, March 2007, http://www.hewittassociates.com/_MetaBasicCMAssetCashe_/Assets/401%20(k)%20PDFs/2007/AssetAllocationChart-04022007.pdf.

15. Jason Zweig, commentary on Benjamin Graham's The Intelligent Investor, 4th rev. ed. (New York: HarperBusiness Essentials, 2004), 102, http:////www.myone1.com/book/the.intelligent.invetor.pdf.

16. Elroy Dimson, Paul Marsh, and Mike Staunton, *Triumph of the Optimists: 101 Years of Global Investment Returns* (Princeton, NJ: Princeton University Press, 2002), 46, 47.

17. Ibid.

18. Jeremy J. Siegel, *The Future for Investors* (New York: Crown Business, 2005), 126.

19. Ari Weinberg, "Dividend All-Stars," Forbes.com, January 7, 2003, http://www.forbes.com/2003/01/07/cx_aw_0107dividend.html.

20. Ibid.

21. Penelope Wang, "Get the Most from Dividend Funds," cnnMoney.com, November 17, 2005, http://money.cnn.com/2005/11/17/funds/dividends_0512/index.htm.

22. Dimson, Marsh, and Staunton, *Triumph of the Optimists,* 46, 47.

23. Ibid., 87–88.

24. David F. Swensen, *Unconventional Success* (New York: Free Press, 2005), 78.

25. Ibid., 66.

26. National Association of Real Estate Investment Trusts, "Why Invest in REITs?" investinreits.com, no date, http://www.investingreits.com/reasons/performance.cfm.

27. Robert F. Shiller, "Irrational Exuberance—again," excerpts from the 5th ed. of Shiller's *Irrational Exuberance,* CNNMoney.com, January 25, 2005, http://money.cnn.com/2005/01/13/real_estate/realestate_shiller1_0502/index.htm.

28. Office of Federal Housing Enterprise Oversight, "House Price Appreciation Continues at Robust Pace," press release, March 1, 2006, http://www.ofheo/gov/media/pdf/4q05hpi.pdf.

29. National Association of Real Estate Investment Trusts, "Why Invest in REITs?"

30. Pacific Investment Management Company LLC, "Real Estate Real Return Strategy Offers More Than an Inflation Hedge," *Product Focus,* January 2005, http://www.pimco.com/LeftNav/Product+Focus/2005/Real_Estate_Real_Return_Approach.htm.

31. National Association of Real Estate Trusts, "Investment Performance of Publicly Traded REITs," NAREIT's web site, April 20, 2007, Exhibit 1, http://www.nareit.com/library/performance/sum0704.pdf.

32. National City Corporation and Global Insight Joint Venture, "House Prices in America, Filings Updated for the 4th Quarter of 2005," National City's Web site, March 2006, 1, http://nationalcity.com/content/corporate/EconomicInsight/documents/rev4Q2005report.

33. Ibid.

34. Michael Larson, "An Early Heads-Up on Another Important Real Estate Trend!" *Money and Markets,* e-letter published by Weiss Research, May 2, 2007.

35. Shawn Tully, "Welcome to the Dead Zone," cnnMoney.com, May 5, 2006, http://money.cnn.com/2006/05/03/news/economy/realestateguide_fortune/index.htm.

36. M. Moosa Khan, "Does Gold Foretell Inflation? A Long-Run Co-Integration Analysis," *Journal of Financial & Economic Practice* 4 (Spring 2004), http://www.bradley.edu/fcba/undergraduate/finance/jfep/issue_4.html; and World Gold Council, "Research Shows Gold as a Leading Indicator of Inflation," press release, November 4, 2005, http://www.gold.org/pr_archive/pdf/Inflation-pr-041105.pdf.

37. Brian M. Lucey and Edel Tully, "Still a Barbarous Relic? Cultural Aspects to Gold Investment," School of Business Studies, Trinity College, University of Dublin, no date, http://www.departments.bucknell.edu/management/apfa/Kilkenny%20Papers/Tully.doc.

38. Brian Lucey, Valerio Poti, and Edel Tully, "International Portfolio Formation, Skewness & the Role of Gold," IIIS Discussion Paper No. 30, School of Business Studies and Institute for International Integration Studies, Trinity College, Dublin, July 2004, 3.

39. World Gold Council, "Consumer Demand in Selected Countries: 2005 and 2006," table 4 of press release "Record Dollar Demand for Gold In 2006," February 15, 2007, http://www.gold.org/pr_archive/pdf/GDT_Q4_06_pr.pdf.

40. Hewitt Associates LLC, "Hewitt 401(k) Index."

41. Dimson, Marsh, and Staunton, *Triumph of the Optimists* 12.

42. Ibid., 15.

43. Burton G. Malkiel, comments from his interview by Christopher M. Wright published in "Capital Markets," National Association of Real Estate Investment Trusts Web site, September/October 2003, http://www.nareit.com/portfoliomag/03sepoct/capital.shtml.

44. Dimson, Marsh, and Staunton, *Triumph of the Optimists,* 110, table 8-2: "Risk and Return Comparisons."

45. Ibid., 110, 111.

46. Population Division, International Programs Center, U.S. Census Bureau, "IDB Summary Demographic Data," census.gov Web site, August 24, 2006, http://www.census.gov.ipc/www/idbsum.html.

47. Ibid.

48. Dimson, Marsh, and Staunton, *Triumph of the Optimists,* 105, table 8-2: "Risk and Return Comparisons."

49. Ibid., 114.

6: *Build Out Your Investment Plan with Funds, Indexes, and Objective Research*

1. Data supplied by Shana Gorsky, Lipper Reuters Research & Asset Management, April 24, 2007.

2. Jeremy J. Siegel, "The 'Noisy Market' Hypothesis," *Wall Street Journal,* June 14, 2006; William F. Sharpe, "The Arithmetic of Active Management," *Financial Analysts' Journal* 47, no. 1 (January/February 1991): 7–9; Thomas P. McGuigan, "The Difficulty of Selecting Superior Mutual Fund Performance," *Journal of Financial Planning,* February 2006; Steve Bergsman, "Indexes: An Investment Strategy or Investment Benchmark," *Real Estate Portfolio* (National Association of Real Estate Investment Trusts), May/June 2006; and John C. Hsu and Carmen Campollo, "New Frontiers in Index Investing: An Examination of Fundamental Indexation," *Journal of Indexes,* January-February 2006, 33.

3. Warren Buffett, "Chairman's Letter to Shareholders of Berkshire Hathaway Inc.," 1966, http://www.berkshirehathaway.com/letters/1996.html.

4. Vanguard Group, "Vanguard 500 Index Fund Fees & Minimums," Vanguard Web site, May 8, 2007, https://flagship.vanguard.com/VGApp/hnw/FundsFeesMinimums?FundId=0040&FundIntExt=INT.

5. William Jahnke, "It's Time to Dump Static Asset Allocation," *Journal of Financial Planning,* June 2004.

6. David F. Swensen, *Unconventional Success* (New York: Free Press, 2005), 222, 223.

7. Vanguard Group, "The Asset Allocation Debate: Then and Now," Vanguard Web site, May 4, 2007, http://global.vanguard.com/international/hIndEN/research/AssetEN.htm; and Yesim Tokat, "The Asset Allocation Debate: Provocative Questions, Enduring Realities," Vanguard Investment Counseling & Research Group, April 2005.

8. Data supplied by Gorsky.

9. Randy Gardner, "Increasing After-Tax Return with Exchange-Traded Funds," *Journal of Financial Planning,* June 2005, http://www.fpanet.org/journal/articles/2005_Issues/jfp0605-art4.cfm?renderforprint+1.

10. Pacific Investment Management Company LLC, "Rob Arnott Discusses the Fundamental Approach to Stock Market Indexing," *Strategic Markets,* June 2005, http://www.pimco.com/LeftNav/Product+Focus2005/ Arnott+Fundamental+Indexing+Interview.htm.

11. Robert D. Arnott, Jason Hsu, and Philip Moore, "Fundamental Indexation," *Financial Analysts' Journal* 61, no. 2 (March/April 2005); Siegel, "'Noisy Market' Hypothesis"; and Robert D. Arnott and John M. West, "Fundamental Indexes: Current and Future Applications," from Institutional Investor's *A Guide to Exchange Traded Funds and Indexing Innovations—Fifth Anniversary Issue,* Fall 2006, http://www .researchaffiliates.com/pubs/pdf/ETF_FA_06_arnott.pdf?PHPSESSID= c68348fb868aaec0f10c6a5e8b50cebf.

12. Pacific Investment Management Company, "Rob Arnott Discusses."

13. Research Affiliates LLC, "Fundamental Indexation," 2005–6, http://www .researchaffiliates.com/strategies/fundamentalIndexation.php.

14. Ibid.

15. Robert D. Arnott, interview by *Wall Street Week* cohost Karen Gibbs, November 15, 2002, http://www.pbs.org/wsw/tvprogram/arnottinterview.html.

16. Penelope Wang, "Get the Most from Dividend Funds," cnnMoney.com, November 17, 2005, http://money.cnn.com/2005/11/17/funds/dividends_0512/index. htm.

17. Elroy Dimson, Paul Marsh, and Mike Staunton, *Triumph of the Optimists: 101 Years of Global Investment Returns* (Princeton, NJ: Princeton University Press, 2002), 8.

18. Ibid.

19. Population Division, International Programs Center, U.S. Census Bureau, "IDB Summary Demographic Data," census.gov Web site, updated August 24, 2006, http:// www.census.gov/ipc/www/idbsum.html.

20. Thomas M. Idzorek, "Strategic Asset Allocation and Commodities," Ibbotson Associates study commissioned by PIMCO, March 27, 2006, iii, http://corporate.morningstar .com/ib/documents/MethodologyDocuments/IBBAssociates/Commodities.pdf.

7: *Get All the Professional Help You Can!*

1. Employee Benefit Research Institute, "Will More of Us Be Working Forever? The 2006 Retirement Confidence Survey," Issue Brief No. 292, April 2006, 21, http:// www.ebri.org/pdf/briefspdf/EBRI_IB_04-020061.pdf.

2. Jump$tart Coalition for Personal Financial Literacy, commentary from the group's Web site, no date, http://www.jumpstart.org.

3. Leslie A. Muller, "Does Retirement Education Teach People to Save Pension Distributions? Perspectives," *Social Security Bulletin* 64, no. 4 (June 2003), 59, http:// www.ssa.gov/policy/docs/ssb/v64n4/v64n4p48.pdf.

4. AllianceBernstein, "Investors Paying a Heavy Price," Morningstar.com, November 2, 2005, http://news.morningstar.com/PR/M11/D02/113090663758.html.

5. Ibid.

6. Internal Revenue Service, Department of the Treasury, *Your Federal Income Tax,* Publication 17, catalog no.10311G, no date, http://www.irs.gov/pub/irs-pdf/p17.pdf; and Internal Revenue Service, Department of the Treasury, *Investment Income and Expenses (Including Capital Gains and Losses),* Publication 550, catalog no. 15093R, no date, http://www.irs.gov/pub/irs-pdf/p550.pdf.

7. Lauren Young, "New Funds: The Value Meal Sequel," BusinessWeek.com, March 9, 2006, http://www.businessweek.com/investing/insights/blog/archives/2006/03/new_funds_the_s.html.

8. Penelope Wang, "Get the Most from Dividend Funds," cnnMoney.com, November 17, 2005, http://money.cnn.com/2005/11/17/funds/dividends_0512/index.htm.

9. Vanguard Group, "How to Select a Mutual Fund," Vanguard Web site, no date, https://flagship.vanguard.com/VGApp/hnw/planningeducation/education/PEdIESelMFChkFundCostsContent.jsp.

10. Data supplied to the author by the Reuters Research & Asset Management Division, April 24, 2007.

11. David F. Swensen, *Unconventional Success* (New York: Free Press, 2005), 223, with attribution to Pace University's Matthew Morey.

12. Employee Benefit Research Institute, "Encouraging Workers to Save: The 2005 Retirement Confidence Survey," Issue Brief No. 280, April 2005.

13. AllianceBernstein, "When It Comes to Asset Allocation, Many Investors Talk the Talk, but May Overstate Knowledge, Behave Badly or, Worse Yet, Do Nothing," AllianceBernstein's Web site, November 2, 2005, 5, https://therightmix.alliancebernstein.com/CmsOjectTRM/PDF/PressRelease_051102_INV.pdf.

8: *Build Income Streams with a Ladder of Annuities*

1. Ron Gebhardtsbauer, Senior Pension Fellow, American Academy of Actuaries, and data from the fully projected UP 94 pension mortality table, which is based on pensioner and group annuitant information, July 26, 2006.

2. Ken Little, *The Pocket Idiot's Guide to Annuities* (Alpha Books, Penguin Group, 2004), 45.

3. Peng Chen and Moshe A. Milevsky, "Merging Asset Allocation and Longevity Insurance: An Optimal Perspective on Payout Annuities," Library of the Society of Actuaries' Web site, February 20, 2003.

4. For example, author Harry S. Dent warns of the likelihood of a sharp stock market turndown beginning in or immediately prior to 2010 caused by the onslaught of boomers into retirement. Nevertheless, Dent predicts strong stock returns until "late 2009," prior to the crisis. Harry S. Dent, *The Next Great Bubble Boom: How to Profit from the Greatest Boom in History: 2006–2010* (New York: Free Press, 2006).

9: *Invest In Health Care Insurance*

1. Henry J. Kaiser Family Foundation, "Medicare Fact Sheet: Medicare at a Glance," September 2005, http://www.kff.org/medicare/upload/1066-08.pdf.

2. Administration on Aging U.S. Department of Health and Human Services, "A Profile of Older Americans: 2004," 15, figure 9, http://www.aoa.gov/prof/Statistics/profile/2004profile.pdf.

3. Kaiser Family Foundation, "Medicare Fact Sheet."

4. Administration on Aging, *"Profile of Older Americans,"* 15, figure 9.

5. Tim Harford, *The Undercover Economist: Exposing Why the Rich Are Rich, the Poor Are Poor—and Why You Can Never Buy a Decent Used Car* (Oxford University Press, 2006), 120.

6. Office of the Assistant Secretary for Planning and Evaluation, U.S. Department of Health and Human Services, "Long-Term Growth of Medical Expenditures—Public and Private," ASPE Issue Brief, May 2005, http://aspe.hhs.gov/health/MedicalExpenditures/ib.pdf.

7. Agency for Healthcare Research and Quality, U.S. Department of Health and Human Services, statistics from the HCUP Nationwide Inpatient Sample, HCUP Web site, http://hcupnet.ahrq.gov/HCUPnet.jsp.

8. Agency for Healthcare Research and Quality (AHRQ), U.S. Department of Health and Human Services, "AHRQ Data Show Rising Hospital Charges, Falling Hospital Stays," AHRQ Web site, October 2002, http://www.ahrq.gov/research/oct02/1002RA28.htm.

9. Joseph L. Matthews and Dorothy Matthews Berman, *Social Security, Medicare & Government Pensions*, 10th ed. (NOLO Publishing, 2005), 11/4.

10. Standard & Poor's Index Analysis and Management Group, "S&P 500: Pensions and Other Post-Employment Benefits," June 6, 2006, 13, 14, http://www2.standardandpoors.com/spf/pdf/index/060606_5OPEB-rpt.pdf.

11. Gallup Organization, "April 10–13 Gallup Poll on Economics and Personal Finances," Gallup Web site, April 25, 2006, http://www.galluppoll.com/content/?ci=22528&pg=1.

12. Kaiser Family Foundation, "Medicare Fact Sheet."

13. Cybele Weisser and Amanda Gengler, "50 Ways to Cut Your Health-Care Costs," CNNMoney.com, November 1, 2006, http://money.cnn.com/magazines/moneymag/moneymag_archive/2006/11/01/8392429/index.htm.

14. Medicare & Medicaid Services, U.S. Department of Health and Human Services, "What is a Medicare deductible?" Frequently Asked Questions section, Medicare Web site; and Kaiser Family Foundation, "Medicare Fact Sheet," 2, figure 3.

15. Richard Wolf, "A 'Fiscal Hurricane' on the Horizon," *USA Today*, November 14, 2005, http://www.usatoday.com/news/Washington/2005-11-14-fiscal-hurricane-cover_x.html.

16. Kaiser Family Foundation, "Medicare Fact Sheet."

17. Employee Benefit Research Institute, "2006 Retirement Confidence Survey: Many Americans' Retirement Hopes Are Filled with Holes," *ERBI News*, PR #733 (Washington, D.C.: April 2, 2006), http://www.ebri.org/pdf_733_4Apr06_2.pdf.

18. National Coalition on Health Care, "Health Insurance Cost," NCHC Web site, April 5, 2006, http://www.nchc.org/facts/cost.shtml; and Fidelity, "Fidelity Estimates $200,000 Now Needed to Cover Retiree Health Care Costs," press release, March 6, 2006, http://personal.fidelity.com/myfidelity/InsideFidelity/index_NewsCenter.shtml?refhp=pr.

19. Henry J. Kaiser Family Foundation, "Talking About Medicare and Health Coverage," foundation's Web site, April 2006, http://www.kff.com/medicare/7067/upload/7076Full.pdf.

20. Centers for Medicare & Medicaid Services, *Medicare & You 2007*, Medicare Web site, 62, http://www.medicare.gov/publications/pubs/pdf/10050.pdf.

21. "Yearly Long Term Care Costs Above $70,000 in 2006, According to Annual Benchmark Study by Genworth Financial, USA," *Medical News Today*, March 28, 2006, http://www.medicalnewstoday.com/medicalnews.php?newsid=40403; and Genworth Financial, "Genworth Financial National Poll Findings," summary of survey conducted February 27–March 1, 2006, Genworth Web site, http://longtermcare.genworth.com/comweb/consumer/pdfs/long_term_care/national_poll_summary.pdf.

22. Peter Kemper, Harriet L. Komisar, and Lisa Alecxih, "Long Term Care over an Uncertain Future: What Can Current Retirees Expect?" *Inquiry Journal* 42, no. 4 (March 1, 2006): 342.

23. Peter R. Orszag, "Strengthening Retirement Security," Retirement Security Project, May 22, 2006, http://www.law.harvard.edu/programs/lwp/PETER%20ORSZAG%20POWER%20POINT.pdf.

24. Kemper, Komisar, and Alecxih, "Long Term Care," 346.

25. Henry J. Kaiser Family Foundation, *"Talking About Medicare: Your Guide to Understanding the Program,"* foundation Web site, April 21, 2006, http://www.kff.org/medicare/med_longterm.cfm?RenderForPrint=1.

26. Genworth Financial, "What Is Long Term Care?" data from the Genworth Financial 2006 Cost of Care Survey, Genworth Web site, 2006, http://longtermcare.genworth.com/overview/what_is_ltc.jsp.

27. David Braze, "Other Long-Term Care Sources," Motley Fool Web site, December 8, 2005, http://www.fool.com/news/commentary/2005/commentary05120609.html?source=irrivslnk4550882.

28. Ibid., 345.

29. Ibid., 341–42.

30. American Association for Long-Term Care Insurance, "1 in 5 LTC Insurance Applicants Are Declined," press release, March 8, 2005, http://www.aaltci.org/subpages/media_room/story_pages/media030805.html.

31. LIMRA (Life Insurance and Market Research Association), "Individual Long-Term Care Insurance: 2005 Sales Supplement."

32. Consumer Reports, *"Do You Need Long-Term-Care Insurance?"* Consumer Reports Web site, November 2003, http://www.consumerreports.org/cro/personal-finance/longterm-care-insurance-1103/overview/index.htm.

33. Ibid.

34. Ibid.

35. Kemper, Komisar, and Alecxih, "Long Term Care," 342

36. "Long Term Care: What Should Retirees Expect?" *Inquiry: Journal of Health Care Organization, Provision, and Financing,* March 1, 2006, http://www.inquiryjournal.org/march_2006.html; and Kemper, Komisar, and Alecxih, "Long Term Care."

10: *The Importance of Periodic Tune-ups*

1. Robert J. Shiller, *Irrational Exuberance* (New York: Broadway Books, 2000), 7.

2. John Mauldin, *Bull's Eye Investing: Targeting Real Returns in a Smoke and Mirrors Market* (Hoboken, NJ: John Wiley & Sons, 2004), 81.

3. Economists have tabulated a number of different "average P/E ratios" for different periods of financial history: 14.6, 15, and more recently 16. We use 15 in the text. Tim Harford, *The Undercover Economist: Exposing Why the Rich Are Rich, the Poor Are Poor—and Why You Can Never Buy a Decent Used Car* (Oxford University Press, 2006), 148; and Mauldin, *Bull's Eye Investing,* 40.

4. Jeremy J. Siegel, *The Future for Investors* (New York: Crown Business, 2005), 14.

5. Jason Zweig, commentary on Benjamin Graham, *The Intelligent Investor,* 4th rev. ed. (HarperBusiness Essentials, 2004), 70, http:////www.myone1.com/book/the.intelligent.invetor.pdf.

6. Mike Sklarz, economist and real estate expert with Fidelity National Financial in Honolulu, conversation with the author on February 28, 2006.

7. Robert D. Arbnott and Peter L. Bernstein, *What Risk Premium Is "Normal"?* Association for Investment Management and Research, University of Texas Web site, March/April 2002, 70, http://www.mccombs.utexas.edu/faculty/keith.brown/Chile Material/ArnottBernstein%20FAJ02.pdf.

8. Siegel, *Future for Investors,* 246.

9. Gregory Zuckerman, "Real Estate Slowdown? No Sign of It in Sector Funds," RealEstateJournal.com, March 6, 2007, http://www.realestatejournal.com/reits/ 20070306-zuckerman.html.

10. Shiller, *Irrational Exuberance,* 198.

11. Marc O. Mayer, quoted in "When It Comes to Asset Allocation, Many Investors Talk the Talk, but May Overstate Knowledge, Behave Badly, or, Worse Yet, Do Nothing," *The Right Mix,* November 5, 2005, 4, https://therightmix.alliancebernstein .com/CmsObjectTRM/PDF/PressRelease_051102_INV.pdf.

12. Leslie A. Muller, "Does Retirement Education Teach People to Save Pension Distributions? Perspectives," *Social Security Bulletin* 64, no. 4 (June 2003); and Joint Economic Committee, "Improving Defined Contribution Pension Plans," Economic Policy Brief, October 2005, http://jec.senate.gov/democrats/Documents/Reports/ dcpensionplans06oct2005.pdf.

11: Tapping Your Home for Retirement Income

1. Kay Bell, "Capital Gains Home-Sale Tax Break a Boon for Owners," Bankrate Web site, October 18, 2004, http://www.bankrate.com/brm/news/real-estate/20041018al.asp.

2. Gallup Organization, "April 10–13 Gallup Poll on Economics and Personal Finances," Gallup Web site, June 26, 2006, http://www.galluppoll.com/content/?ci= 23488&pg=1.

3. Ibid.

4. Dennis Jacobe, "Americans Are Hooked on Home Equity Loans/Lines," commentary on the findings of the Experian/Gallup Personal Credit Index Survey of October–December 2006, Gallup Web site, February 12, 2007, http://www.galluppoll.com/ content/?ci=26488&pg=1.

5. Mortgage Bankers Association, "The Residential Mortgage Market and Its Economic Context in 2007," MBA Research Monograph Series, January 30, 2007, 3, http:// www.mortgagebankers.org/files/News/InternalResource/48215_TheResidentialMortgage MarketandItsEconomicContextin2007.pdf.

6. Ibid.

7. Alan Greenspan, "Remarks to the American Bankers Association" (speech to the American Bankers Association Annual Convention, Palm Desert, CA, September 26, 2005), Federal Reserve Web site, http://www.federalreserve.gov/boarddocs/speeches/ 2005/200509262/default.htm.

8. Christopher L. Cagan, "Mortgage Payment Reset: The Issue and the Impact," (Santa Ana, CA: First American CoreLogic, March 19, 2007), 2, http://www.firstamres .com/pdf/200770048_reset_study_03062007_RV5.pdf.

9. Dean Baker, "The Housing Bubble Fact Sheet," Center for Economic and Policy Research Issue Brief, July 2005, http://www.cepr.net/publications/housing_Fact_2005 _07.pdf.

10. Cagan, "Mortgage Payment Reset," 2.

11. Wilshire Associates, "2006 Report on City & County Retirement Systems: Funding Levels and Asset Allocation," September 14, 2006, 1, http://www.wilshire.com/BusinessUnits/Consulting/Investment/2006_City_County_Funding_Report.pdf.

12. Wilshire Associates, "2007 Wilshire Report on State Retirement Systems: Funding Levels and Asset Allocation," March 5, 2007, 1, http://www.wilshire.com/BusinessUnits/Consulting/Investment/2007_State_Retirement_Funding_Report.pdf.

13. John Mauldin, *Bull's Eye Investing: Targeting Real Returns in a Smoke and Mirrors Market* (Hoboken, NJ: John Wiley & Sons, 2004), 129.

14. Harry S. Dent Jr. and Michael A. Burns & Associates, Public Relations Agency of Record, "HS Dent Publishing Issues 'Death of Pensions,'" press release, HS Dent Foundation Web site, December 5, 2006. http://www.hsdent.com/newsreleases.php.

15. Kenneth R. Harney, "Baby Boomers: Greatest Real Estate Generation?" Homes101 Web site, October 26, 2006, http://www.homes101.net/news/n2034; and National Association of Realtors, "Baby Boomer Survey Shows Big Appetite for Real Estate," press release, May 18, 2006, http://www.realtor.org/press_room/news_releases/2006/babyboomerstudy06.html.

16. Harris Interactive, "WSJ.com/Harris Interactive Survey: Majority of Adults Expect Retirement Income to Include Social Security," February 22, 2007, table 1A, http://www.harrisinteractive.com/news/allnewsbydate.asp?NewsID=1183.

17. National Association of Realtors, "Baby Boomer Survey."

18. U.S. Census Bureau, "IDB Summary Demographic for United States," April 2005, http://www.census.gov/cbi-bin/ipc/idbsum.pl?cty=US.

19. Dennis Jacobe, "Many Americans Banking on Real Estate for Retirement Income," Gallup Web site, July 12, 2005, http://www.galluppoll.com/content/?ci=17284&pg=1.

20. Howard Godfrey and Edward Malmgren, "Going Forward with Reverse Mortgages," *Journal of Accountancy* 202, no. 1 (July 2006), American Institute of Certified Public Accountants Web site, http://www.aicpa.org/PUBS/jofa/jul2006/godfrey.htm.

21. National Reverse Mortgage Lenders Association, "Record Number of Reverse Mortgages Made in February," NRMLA Web site, March 19, 2007, http://www.reversemortgage.org.

22. Lisa N. Davis, "Paying for Staying at Home: Reverse Mortgages," *Connecticut Bar Association Elder Law Section Newsletter,* Summer 2002, revised June 8, 2005, http://www.sharinglaw.net/elder/paying_for_staying_at_home.htm.

23. AARP, "Session 3—Overview of Reverse Mortgages," Homemade Money: A Consumer's Guide to Reverse Mortgages, online reverse mortgage seminar, 2003, http://www.aarp.org/learntech/personal_finance/Articles/a2003-05-12-revmortoverview.html15. AARP's excellent educational materials contain details about the specific kinds of properties that qualify for reverse mortgages.

24. Blake Fetrow, "Reverse Mortgages—What Are They? Is One Right for You?" People's Law Web site, July 22, 2004, http://www.peoples-law.org/housing/home-ownership/fetrow_reverse_mortgage_information.htm. The author likewise used online calculators to determine different loan amounts under different age and property-location scenarios.

25. Godfrey and Malmgren, "Going Forward with Reverse Mortgages."

26. Ibid.

27. Doug Foust, "Reverse Mortgages: Shift into High Gear," *Business Week,* July 31, 1997, http://www.businessweek.com/1997/32/b3539125.htm.

28. Godfrey and Malmgren, "Going Forward with Reverse Mortgages."

29. Bureau of Consumer Protection, Federal Trade Commission, "Reverse Mortgages: Get the Facts Before Cashing In on Your Home's Equity," FTC Facts for Consumers, June 2005, http://www.ftc.gov/bcp/conline/pubs/homes/rms.pdf.

30. FSO Technologies, "Reverse Mortgages: How They Can Enhance Your Retirement," Financial Strategies Online, 2003, http: www.gofso.com/Premium/LE/20_le_ir/fg/fg-Reverse_Mortgage.html.

31. Robert F. Shiller, "Irrational Exuberance—Again," excepts from the latest edition of Shiller's book *Irrational Exuberance,* CNNMoney.com, January 25, 2005, http://money.cnn.com/2005/01/13/real_estate/realestate_shiller1_0502/index.htm; and Dr. Shiller's letter to the author, dated September 12, 2007.

32. Ibid.

33. Rebecca Boreckzy, "Boomers Spark Second-Home Sales Surge," *Washington Times,* October 6, 2006, http://www.washingtontimes.com/fhg/20061004-083346-3443r.htm; and National Association of Realtors, "Baby Boomers and Real Estate: Today and Tomorrow," results of the nationwide Harris Interactive survey, October 2006, http://www.realtor.org/Research.nsf/files/BBPreview10Page.pdf/$FILE/BBPreview10Page.pdf.

34. National Association of Realtors, "Second Home Sales Hit Another Record in 2005; Market Share Rises," press release, NAR Web site, April 5, 2006, http://www.realtor.org/press_room/news_releases/2006/secondhomesales05.html.

35. National Association of Realtors, "Second-Home Market Surges, Bigger Than Shown in Earlier Studies," press release, NAR Web site, March 1, 2005, http://www.realtor.org/press_room/news_releases/2005/seconghomemktsurges05.html.

36. Paul Bishop, "Second Home Sales: Another Record in 2005," *Real Estate Insights,* April 2006, 10, http://www.realtor.org/reioutlook.nsf/files/currentissue.pdf/$FILE/currentissue.pdf.

37. National Association of Realtors, "Baby Boomers and Real Estate."

12: When to Get Defensive

1. Jeremy J. Siegel, in Mark Skousen, "Dr. Skousen Interviews the Author of *The Future for Investors* and a Proponent of 'Buy and Hold' and Dividend-Paying Stocks," Investment U e-letter #585, September 26, 2006, http://www.invetmentu.com/IUEL/2006/20060926.html.

2. David F. Swensen, *Unconventional Success* (New York: Free Press, 2005), 48.

3. Daniel Kadlec, "Inflation Tips Wanted," *Time* 167, no. 11 (March 13, 2006), 65.

4. Morningstar, "U.S. Government Agency Bonds," Morningstar's Interactive Classroom, 2006, http://news.morningstar.com/classroom2/printlesson.asp?docId=5482&CN=COM.

5. Swensen, *Unconventional Success,* 93.

6. Ibid., 104.

7. Standard & Poor's Index Services, "S&P 500 Monthly Returns," Standard & Poor's Web site, March 30, 2007, http://www2.standardandpoors.com/spf/xls/index/MONTHLY.xls.

8. Richard H. Thaler, "The End of Behavioral Finance," Association for Investment Management and Research, November/December 1999, 13, http://faculty.chicagogsb.edu/richard.thaler/research/end.pdf.

9. Jeremy J. Siegel, in Ira Carnahan, "Should You Still Be a Bull?" Forbes.com, April 19, 2004, http://www.forbes.com/forbes/2004/0419/096-print.html.

10. Jason Zweig, commentary on Benjamin Graham, *The Intelligent Investor,* 4th rev. ed. (New York: HarperBusiness Essentials, 2004), 70, http://www.myone1.com/book/the.intelligent.investor.pdf.

11. Carnahan, "Should You Still Be a Bull?"

12. Robert J. Shiller, updated stock market data used in Dr. Shiller's book *Irrational Exuberance,* Yale University Web site, http://www.econ.yale.edu/~shiller/data/ie_data .htm.

13. Floyd Norris, "Looking Back at the Crash of '29," *New York Times,* no date, http://www.nytimes.com/library/financial/index-1929-crash.html.

14. Robert J. Shiller, *Irrational Exuberance* (New York: Broadway Books, 2000), 11.

15. Matthew Spiegel, "2000 Bubble? 2002 a Panic? Maybe Nothing?" Yale University Web site, October 28, 2002, http://som.yale.edu/~spiegel/editorial/CrashorPanic .pdf.

16. Shiller, updated stock market data.

17. Ibid.

18. Jeremy J. Siegel, "Stock Prices," *Concise Encyclopedia of Economics,* Library of Economics and Liberty Wet site, no date, http://www.econlib.org/LIBRARY/Enc/StockPrices.hmtl.

19. Standard & Poor's Index Services, "S&P 500 Monthly Returns."

20. Shiller, *Irrational Exuberance,* 7–8.

21. Tim Harford, *The Undercover Economist: Exposing Why the Rich Are Rich, the Poor Are Poor—and Why You Can Never Buy a Decent Used Car* (Oxford University Press, 2006), 146–47.

22. Standard & Poor's Index Services, "S&P 500 Monthly Returns."

23. Robert Arnott, "Bull vs. Bear Debate" (presentation to the Securities Industry Association, Boca Raton, FL, November 10, 2005), http://www.sia/com/boca2005/pdf/RobArnott.pdf.

24. Jeremy J. Siegel, *The Future for Investors* (New York: Crown Business, 2005), 42; and Jeremy J. Siegel, in Pablo Galarza, "Siegel: How to Invest Now," *Money,* November 30, 2004, http://money.cnn.com/2004/11/30/markets/siegel_0412/index .htm.

25. John Mauldin, *Bull's Eye Investing: Targeting Real Returns in a Smoke and Mirrors Market* (Hoboken, NJ: John Wiley & Sons, 2004), 16.

26. Paraphrased remark attributed to Cliff Asness, managing principal of AQR Capital Management, in Justin Lahart, "The Broken Model," CNNMoney.com, February 13, 2003, http://money.cnn.com/2003/02/13/markets/fedmodel.

27. Joshua Gallin, "The Long-Run Relationship Between House Prices and Rents," Finance and Economics Discussion Series, Divisions of Research & Statistics and Monetary Affairs, Federal Reserve Board, Washington, D.C., September 2004, http://www.federalreserve.gov/pubs/feds/2004/200450/200450pap.pdf.

28. Janet L. Yellen, "Views on the Economy and Implications for Monetary Policy" (speech by the president and CEO of the Federal Reserve Board of San Francisco, July 29, 2005), Federal Reserve Bank of San Francisco Web site, http://www.frbsf.org .news/speeches/2005/0729.html.

29. Craig Woker, "Real Estate Is the Next Dot-Com," Morningstar Web site, May 27, 2005, http://news.morningstar.com/article/article.asp?id=135312&_QSBPA =Y.

30. Ellen Florian Kratz, "Could Renting Be Smarter?" *Fortune,* December 19, 2005, http://money.cnn.com/2005/12/15/real_estate/4questions_rent_fortune_122605/index.htm.

31. Yellen, "Views on the Economy."

32. Gallin, "Long-Run Relationship."

33. Steve Sjuggerud, "How to Value Any Piece of Real Estate ('Real' Real Estate Advice for Today's Investor)," InvestmentU.com Web site, April 10, 2006, http://www.investmentu.com/realestateinvestmentadvice.html.

Index